CW01509911

Dave Tabler

ISBN: 979-8-9921667-2-9

Library of Congress Control Number: 2025915175

Cover Design: Ben @BenCreatesBooks

Printed in the United States of America

www.davetabler.com

Dedicated to

EM

My partner in crime

With love,

DT

DELAWARE
BEHAVING BADLY

FIRST STATE, TRUE CRIMES

Dave Tabler

TABLE OF CONTENTS

PREFACE

Crime happens every day. Some cases barely make the news cycle, buried beneath the weight of routine arrests, petty frauds, and domestic squabbles. But every so often, a crime shatters the expected, sending shockwaves through a community. When that happens, media outlets do what they do best—they make it their lead story.

This book is about those crimes.

From the colonial era to the dawn of the 21st century, crime has shaped Delaware's history, challenged its values, and sometimes changed its laws. These aren't just sensational headlines—they're windows into the First State's evolving identity, reflecting shifts in power, race, class, and justice across generations.

Some crimes shake the structure of society itself. Consider the 1897 Boggs embezzlement scandal, when a respected Dover banker vanished with $107,000—enough to cripple a financial institution and implicate a sitting U.S. Senator. Or the tragic case of Anne Marie Fahey, whose 1996 murder by a prominent attorney exposed the dark underside of Delaware's political power structure. Other stories involve desperate bids for freedom, like the Dover Eight's daring 1857 escape from slavery, which triggered a multi-state manhunt and became a powerful symbol in the abolitionist movement.

Delaware's criminal history contains both brutality and absurdity. There's Harley G. Brown's 1878 train derailment, where a desperate former railroad worker placed an obstruction on the tracks hoping to "heroically" discover it and earn his job back—instead causing four deaths when an unexpected express train came through. Then there's the attempted 1891 police raid on Ada Winters' Wilmington brothel that devolved into a farcical brawl involving constables, a furious mayor, and an officer accused of choking the city's chief executive.

Race and power shaped many of these stories, from the bold action of New Castle Catholics who disrupted a 1923 KKK cross-burning, to the courts that systematically failed to protect Black victims like Peter "Cooch" Turner, whose 1872 murder became a stark example of justice denied. Even Delaware's witchcraft laws, which remained on the books until 1953, were weaponized against Black practitioners, immigrants, and Roma fortune-tellers while sparing their white counterparts. Similarly, the early 19th-century crimes of Patty Cannon and her gang, who kidnapped free Black men, women, and children to sell into slavery, are a chilling reminder of how criminal enterprises thrived when law enforcement looked the other way.

Waves of moral panic and economic necessity reshaped the state's criminal landscape. During World War II, ration coupon counterfeiters drained millions of gallons of gasoline from the war effort. In the late 19th century, oyster pirates violated Delaware Bay restrictions, leading to armed confrontations that sometimes turned deadly. In the 1970s, the Matherly gang graduated from stealing tractors to orchestrating Delaware's most significant art heist.

Throughout Delaware's history, law enforcement and criminals have pushed and pulled against each other in a complex dance. Some, like respected citizens who spoke fondly of "my bookie" while lunching with journalists in 1950, saw certain crimes as acceptable vices. Others, like Cheney Clow in the Revolutionary War era, became caught in the shifting definitions of loyalty and treason as the young nation found its footing.

Delaware may be small, but its criminal history contains multitudes. These stories span a spectrum—from blood-chilling murders that haunted generations to curious capers lost in dusty archives, from soul-crushing injustices that demanded reform to schemes so preposterous they strain credulity. What unites them all is their ability to captivate public attention—the recognition that, for a moment, they changed something fundamental about how Delaware understood itself.

Whether the courts delivered justice, whether history preserved the truth, whether the guilty paid or walked free—these chapters explore those questions. What's undeniable is that when news outlets spotlighted these crimes, they revealed not just individual moral failures, but the character of Delaware itself—its prejudices and principles, its corruption and courage, its darkness and its daylight.

Delaware may pride itself on being the first state to ratify the Constitution, but these headline-making stories expose a different kind of distinction—times when Delaware grappled with the darker aspects of its own history. And perhaps nowhere is a place's true character more honestly revealed than in its most prominent news coverage, where the stories that shake a community force us to see what lies beneath the carefully maintained surface of civic life.

1

WHEN SPELLS BECAME CRIMINAL ACTS

A look at Delaware's early supernatural accusations.

While the infamous Salem Witch Trials of 1692 have become synonymous with colonial America's relationship to witchcraft, Delaware's experience with supernatural accusations and prosecutions followed a markedly different path. When hysteria gripped Massachusetts, settlers had already established Delaware for 54 years, shaping it under distinctly different cultural influences. A powerful Puritan presence never took root in Delaware, leaving the colony's religious and legal landscape distinct from New England's. Instead, a mix of Anglicans, Quakers, Dutch Reformed Church members, Lutherans, and Mennonites shaped the region. Their presence fostered a more diverse and religiously tolerant environment that contrasted sharply with the rigid orthodoxy of Puritan New England.

Nevertheless, when the settlement transitioned to English control in 1664, King James I's Witchcraft Act of 1604 reshaped Delaware's approach to sorcery accusations for centuries.

The 1604 Act was unequivocal and severe, declaring that any person "invoking any evil spirit or consulting, covenanting with, entertaining, employing, feeding, or rewarding any evil spirit; or taking up dead bodies from their graves, to be used in any witchcraft, sorcery or charm, or enchantment; or killing or otherwise hurting any person by such infernal arts, should be guilty of felony without benefit of the clergy, and suffer death." The statute's application in Delaware, however, proved far less zealous than in New England.

To grasp the colony's later development, one must first examine how Delaware's early settlers conceptualized and responded to supposed witchcraft. Rev. Joseph Doderidge's seminal work, *Notes on the Settlement and Indian Wars in Pennsylvania and Virginia* (1824), offers valuable insights into these early beliefs. According to Doderidge, people commonly attributed certain childhood afflictions, particularly "dropsy of the brain and the rickets," to supernatural intervention. These conditions, being neither fully understood nor curable by contemporary medicine, naturally invited occult explanations.

Colonial Delawareans proposed equally fascinating remedies for such bewitchment. Doderidge described an elaborate ritual where "the picture of the supposed witch was drawn on a stump or piece of board and shot at with a bullet containing a little bit of silver. This silver bullet transferred a painful and sometimes mortal spell on that part of the witch corresponding with the part of the picture struck by the bullet." This practice reflects both the desperation of parents facing inexplicable childhood illnesses and the detailed metaphysical framework early settlers constructed to explain their world.

Delaware's folk customs surrounding witchcraft extended far beyond medical concerns. Early settlers developed an intricate system of protective measures against otherworldly interference. Parents placed psalm books beneath their newborn children's heads, trusting this act would stop witches from swapping their infants for "elf children."

Colonists assigned protective power to practical household items— for example, carving crosses into broom handles to stop witches from using them for transportation. Caretakers gave livestock magical protection by feeding cattle the crumbs from each course of Christmas dinner to guard against hexing.

Witchcraft accusations reached the highest levels of colonial administration. During the governorship of Johan Printz (1643-1653), two Finnish settlers, Karim and her husband Lasse, faced accusations of what was then called witchery. Printz punished them severely, banishing them from New Sweden's main settlements and confiscating their Chester County, Pennsylvania farm. This incident demonstrates how witchcraft charges could serve as tools of political and social control, even in Delaware's pre-English period.

By the mid-nineteenth century, educated Delawareans increasingly dismissed witchcraft practices as antiquated superstitions, though some communities still clung to these beliefs.

An 1869 letter to the *Delaware Tribune* from "B.V." of Brandywine Hundred captured this cultural tension. The writer described a disturbing incident where a woman, after noticing her hens were unproductive, concluded someone had bewitched them. Her solution – binding two live hens together and throwing them into a ritual fire to force the "witch" to reveal itself – struck the letter writer as particularly irrational. The fire consumed both, offering pointed commentary on the futility of these beliefs. B.V.'s exasperation that such practices continued in the community reflects the growing divide between educated skepticism and persistent folk superstitions.

During the 1880s, several high-profile cases revealed how witchcraft finger-pointing often overlapped with racial and ethnic tensions in Delaware's urban centers. The 1883 case of Hannah Lloyd, a Black woman living on Wilmington's Greeley Street, particularly illuminates these dynamics. Lloyd suffered from an unidentified illness that manifested in dramatic fashion – she "would terrify the whole neighborhood with her screams, and at the next she would be singing and shouting." Her accusation that another Black woman, known as "Big Lizzie," had bewitched her sparked a community crisis. The *Daily Republican* depicted Greeley Street's Black community as prone to "fights and quarrels," while barely concealing its derision in descriptions of residents gathering nightly for "weird spells and incantations" to drive out evil spirits.

A white physician's dismissive diagnosis of "bad whiskey and hysteria" reflected both the medical and racial prejudices of the time. Lloyd's death and the community's threats against "Big Lizzie" revealed how witchcraft allegations could still ignite dangerous tensions even in supposedly "modern" times.

Delaware's colonial-era witchcraft charges lacked obvious racial overtones. The surge of cases beginning in the 1865–1920 period, by contrast, reflects profound social changes. The emancipation of enslaved people had fundamentally altered the South's social and economic landscape. Newly freed Black Americans, viewed as both economic competition and a challenge to white supremacy, faced an intense backlash in the form of Jim Crow laws and other mechanisms of social control.

In this context, the 1888 case of an unnamed Black man who approached the *Daily Republican* office takes on darker implications. His written complaint claimed that a "highly respectable family" subjected him to "preternatural influences," making him "incapable of working or earning a living." The newspaper's response was telling – rather than investigating his claims of harassment, they focused patronizingly on his writing style and "orthography," suggesting these "probably date further back than a recent exercise of prenatural [sic] powers."

This dismissive treatment reveals how the press wielded claims of superstition to reinforce racial hierarchies during the Jim Crow era. By portraying Black citizens as prone to paranormal thinking and questionable literacy, such coverage helped justify their continued marginalization. The Daily Republican reframed the man's complaint that authorities had prevented him from working—a common experience for Black Americans facing systematic economic discrimination—as evidence of his own irrationality, dismissing the complaint instead of recognizing the letter as testimony to the very real "preternatural influences" of systemic racism.

Wilmington's courts addressed a case in 1891 that highlighted how witchcraft laws could be weaponized to target both racial and religious groups deemed undesirable by society. Every Evening described Herman Zutler with casual antisemitism as a "tall, nervous-looking Jew." Following his brief but profitable stay in Wilmington, he faced charges of conjuring.

His scheme involved an elaborate ritual: he would take a $5 note from his "patient," roll it in a handkerchief, pass it around the afflicted body part while murmuring prayers, and promise the disease would vanish—but in the end, it was the patient's money, not the ailment, that disappeared.

His victim, a Jewish woman living near Front and Shipley streets, ended up not only unhealed but hungry, since the $5 he stole was all she had for food. Zutler's other supposed cures included a bizarre prescription instructing sufferers to steep a piece of leather in water at Third Street bridge for eleven days, then drink the liquid as a remedy for stomach ailments.

When the case reached court, Judge J. Frank Ball ordered Zutler to return the money, but the self-proclaimed healer had none to give. After authorities ordered Zutler to leave the city, his wife met him outside the courthouse. In a touching, if ironic, gesture, she "grasped him affectionately and kissed his hand." Acting City Solicitor William Lynam had to search through antiquated legal records to find applicable law, suggesting how rarely such charges were prosecuted.

The case drew significant attention; *Every Evening* noted that "nearly the whole Hebrew population of the city" took interest, since both Zutler and his victim belonged to the same community. Officer Simon Cohen, himself a member of the Jewish community, played a key role in bringing Zutler to justice—a gesture that underscored how some within the community took active steps to protect their own from exploitation.

The *Daily Republican* reported a troubling 1895 case of false charges. Authorities jailed Mr. and Mrs. S. S. Baldwin—performers known for their "mystifying demonstrations" before Wilmington audiences—in Wilkes-Barre, Pennsylvania, on allegations of witchcraft and necromancy.

The subsequent discharge and the arrest of their adversaries on blackmail charges revealed how unscrupulous citizens wielded supernatural denunciations as leverage for extortion. Arthur Miller later dramatized this pattern of unfounded claims for ulterior motives in his 1953 play *The Crucible*, using the Salem witch trials as an allegory for McCarthyist persecution.

Delaware's press and legal system increasingly solidified their framing of witchcraft cases in the early twentieth century. By consistently equating witchcraft with "voodoo" —a practice exclusively associated with the Black community—newspapers effectively racialized all supernatural practices. This rhetorical sleight-of-hand suggested that witchcraft itself was inherently tied to Black practitioners, conveniently erasing centuries of European witchcraft traditions.

The 1905 case of Daniel Hector documents this dynamic perfectly. When Hector appeared before the Court of General Sessions on formal charges of "witchcraft and fortune telling," *Every Evening* repeatedly characterized his practices as "voodoo business." The newspaper noted that Hector had "fleeced" about twenty-six witnesses of sums ranging from $3 to $15. Chief Justice Charles Lore's pronouncement that "fleecing of the people under misrepresentation shall not be encouraged" reflected how the legal system viewed these practices primarily as fraud rather than genuine otherworldly beliefs.

Around the same time, press coverage explicitly labeled Lawrence Maltro Durham, a self-proclaimed healer in Sussex County, as "negro" and Daniel Hector as "colored," framing their practices as "voodoo."

Durham systematically approached families with chronically ill members, convincing them that doctors "could never do them any good" because their ailments stemmed from spells. When John Purnell Fitzgerald, a prominent farmer in Cedar Neck (whose race went unmentioned in the press, indicating his whiteness), sought help for his wife's two-year illness, Durham promised a nine-day "faith cure" for $50. He meticulously structured the payment plan: he required a $10 down payment and had the client sign a note for the remaining $40, which he would collect once he delivered the promised results. Durham later managed to convert this note into "bankable" form, which he promptly cashed out for $20 in clothing and $20 in cash at a local merchant.

Durham extracted $100 from another victim at Cedar Creek and accumulated several other payments before his arrest. His testimony in court about Fitzgerald's wife being under a spell turned the proceedings into a near-theatrical spectacle. The *Milford Chronicle* noted the "considerable humor" in the courtroom, pointedly adding that this witchery charge was "perhaps the first of its kind ever known in this section of Delaware"—a claim that ignored numerous earlier witchcraft cases but reinforced the idea that such practices were foreign to white Delaware.

Most Delawareans by the 1920s regarded witchcraft charges as relics of a less enlightened age. Wilmington Deputy City Solicitor P. Warren Green hesitated to bring sorcery charges against one Frank Bias in 1921, admitting his reluctance in "these modern times."

Bias convinced Julian Jumbo to give him $100 to help recover $660 that had been stolen. He supplied Jumbo with a bottle of medicine, meant to be slipped into the thieves' water or coffee, while promising to cast a spell over them. Another victim, Agretta Capelle, paid Bias $80 to cure her rheumatism. He gave her a $20 charm made of green string to wear against her skin, a caustic salve that "took the skin off her legs," and a medicinal liquid so potent he instructed her to take only nine drops three times daily.

Instead of pursuing witchcraft charges, Green charged Bias with practicing medicine without a license, illustrating how professionalized healthcare increasingly displaced supernatural practices. The case showed how Bias systematically targeted immigrant communities, particularly Italians, whose recent arrival and cultural backgrounds left them more vulnerable to such scams.

That same year, the case of Mary Burke came to light—a young mother who sold "charm powder," black dust mixed with salt, to desperate gamblers. Her client William F. Lambert testified that he paid $5 for the powder, rubbed it on his hands as instructed, and exclaimed, "Don't cha know, the first game I got into...I 'crapped' 'leven straight times."

"It's all foolishness, that powder — but I didn't sell it. I gave it away to keep the peoples' trade."

MARY BURKE

When his luck turned sour, Burke explained that one of Lambert's opponents was stronger than him because "he had bought more of the dust" and suggested Lambert had "rubbed it on his hands wrong." Despite losing so badly he had to borrow money, Lambert bought the powder a second time.

Burke, cradling her infant in court, denied selling the powder, claiming instead that she gave the mixture away to maintain relationships in her work for the Spiritualists. "It's all foolishness, that powder," she explained, "But I didn't sell it—I'm not guilty of that. I gave it away to keep the peoples' trade for the Spiritualists." Her desperate circumstances emerged in her testimony: her husband, a veteran, had been jobless for two months, and "many nights she walks the floor with her baby, having no food for it." Although authorities charged Burke and set her bail at $1,000, the judge acknowledged her difficult circumstances and allowed her to sign her own bond, balancing punishment with leniency in light of her economic hardship.

As Delaware's aging witchcraft statutes entered their final decades, authorities increasingly deployed them against a widening circle of marginalized communities. Officials underscored this shift when they arrested Rosie John, a young Roma woman who operated a fortune-telling establishment at 217 Market Street in Wilmington. The case centered on an encounter with Luigi Matheno, who accused her of stealing $11 from his $68 roll during a palm reading. Matheno testified that John used a classic fortune-teller's philosophical misdirection, telling him that "it is good luck to make money but bad luck to save it" before requesting to hold his money.

He claimed she "diverted his attention" during the reading, and he only discovered the missing money later at the bank. Deputy Judge John Lynn held her on $500 bail for both witchcraft and larceny charges. Rosie John's arrest revealed how deeply ingrained fears of the supernatural fueled prejudice well into the 20th century.

Delaware closed the final chapter in the state's legal relationship with witchcraft in 1953. That spring, Andrew W. Christie, Executive Director of the Legislative Reference Bureau, spoke to the Kent County Republican Women's Club in Dover's Legislative Hall, explaining how the bureau modernized and streamlined state laws. He noted with a smile that the commission struck down the state's power to prosecute witchcraft, labeling the statute one of the "ancient and obsolete" laws. His lighthearted delivery underscored how the old edict, like the beliefs it once governed, had faded into mere historical curiosity.

Delaware's witchcraft history evolved from colonial-era fears to twentieth-century frauds, revealing how society weaponized supernatural beliefs for social control or exploitation. Though educated Delawareans dismissed these beliefs by the mid-1800s, supernatural explanations endured in vulnerable populations. This persistence reveals a timeless human need to find meaning in chaos. Mystical frameworks offered ways to explain suffering and express power, leaving a lasting mark on how communities confront the unknowable.

2

CHENEY CLOW'S REBELLION

The defiant actions and legal battles of Cheney Clow.

The crowd did not expect the hymn. A moment of serene melody rising from a man about to die, suspended between condemnation and compassion. On the day of his execution in 1788, Cheney Clow walked to the gallows singing, threading through the silence of a crowd unsure whether they watched justice or tragedy unfold. Was he a traitor? A victim? A principled man or a dangerous provocateur? Even as the rope tightened, Delaware remained divided.

Cheney Clow's story carried tension beyond a simple tale of one man's rebellion. American society fractured along a profound and bitter schism during the revolutionary struggle, observed J.B. Turner in *Cheney Clow's Rebellion*. Throughout the war, nearly a third of Delaware's population wrestled with divided loyalties, caught between the revolutionary cause and allegiance to the British crown. While revolutionaries celebrated their fight for independence, Loyalists believed they were safeguarding an essential political and social order.

Loyalists, or Tories, were not merely passive dissenters, but individuals with complex motivations, some driven by genuine belief in the British system, others by economic interests, family ties, or deep-seated conservative principles. They saw themselves not as traitors, but as faithful subjects preserving a political and social order they believed essential.

For many, the revolution represented not a noble struggle for liberty, but a dangerous upheaval that threatened social stability, property rights, and long-standing communal bonds. But the revolutionary leadership instead understood Loyalists as critical assets to the British war effort. Their existence transformed political disagreement into something far more dangerous: a potential mortal threat to the fragile new republic. Tories actively smuggled provisions to British troops, spied on American forces, steered British ships through local waters, and recruited soldiers to fight against the revolutionaries.

In Kent County, where Clow made his stand, few Loyalists remained, as the predominantly Scotch-Irish population strongly backed the revolutionary cause. The county mirrored Delaware's broader political landscape, where a minority of Tories still wielded enough influence to create meaningful havoc within the emerging

American society.

A dense forest surrounded Cheney Clow's homestead in western Kent County, an isolated clearing where Delaware met Maryland. Clow's position on the border between Delaware and Maryland meant more than just where his house stood—the line between states shaped his identity, his loyalties, and ultimately, his defiance. Though his house sat 200 yards inside Delaware's borders, he insisted it lay within Maryland's jurisdiction. This was no mere quibble over property lines. Clow had deep family ties across the border in Maryland, and the recent settling of a boundary dispute in 1775 had forced many residents to shift their allegiance from one colony to another. Such territorial tensions only heightened the coming conflict between Clow and Delaware authorities.

On April 18, 1778, recently elected Delaware President Caesar Rodney wrote urgently to his predecessor Thomas McKean about the growing threat: "The night before last a part of the Militia of this County which I ordered out under Lt. Col. Pope of Delaware, against Genl. China Clow, and his army of Refugees, came up with them on the Western Borders of this County, and verry soon routed Mr. Clow and his Army, and burned the Fort."

Rodney added that "This Villain Clow had about one hundred and fifty men, they left in the fort about a thousand weight of Bacon and two barrels of flower which they stole." Ten days later, on April 28, Rodney informed Continental Congress president Henry Laurens that the military had crushed what could have grown into a greater threat to the Revolutionary cause in Delaware. "They increased verry fast," he warned, "and I believe, if they had not been opposed very suddenly and with Spirit, they would have become formidable in a Little time."

In 1782, four years after the fort incident, authorities launched another attempt to capture Clow. Based on the court records cited in the *Delaware Register*, Sheriff John Clayton, anticipating resistance and knowing Clow's reputation for courage, assembled a well-armed posse before proceeding to Clow's house at night, approx-imately twelve miles from Dover. When they arrived, they found the door closed and barred. Clayton identified himself and his official business, demanding that

Clow surrender himself as a prisoner.

Gunfire erupted immediately from the house. Both sides exchanged volleys, as shots splintered through the structure. The violent confrontation left a militiaman named Moore dead. According to the *Delaware Register* account, Clow fired so rapidly that Clayton's men believed multiple defenders occupied the house. When the posse finally breached the door, forcing their way past barricaded furniture, they found only Clow and his wife Elizabeth. Despite a wound in her breast, she molded bullets and loaded guns for her husband throughout the confrontation.

After Sheriff Clayton's men forcibly seized Clow following the violent confrontation at his home, they prepared to escort him under armed guard to Dover. Just before this forced march, Clow requested permission to don his British Army captain's uniform, a final assertion of his allegiance. Clayton, recognizing the charged symbolism yet adhering to protocol, granted Clow's request. He placed Clow on a horse and started toward town, but a militia captain soon rode up in a fury, vowing to "hang the d—d traitor on the nearest tree." Clayton countered this outburst "with a wrath as generous as his determination to maintain the supremacy of the civil power against the military arrogance of the noisy officer," reported *The Philadelphia Times*. Backed by his men, he refused to surrender Clow. The militia captain's attempt to subvert legal procedure exemplified the broader clash between Delaware's civil and military authorities, a divide that ran deep throughout the Revolutionary War.

Clow proceeded with measured steps to Dover under Clayton's custody to face trial. He appeared before the Court of Oyer and Terminer on December 10, charged with treason. Justices William Killen and David Finney presided over a fraught proceeding. Clow confronted the magistrates, pleaded "not guilty," and then reached into his coat to produce his captain's commission in the British Army.

Clow argued that, as an officer in the King's service who had never sworn allegiance to any other government, he was not answerable to the court and must instead be "upon the footing of a prisoner of war."

The law was plain: as an enemy officer, he was a prisoner of war, not a traitor. The judges, after deliberation, acquitted him on the treason charge. However, the court immediately imposed an extraordinary condition—Clow had to enter into a recognizance of ten thousand pounds, with two sureties of five thousand pounds each, to ensure his "good behavior" for the duration of the war. In effect, while legally free, Clow remained imprisoned, as he could not possibly meet such an exorbitant bail.

Five months after his acquittal on the treason charge, prosecutors filed a new indictment for Moore's murder. On May 5, 1783, Clow once again stood before the Court of Oyer and Terminer, this time facing a trial that would seal his fate. Sheriff Clayton testified that Moore had most likely been shot accidentally by his own compatriots during the chaotic raid, killed by a stray bullet fired in the rear of the attacking party.

Colonel Charles Pope, who had led the original militia attack on Clow's fort in 1778, grew visibly agitated by the proceedings. During the trial, according to The Philadelphia Times, he "officiously drew up a troop of horse before the door of the Courthouse with a view, it was thought, of intimidating the jury. A great clamor was raised outside for Clow's conviction."

Clow undertook to defend himself, arguing that it had not been proven he killed Moore—and that even if he had, the shot was fired without malice, in the act of defending himself against an armed assault. As a British officer, he claimed he had the right to defend himself "to the last extremity" against citizens or soldiers attempting to deprive him of his liberty.

Nevertheless, the jury convicted Clow. Sentenced to hang, he returned to his cell. Governor Nicholas Van Dyke questioned the conviction. He delayed, issuing reprieve after reprieve, and confronted a citizenry divided on the question of mercy. Some wrote directly to him urging commutation or banishment in lieu of execution. Others believed Clow's actions warranted nothing less than death. Two petitions, both printed in the September 3, 1783 issue of The Freeman's Journal, capture these opposing opinions in strikingly passionate language.

The petition that sought mercy focused on the legal issue of whether Clow's killing of Moore constituted murder. The signers conceded Clow's poor reputation yet insisted he did not display "malice aforethought," which they viewed as essential to a murder conviction:

"We, therefore, on a due consideration of the whole premises, and full conviction that this unhappy man's crime did not amount to murder, in the estimation of the law, do most respectfully and earnestly recommend him to your excellency for mercy, that you would be pleased to grant him a reprieve, if it can be done with propriety, on condition that he be banished this country."

They stressed the contradictions in eyewitness testimony and worried about a dangerous precedent:

"It was a mere casuality that Mr. Moore was the unhappy man that fell—that any other who had been foremost in the onset, would have shared the same fate."

A second petition flatly rejected that reasoning. The document's signers believed the legal process had been thorough and correct, citing the careful examination of evidence and the unanimous verdict of the jury. Taking offense at any suggestion of court error, they wrote:

"If the petitioners had done this, every code of criminal law would have instructed them, that if the bullet maliciously aimed at the heart of one innocent man, should give a mortal wound to another . . . it would be equally murder in the aggressor as if he had sacrificed the original victim of his will."

They referenced Clow's long history of opposition to the new government:

"But when an abandoned man whose crimes have run parallel with his years . . . crowns his career with an additional murder, God forbid it should be supposed that the power of pardon was ever given to screen such offenders from the sword of justice."

They urged that showing mercy to a "wicked" man amounted to cruelty toward the larger community.

These two petitions sat on Governor Van Dyke's desk, each articulating a vision of justice. The opposing views reflected the broader public divide over Clow's fate. This division continued through Van Dyke's term and into that of his successor, Thomas Collins, who also granted multiple reprieves. By 1788, with the debate still unresolved after six years, Collins felt compelled to enforce the law.

Clow, too, had tired of waiting. In a final plea, he wrote to Collins, declaring that "Life under these circumstances is worse than death." He demanded either a pardon or the swift conclusion of his sentence. That letter became his undoing. Collins signed the death warrant and set the date. "It is said that Clow heard the news of his fate with the utmost composure ... No more he asked for mercy; he complained of his fate no more," reported the *Delaware Register and Farmers Magazine*.

Cheney Clow faced the gallows in the fall or early winter of 1788. He advanced with unwavering resolve, singing a hymn as he ascended the wooden steps. He dropped through the trapdoor, his melody dissolving into stillness. "The effect of the hanging was to immediately turn public favor to his side," the *News Journal* later reflected. "He will go down in history as a victim of party feeling, whose only sin was his reluctance to desert his native land, or at least to curb his tongue."

Cheney Clow's rebellion ended at the end of a rope, but the questions he embodied lingered. The tensions of revolution—loyalty, justice, and mercy—haunted the young nation's struggle to define itself, long after combatants fired the last shots of war.

3

PATTY CANNON, QUEEN OF KIDNAPPERS

A ruthless woman profited from human trafficking.

"She died a most terrible and awful death. After the effects of the poison which she had taken began to take effect, she raved like a maniac, tearing the clothes from off her body, and tore the hair from her head by handfuls, attempting to lay hold and bite everything within her reach, cursing God and the hour that gave her birth."

John Griffin, an alleged associate, provided this dramatic account of Patty Cannon's final hours in the 1841 *Narratives and Confessions of Lucretia P. Cannon*. Like much of the *Narratives*, the scene reflects the exaggerated crime literature of the time—early American pulp stories designed to thrill readers while moralizing on vice and criminality. Folklore and sensationalism have often obscured the real details of Cannon's life and crimes. No author blurred that line more lastingly than Georgetown native George Alfred Townsend, whose 1884 novel *The Entailed Hat* wove Patty into a melodrama of attic dungeons and midnight rides, cementing the lurid version that still circulates today.

The *Narratives* refer to her as "Lucretia," but verified sources, including an indictment published in Oswald Tilghman's 1907 book *Tales of Old Maryland*, name her as Martha Cannon. Likewise, the *Narratives* refer to her husband as "Alonzo," though most historical records name him as Jesse or Jessie Cannon. The *Narratives* also distort other family connections, for example regarding Joe Johnson, who was actually married to her daughter, not her fictional "Lucretia" character.

Patty's daughter Mary, "a noted beauty," married Harry Brereton. The state hanged Brereton in 1814 for murdering a slave trader named Ridgeway. After Brereton's execution, Mary married Joe Johnson, who became Cannon's primary business partner. Together, Cannon and the Johnson brothers, Joe and Ebenezer, ran what court papers reveal to be a family enterprise: a November 1821 indictment named six defendants—Joe Johnson, his wife Mary Cannon Johnson, Patty (listed as Martha), her husband Jesse Sr., their son Jesse Jr., and accomplice John Stevenson—all charged with kidnapping a free Black man, Thomas Spence. Joe Johnson operated a tavern near Patty's home, which became a gathering place for slave traders and was a key part of the kidnapping operation.

Patty's son Jesse, according to contemporary accounts, was "nearing the age of manhood... little better even at this age than a perfect sot." He disappointed his mother by associating with "a set of low, drinking, gambling, and licentious persons."

Patty Cannon was a striking woman of formidable strength and presence. The *Baltimore Sun* described her as "a large and handsome woman who found life extremely well worth living." She had "thick black hair, flashing black eyes, and walked with a swaying, swashbuckling gait" as she served drinks in Johnson's tavern.

Legends of her physical prowess abounded. Though of average height, she was "so powerful that she often threw a towering slave and tied him securely." She could also "lift a full bag of wheat off the ground and put it in a cart while standing in a bushel basket." Her handbag was a deep pocket in her petticoat, where she kept a rope and pistol "always ready," drawing them with remarkable speed.

Beyond brute strength, she took pleasure in wrestling, personally ejecting troublemakers and subduing strangers in public challenges. During kidnappings, she would hogtie men with the ropes concealed in her skirts. "Woe to the darkey who happened to meet her alone on the county road," warned the *Baltimore Sun*, for she could "grapple with a strapping negro, tie him hand and foot and throw him unaided into a wagon."

The freed slaves kidnapped by Cannon and her gang endured horrific conditions. Captors imprisoned victims in a "n-keep" in the attic of Johnson's tavern—a dungeon "twelve feet square, built of heavy oak" with ring bolts where they chained captives.

The kidnappers divided the space into two rooms, leaving the back one completely windowless. A barred transom above the double door provided the only ventilation, while heavy iron fastenings reinforced the entrance.

Cannon's own house contained a similar makeshift jail. Her gang disposed of any infants born to imprisoned women who were too young to be sold, burying their small bodies in Cannon's personal graveyard in her garden among the other victims.

Escaping these confines proved nearly impossible. Only one man ever got out, prying open the attic trapdoor while briefly left unattended and "making his way to the town of Seaford still shackled before his chains were finally cut off." For the others, a horrific fate awaited: sale into slavery in the South or death at Cannon's hands to silence them.

Patty Cannon's rise began amid the chaos of the War of 1812. She and her crew kidnapped Black men whom the British had recruited to fight against the Americans, according to the News Journal. The British had promised freedom and resettlement to these soldiers, but many found themselves stranded and vulnerable after the war.

Cannon and followers exploited this situation, capturing and selling them into slavery. These British-trained men, unfamiliar with the region and lacking local allies, became easy targets. While local authorities could not officially sanction such kidnappings, they allegedly turned a blind eye when these soldiers vanished. The gang profited by selling them to Georgia slave dealers, with Johnson's Tavern, named for Cannon's son-in-law, as the central hub for these transactions.

Cannon's ruffians sought new opportunities to expand their reach. They initially faced little effective opposition from the law despite the horrific nature of their crimes. Legal authorities attempted to stop them, but their efforts largely failed. This sense of impunity emboldened the miscreants to prey on other victims, including operatives within the slave trade.

Cannon selected a more audacious target in 1814: a slave trader named Ridgeway, who had recently stopped at the tavern. Finding no slaves for sale, Ridgeway continued toward Laurel, carrying a large sum of money. Patty Cannon, the Griffin brothers, and her son-in-law Harry Brereton spurred their horses forward, galloping ahead to Slabtown, a mile above Cannon's Ferry. They crossed the river in a skiff and reached a bend in the road before Ridgeway arrived. There, they piled brush and saplings across the path to force him to stop.

Patty, disguised as a man, urged the gang on. As Ridgeway's wagon slowed, they emerged from the shadows and opened fire, striking Ridgeway and wounding his horse. The animal panicked, bolting forward as Ridgeway, mortally wounded, struggled to draw his pistol. "Before he could fire, his horse reared and crashed through the brush, dragging his lifeless body toward Laurel Town. Ridgeway clung to life until the next day before succumbing to his wounds."

This murder, while shocking, did not immediately lead to Cannon's own downfall. But law enforcement could not ignore the killing of a white man in the slave trade. Investigators eventually traced Ridgeway's killing to the Griffin brothers, Brereton, and other unnamed accomplices. They captured Brereton, tried him, and hanged him in 1814, yet Patty Cannon remained at large, continuing her crimes for another fifteen years. In 1822 the law finally caught up with her son-in-law Joe Johnson. A Georgetown jury convicted him of kidnapping; on 4 June the sheriff administered thirty-nine lashes and an hour in the pillory with his ears nailed to the boards, the planned ear-cropping spared only by a last-minute gubernatorial reprieve.

Not long after the Ridgeway murder, another potential victim walked into Patty Cannon's trap. A slave trader seeking to buy kidnapped slaves arrived at her house and let slip that he carried $15,000 in cash. That night, as he sat with his back to an open window, eating supper, Patty Cannon slipped up behind him from the yard and shot him in the head with a horse pistol. She and her henchmen buried him in the garden. Cyrus James, a bound servant boy, witnessed the burial but kept silent. (Accounts differ on whether James was Black or a white indentured servant; if he was white, his testimony would have been admissible under 1829 Sussex rules that barred Black witnesses against former masters.) Years later, when lawmen finally arrested Patty Cannon, James testified about what he had seen.

Cannon, along with members of her gang, faced trial in 1821 for kidnapping. But the charges didn't stick. The difficulty of enforcing anti-kidnapping laws during this period appears in cases like that of three free Black apprentices from Delaware— Samuel, James, and Hannah—who disappeared under suspicious circumstances in 1820. W. P. Goslin held them in Fredericksburg, Virginia, and claimed ownership based on a purported bill of sale from his brother-in-law, John Anderson. These two traffickers, the *Baltimore Morning Chronicle* reported, had "taken these blacks clandestinely from their homes and firesides" and fabricated papers "for the purpose of giving color to such outrageous enormity," targeting the apprentices not out of personal animus but "in defiance of the laws of humanity, and in contempt of the ties of domestic life."

A habeas corpus proceeding before Judge John W. Green of Virginia's Superior Court of Chancery exposed the fraud. Green, exercising authority in the absence of action from Delaware's courts, ruled that the captives had been wrongfully held and ordered that each "be forthwith discharged from imprisonment."

Two private citizens from Delaware, Henry M. Goodwin and Tristram McCauley, appeared to support the captives' case and assist in presenting evidence of their free status. Although justice prevailed in this instance, the case revealed how traffickers like Cannon colluded to fabricate legitimacy—and how rarely victims found recourse when left to the fragile protections of their home states.

Cannon and her son-in-law Joe Johnson had built their homes strategically on the Delaware-Maryland border, exploiting jurisdictional loopholes. If Maryland authorities sought to arrest them, they would simply step across into Delaware, and vice versa. This geographic advantage allowed them to operate with near impunity for years.

The Cannon gang's activities reached a frenzied peak between 1825 and 1829. They kidnapped men, women, and children, often transporting them to Cannon's property before shipping them south. Her operation extended far beyond local kidnappings. The Cannon network employed mixed-race accomplices who worked as recruiters in northern cities, luring unsuspecting free Black people onto vessels bound for slavery.

In the summer of 1826, as Cornelius Sinclair walked through Philadelphia, a mixed race man approached him and offered work unloading melons from a sloop. The opportunity seemed like an innocent chance to earn a few coins. Instead, once aboard, captors seized Sinclair, took him below deck, and confined him. They "carried [him] first to the line of Delaware and Maryland and thence transported [him] by land and water to Alabama," reported the *National Gazette* on June 30, 1826.

Johnson and Cannon's operation used this vessel as a floating prison, moving human cargo down the coast.

Sinclair's harrowing experience was part of a larger coordinated abduction. During the same 1826 operation, Cannon's network kidnapped several other individuals alongside Sinclair: Enos Tilghman, Alexander Manlove, Samuel, and Joe (a chimney sweep). The group suffered a brutal journey southward through Cannon's trafficking pipeline. Tragically, Joe never reached freedom. He "died at Rocky Spring, in consequence of the cruel beating he received from Abraham F. Johnson, one of the kidnappers," said the National Gazette.

Sinclair, who faced the threat of vanishing into the brutal southern slave system after his sale in Tuscaloosa, Alabama, returned to freedom after an intense rescue campaign. The United States Gazette stated on July 4, 1826, that a widely publicized search had located him and that he was "now on his passage" back to Philadelphia.

The Gazette went on to credit Philadelphia Mayor Joseph Watson with securing the freedom of Tilghman and Manlove as well, praising his "indefatigable and charitable zeal." "Kidnappers took Alexander Raymon, alias Manlove, Enos Tilghman, and Samuel Scamps months ago, but the Mayors of Natchez and Philadelphia worked to restore their liberty," said the paper. "This morning, they returned home in the brig Catharine from New Orleans."

These two mayors did not intervene because the kidnapped men held positions of power; rather, they acted in response to the widespread trafficking of free African Americans. Philadelphia Mayor Watson had launched an ongoing campaign to confront kidnapping rings that targeted free Black Northerners for sale into slavery. His efforts extended well beyond the Sinclair case, involving coordinated investigations, correspondence with southern officials—including in Natchez—and repeated attempts to reclaim the abducted. Such cooperation proved rare and often depended on the willingness of local authorities to uphold justice across state lines.

Women kidnapped by Patty Cannon's gang confronted additional dangers, especially those traveling alone, like Mary Fisher. Abductors seized the middle-aged, unmarried Fisher near Elkton, Maryland—despite her having lived free for years—and transported her south. With no male companions who might have resisted her captors, and likely facing threats of sexual violence common to female captives, Fisher had few options for escape or self-defense during her ordeal.

J.W. Hamilton of Rocky Spring, Mississippi, who would later offer her sanctuary, wrote a letter to verify Fisher's identity and free status. Published in the *United States Gazette* on March 3, 1826, Hamilton's letter described her in detail: "MARY FISHER, aged from 40 to 50 years, says she was set free by William Berry in Dover... She is known to John Dill, Frederica -- John Lape, Esq Smyrna -- Isaac Wright, North West Fork. She has lived with Widow Anderson, Elkton. Her father's name Benjamin Davis -- freed by Benjamin Tow -- was taken from Delaware by said Johnson, fall past was a year. -- Her height about 5 feet 5 inches, stout made."

The *National Gazette* noted on June 30: "The woman, Mary Fisher, has been restored to freedom, and is under the protection of J. W. Hamilton, of Mississippi, where she chose to remain rather than encounter the sufferings of a sea voyage home."

The ordeals of Sinclair, Tilghman, Manlove, and Fisher were not the only stories to emerge from Cannon's reign of terror. The *National Gazette* published Peter Hook's tale on January 27, 1827, offering perhaps the most detailed first-person account. Born in Philadelphia to Peter and Betsey Hook, Peter grew up in Currant Alley between Walnut and Locust Streets. His father had once worked as a coachman for Mr. Hartman Kuhn.

In June 1825, kidnappers seized Peter Hook, the son, when he met "a black man whom they called John" who persuaded him to go to a schooner near Arch Street wharf for a drink. There, a white man named Joe Johnson confronted him, drew a long knife across his throat and said, "if you halloo, god damn you, I'll kill you," before dragging him below deck and tying and chaining him to the pump.

"That same night, two more boys—William Miller, who lived on South Street, and Milton Trusty, a chimney sweep from Eighth and Spruce Streets—were brought aboard and chained alongside Hook," reported the Gazette. "The next evening, two additional black boys, Clement Cox and William Chase, joined them, all secured below decks. After three days at anchor, the vessel sailed out of the harbor, and the captives saw the lighthouse at Cape Henlopen before landing a day later.

"The five boys were then taken by night in a carryall and gig," continues Hook's story, "passed Lewistown [Lewes] about day light, and stopped at Joe Johnson's house, a tavern, on the road six miles from Lewistown, saw Abraham F. Johnson, Joe's Brother, and his wife, there, where all five were chained to a staple in the floor of the garret."

Over the next several weeks, more captives arrived: John Jacobs, a cart driver from Philadelphia; James Bayard, a chimney sweep; Benjamin Baxter from South Street; "Little Jack," a small black boy; Ephraim Lawrence and "little (hopping) John," who had both worked for a Mr. Hurst in Philadelphia; and "black Henry," a young man. "The 12 were all chained to the same staple," Hook related.

The Cannon gang kept the captives imprisoned in the attic prison for approximately six months before moving them again. One night, "the twelve boys and two girls were taken down, walked six or seven miles, and were put on board a ship by Joe Johnson, and set sail." After a six-day journey, they landed somewhere near the Chesapeake Bay and then spent a month traveling overland until they reached Rockingham, Virginia.

Johnson "chained the large boys two and two, but not the small ones. They travelled generally on bye roads. Were not permitted to talk to any one they met; always encamped out. Were severely whipped by Johnson, for saying we were free; though he never whipped me," Hook recounted.

Johnson sold the captives to "Mr. Miller and Josias Sutler, near Rockingham," who transported them to Mississippi. According to Hook, he and three others—William

---

"The twelve were all chained to the same staple, ... where they remained for six months."

PETER HOOK

Miller, John Jacobs, and James Bayard—"were sold to Mr. Perryman, for $450 a piece, last winter" while "the other six free ones were taken on by Sutler.

Hook's vivid recollections, along with the stories of Sinclair, Fisher, and the others, provide a rare and devastating glimpse into the human toll of Cannon's criminal enterprise. Each represents not just a statistic but a life interrupted—people with families, connections, and futures violently redirected into the brutal southern slave system. Their return to freedom demonstrated not only the captives' extraordinary determination and fortitude but also the potential of coordinated law enforcement efforts. When properly motivated, authorities could reach across state lines to restore justice. The beginning of Cannon's end came in the spring of 1829. A tenant on her farm, clearing brush from a low-lying area, noticed his horse sinking into the ground. As he investigated, he uncovered a chest filled with human bones. The grisly discovery led to further excavations, revealing multiple graves and dismembered remains.

Witnesses soon came forward. One man, arrested in Maryland, confessed that Cannon and the Johnson brothers "did kill and murder, against the Peace and Dignity of the State," then buried numerous individuals on the property. Their victims included travelers who carried large sums of money, as well as kidnapped free Blacks whose deaths ensured silence.

Prosecutors filed an indictment against Cannon on April 13, 1829, charging her as an accessory "not having the fear of God before her eyes, but being moved and seduced by the instigation of the Devil." The bill alleged her role in the murder of a young Black boy (Sussex Co. Indictment, April Term 1829). The following month the Sussex County grand jury also charged her with the deaths of three infants seven years earlier, alleging she "with both her hands, about the neck of the said infant female child ... did choke and strangle," then buried the bodies in her garden.

The court also indicted Joe Johnson and Ebenezer Johnson on separate murder charges, alleging they "feloniously, wilfully, and of their malice aforethought" beat their victim to death with a wooden club. Sussex County held Cannon in custody and scheduled her trial for the Court of Oyer and Terminer in October.

Georgetown police jailed her while she awaited trial. But true to her nature, she would not let the law decide her fate.

Cannon allegedly took poison one day before her scheduled execution. She refused to relinquish control, even in her demise. The United States Gazette (May 22, 1829) confirms her death in prison but does not describe her final moments in the manner recorded in the 1841 Narratives and Confessions of Lucretia P. Cannon. The Narratives, not a verified contemporary news source, created the dramatic details—raving, tearing at her hair, and cursing.

With her passing, one of the most brutal criminal enterprises in Delaware history ended. Patty Cannon and her hooligans left lasting scars on the lives of the kidnapped and the region's collective memory.

For the free Black men, women, and children who survived, the trauma of their ordeal did not vanish with Cannon's undoing. Families torn apart were never made whole. The system that enabled her crimes endured, the violence shifting forms but never fully disappearing.

Stripped of lurid embellishments, Cannon's story reveals more than just one woman's wickedness. Her saga testifies to how lawlessness festers when cruelty is tolerated, when profit justifies human suffering, and when the powerful turn away.

Nearly two centuries later, the echoes of her crimes still linger along the banks of the Nanticoke River. If these waters could speak, they would tell us what we already know: that justice delayed is often justice forever denied, leaving only memory to bear the burden where the law could not.

4

THE
DOVER
EIGHT

The daring escape of eight freedom seekers.

Eight freedom seekers from Dorchester County, Maryland, slipped into Dover on Tuesday, March 10, 1857, braving the sharp chill of a moonlit night. After two days of hard, backwoods travel, they reached this strategic waypoint on their carefully planned route of safe houses leading north toward Philadelphia. They all fled the Bucktown area of Maryland.

Among them were Thomas Elliott and Denard Hughes, who had escaped the plantation of Pritchett Meredith. In his testimony to William Still, a Philadelphia abolitionist whose meticulous records preserved countless Underground Railroad stories, Hughes described Meredith as "the hardest man around." Hughes painted a particularly harsh picture of life under the Merediths, noting that his mistress, at eighty-three years of age, "drank hard" and was "very stormy," despite being a member of the Methodist Church.

Henry Predeaux a twenty-seven-year-old man described by contemporaries as a "giant," had fled from Judge Ara Spence's property after threats of being sold south. Among the group were two married couples: William Kiah, who belonged to Benjamin G. Tubman (no relation to Harriet), and his wife Emily, owned by Ann Craig of the Lake family in Vienna, Maryland; and James and Lavinia Woolfley. An eighth person, whose name has been lost to history, completed the group. They had armed themselves with "cudgels and pistols," knowing well the dangers that lay ahead, said The Dover Reporter (March 13, 1857).

They traveled through the marshy terrain of Maryland's Eastern Shore, finding brief sanctuary with trusted allies. The Reverend Samuel Green, a free Black minister in East New Market, provided temporary shelter. From there, they made their way to Poplar Neck, where Ben Ross, Harriet Tubman's father, concealed them in his cabin. Harriet had likely shaped their escape route, as she knew the Bucktown area intimately from her own childhood in slavery.

Relying on trusted couriers, she had provided detailed instructions on which safe houses to seek and which conductors to trust along the Underground Railroad. One such conductor, William Brinkly, later wrote to the Philadelphia Vigilance Committee, the abolitionist network aiding fugitive slaves, about the perils of his work: "We put them throug, we hav to carry them 19 mils and cum back the sam night wich maks 38 mils. It is tou much for our littel horses. We must do the bes we can, ther is much Bisness dun on this Road. We hay to go throw dover and smerny, the two wors places this sid of mary land lin."

The Dover Eight's escape unfolded on the very eve of the Supreme Court's Dred Scott decision, which was handed down on March 6, 1857—just two days after the group reached Dover. In that ruling, Chief Justice Roger B. Taney declared that no Black person, whether enslaved or free, could claim U.S. citizenship, and that Congress held no authority to prohibit slavery in federal territories.

The decision emboldened slaveholders and outraged abolitionists, deepening sectional tensions and sowing widespread fear among free and fugitive Black communities alike. Though not directly linked to the Dover Eight's ordeal, the decision sharpened the stakes of every escape attempt. The ruling signaled that the federal government, far from acting as a neutral arbiter, had aligned itself with the interests of slaveholding power. Against that backdrop, the daring flight of eight men and women through Delaware's contested ground carried even greater urgency.

Word of the Dorchester County freedom seekers' escape spread quickly. Pritchett Meredith placed an advertisement in the *Baltimore Sun* as early as March 11, offering $600 for the return of Elliott and Hughes alone. He suspected they might seek help from Elliott's uncle, Moses Pinket, who lived in Wilmington. Together, the combined bounty totaled $3,000—a sum that, in today's terms, would amount to nearly $100,000.

Thomas Otwell, a free Black man living near Milford, had previously proven himself as a reliable conductor on the Underground Railroad, helping other freedom seekers navigate the dangerous passage through Delaware. His home had served as a waystation. But the promise of such a substantial reward proved too tempting.

U.R. operative Thomas Garrett, one of the most important conductors in the mid-Atlantic region, received the news. Operating from his home in Wilmington, Garrett had established himself as a vital link in the network of safe houses stretching north toward Philadelphia. His position in Wilmington was strategically crucial—the city served as one of the last major stops for freedom seekers before reaching Pennsylvania. Through his network of trusted messengers and fellow conductors, Garrett helped coordinate the dangerous passage of escapees through Delaware, often racing against slave catchers and hostile authorities.

On March 13, Thomas Garrett urgently wrote to his cousin Samuel Rhoads: "I have a letter this day from an agent of the Underground Rail Road, near Dover, in this state, saying I must be on the look out for six brothers and two sisters, they were decoyed and betrayed, he says by a colored man named Thomas Otwell, who pretended to be their friend, and sent a white scamp ahead to wait for them at Dover till they arrived; they were arrested and put in Jail there, with Tom's assistance, and some officers."

The treacherous trap snapped shut around 4 a.m. Tuesday morning. Only once the eight freedom seekers were inside and climbing the jail stairs did "they discover[ed] the iron bars and the fact that they had been betrayed," wrote William Still in his 1872 account of the event. The contemporary account in *The Dover Reporter* provides additional detail: "While the Sheriff was dressing, they all entered the jail, went up stairs (in the dark), found an open room, and went into it, but there being no fire, they came out into the entry."

Otwell had callously remarked they would "soon have a good warming," a cruel double meaning—ostensibly referring to the promised fire but also invoking the common mid-nineteenth century jail slang for a severe beating. Henry Predeaux's suspicions were immediately aroused. He declared he "did not like the looks of the place." Sheriff Robert Bell, seeing his ruse beginning to unravel, retreated to his quarters to retrieve his pistol.

Chaos unspooled. The group pressed after the sheriff into his private quarters, where his wife and children lay sleeping. There, according to *The Dover Reporter's* contemporary account, Predeaux seized a shovel of fire from the fireplace and scattered the hot coals across the floor. The sheriff's family awoke in panic, adding to the commotion of the scene.

The fugitives seized their chance. Back in the hallway, one member of the group bolted for a window. While the sheriff struggled with this first escapee, the others burst through a second window. Predeaux grabbed a heavy andiron from the fireplace and smashed out the remaining glass and frame of the second window to ensure a clear escape path. They all dropped twelve feet to the ground below. They faced yet another obstacle—"a high wall that seemed to promise recapture." Driven by desperation, they scaled it. The sheriff attempted one last shot at Predeaux as he climbed, but his pistol misfired, allowing the final escapee to disappear into the night.

Now scattered, the Dover Eight faced crucial decisions. Six of them, including Elliott and Hughes, backtracked along their route and encountered Otwell again. "It is a wonder that they acted with so much coolness and discretion," Thomas Garrett later observed in a letter documented by William Still. "One of the men told me he would have killed [Otwell] at once had he not thought, if he did do it, he would have less chance to escape than if they committed no act of violence, which no doubt was a correct view."

"Six of them were tracked to a house in Camden, but the officers could not enter for the want of authority," said *The Dover Reporter*. "The magistrates said they had no power to give."

Armed with their knives and pistols, the freedom seekers forced Otwell to lead them toward Willow Grove. By nightfall, they had reached William Brinkly's home, preparing for the next leg of their journey.

Lavinia Woolfley lost contact with her husband James during the getaway. She "managed to stay in hiding in Delaware for several months before finally finding her way into Pennsylvania" and would eventually reunite with James in Canada, according to William Still's records.

Thomas Garrett was already coordinating their passage, writing an urgent letter to his cousin Samuel Rhoads warning that the fugitives' owners had "persons stationed at several places on the road watching." Brinkly and his associates prepared to move the group to Garrett with calculated, swift movements. Each moment could mean the difference between freedom and recapture. The freedom seekers did reach Garrett safely, guided through the final stretch by their Delaware allies under cover of darkness and constant threat.

Meanwhile, Predeaux had struck out alone toward Wilmington, eventually finding his way to Thomas Garrett's home.

The aftermath of the escape reverberated throughout the region. "Our town was thrown into considerable excitement," exclaimed *The Dover Reporter*, "in consequence of an almost successful attempt to capture eight runaway slaves." But the implications reached far beyond Dover. Slaveholders in Maryland convened emergency meetings, demanding stricter patrols and harsher penalties for "runaways." On April 14, 1857, a group of prominent Dorchester County slaveholders convened a hasty meeting to "devise means for a better protection of the slave property [sic]."

Sheriff Bell descended on Reverend Samuel Green's house with a search warrant that same month. Green, a free Black man living in Dorchester County, Maryland, had long been suspected of aiding freedom seekers, and rumors of his involvement had circulated even before the Dover Eight's escape. The discovery that the group had passed near his home only deepened that suspicion.

Bell crossed state lines to pursue Green—an extraordinary move in an era before state police or formal extradition protocols. His actions reflected the improvisational nature of antebellum law enforcement, when sheriffs often exercised wide latitude, driven as much by local loyalties and political pressure as by legal precedent.

During the search, officials found items they claimed implicated Green in Underground Railroad activities: a map of Canada, letters from runaway slaves in Ontario, several railroad route schedules through New Jersey, a letter from his son Samuel Green Jr. (who had fled bondage three years earlier), and a copy of *Uncle Tom's Cabin*. Though they lacked direct evidence linking him to the Dover Eight, Maryland prosecutors used the possession of abolitionist literature as a pretext for arrest. A Dorchester County court sentenced Green to ten years in the Maryland State Penitentiary, though he ultimately served just over five. Maryland Governor Augustus W. Bradford pardoned him in March 1862, on the condition that he leave the state within sixty days.

The Dover Eight's escape also placed Harriet Tubman's family in immediate peril. Her father, Ben Ross, had sheltered the eight runaways in his cabin at Poplar Neck. Garrett later wrote that the original party might have been nine, noting they were "betrayed by one who started with the rest," who "turned back and informed on the man who piloted them, and told where they went to stop over the first day" at Ben's house. As rumors of Ross's involvement circulated, someone warned him that authorities would likely arrest him. Recognizing danger, Tubman acted swiftly. She returned to Maryland in summer 1857 to rescue her elderly parents and relocate them to Canada, protecting them from potential arrest and re-enslavement.

The Dover Eight dispersed across the northern United States and Canada, their paths reflecting the broader migration of freedom seekers. Thomas Elliott and Denard Hughes settled initially in St. Catharine's, Ontario. Harriet Tubman considered recruiting Hughes to potentially support John Brown's anti-slavery efforts. Elliott later moved to Auburn, New York, where he married Tubman's great-niece Ann Marie Stewart and had two daughters. William and Emily Kiah, who adopted the surname Williams, also settled in Auburn, returning to Philadelphia in 1860 to help their daughter Mary escape to freedom.

James and Lavinia Woolfley reunited in Canada after Lavinia's harrowing separate journey, during which she hid in Delaware for months before finding her way north. Henry Predeaux, celebrated for his quick thinking during the escape, seems to have disappeared from historical records after 1857, with his fate remaining unknown. The eighth member remains entirely anonymous, their name and subsequent life unrecorded in the available historical documents.

The Dover Eight's escape joined many daring flights to freedom that revealed cracks in the institution of slavery. Their story, widely circulated in abolitionist newspapers, reinforced the constant danger faced by those seeking liberty and those who aided them. The flight also highlighted the fragility of trust along the Underground Railroad, where betrayal could come from unexpected places.

Though the escape did not alter history on its own, the episode was part of a wider resistance that, in the years leading up to the Civil War, made slavery harder to enforce. The Dover Eight, like many others who took freedom into their own hands, intensified the growing pressure that ultimately forced the nation to confront the question of freedom on a far larger scale.

5

DECAPITATION FOR INSURANCE MONEY

A calculated crime revealed underlying racial tensions.

In the broader context of post-Reconstruction Delaware, Isaac C. West's actions cannot be seen in isolation. Delaware, positioned in a region still grappling with the legacy of the Civil War, operated under a legal system steeped in racial prejudice. The state had symbolically rejected the Thirteenth Amendment in 1865 (though Congress ratified it nationally), signaling its resistance to racial progress. Societal norms and state policies continued to perpetuate inequality in Delaware right into the early 1870s. That climate enabled a well-connected white man to escape full accountability for an 1872 murder, while his victim, a Black laborer named Peter "Cooch" Turner, carried no weight in the eyes of the law.

After completing degrees in both law and medicine at Dickinson College in 1868, 25-year-old Isaac C. West returned to his native Dover and took work as an assistant teacher at a private prep school that the Methodist Episcopal Church operated. The pay wasn't to his liking, though, and he bragged to friends that a Milford prep school had dangled $1,200 a year in front of him, and that he would surely get rich from that salary. He never moved to Milford.

By 1872 Isaac West had hatched the idea of starting a museum of curiosities and acquired a mummified human arm and other pieces of jetsam and flotsam for this latest project. All sat in boxes in his house.

That same year West opened a medical storefront in Dover, offering a gaseous treatment that he claimed cured tuberculosis. "The real purpose of the gas, it seems, was its inhalation for its wonderful exhilarating effects, it being nothing more than nitrous oxide gas disguised with a color," snorted *The New York Herald* at West's trial.

By now, West's grandiosity had plunged him into financial trouble. He needed cash fast. In the summer of 1872, he took out a $25,000 life insurance policy payable to his new wife Mary. The townsfolk knew he dealt with gasses that were highly flammable. What if, one day, his medical storefront exploded and killed him, causing a fire that burned down the building? That would be believable, wouldn't it? He could plan a rendezvous point with Mary far from Dover and meet her once she had collected the insurance money.

The problem was he needed a dead body found after the explosion. And so, in the early fall of 1872, he hired a poor itinerant worker, a Black man named Peter "Cooch" Turner, as an assistant. Turner lived alone and, as far as records show, had no immediate family nearby. Problem solved.

Ah, but the authorities would find body parts after the "explosion," and realize they were looking at the body of a Black man, not a white man. West would have to skin Turner's body, and remove head, hands, and feet in order for the discovered parts to pass as white. Then he'd bury the leftovers far from the scene.

In November, West got as far as killing Turner, skinning the body, removing the head, and burying it in his planned spot. However, he made a crucial mistake. After the murder, he'd gone to a local hardware store and purchased gunpowder and a large auger drill, which raised the suspicions of the shopkeeper. West's plan was to bore holes in the floor, put the gunpowder beneath, light a fire on the top floor, and have fuses to the gunpowder just at the opening of the holes. By the time the whole place blew, the gunpowder wouldn't leave an obvious trace.

Police started poking around. West skinned Turner and removed his hands and feet but ran of time to bury them. Knowing he was hours, if not minutes, away from being caught, he threw everything into a large duffel bag, started the fire on the second floor, and grabbed a train headed south.

Fire authorities contained the blaze before it reached the first floor. Police found the mangled body, the holes, the gunpowder, and realized they were looking at a "put up job" (i.e. a staged event). The search for a murderer began.

West got as far as Salisbury. His jittery demeanor and the rank smell of his damp duffel bag gave him away, and authorities seized him within hours. He confessed to killing Turner, and officials returned him to Dover for trial.

West leveraged his family connections to hire the best lawyer available: ex-Delaware senator Willard Saulsbury. The trial caused a sensation, and newspapers nation-wide followed it closely. The affair "brought out many ladies and spinsters of high degree, and many dowagers of blooded ancestry that Dover and its environs boast," trumpeted The New York Herald correspondent dispatched to cover the melodrama.

And the *Wilmington Daily Commercial* observed the presence of Anna E. Dickinson, her mother and brother, who "occupied seats to the left of the Judges during the trial." These were Dickinsons descended from Revolutionary War hero John Dickinson, and benefactors of Dickinson College.

The trial stretched over a full week. The eloquent and highly regarded Saulsbury persuaded the jury that, while West had technically murdered Turner, he had acted in self-defense. The court acquitted him on June 10, 1873.

The proceedings exposed a judicial system that prioritized social status over fairness. With white character witnesses and an all-white jury—as Delaware barred Black citizens from jury service until the 1880s—West's well-established connections tipped the scales in his favor.

Howls of protest rose immediately everywhere outside of Dover. Said a letter to the editor in *The Daily* Gazette [Wilmington] of June 11: "If Cooch Turner had been a white man and Isaac C. West a negro there would have been no difficulty about conviction for so terrible a crime."

"The only conclusion that can be arrived at," cried the *Philadelphia Enquirer* that same day, "is that the hawbucks of Delaware, the passionate advocates of the tortures of the whipping post and pillory, do not regard it as a crime for a white man—especially a white man of good social position—to kill a negro."

And the *Baltimore Sun*: "Justice, which is popularly supposed never to sleep, was slumbering this time, or rather, its accredited representatives were in the arms of Morpheus."

Isaac West still stood trial later that year for the arson connected with the case, potentially a capital crime if lives were lost as a result. Since Turner was already dead at the time West set his storefront aflame, the court sentenced West to only two years in prison and fined him $500. His wife Mary left him.

After his release, Isaac West fled to Dallas, Texas, seeking distance from the scandal that ruined his reputation. He established a more traditional medical practice by 1890, married Willie Boales in 1900, and remained free until his death in 1913 at age 71.

The Turner-West case reminds us that when justice becomes contingent on identity, it ceases to be justice at all, becoming instead another tool of oppression. This 1872 murder illustrates how the state's legal institutions sanctioned racial violence through calculated leniency, leaving a stain of inequity that echoes into the present day.

6

SMUGGLERS IN LEWES

Coastal gangs test local law enforcement.

Major James B. Morris knew he had stepped into something big. In the winter of 1876, during a seemingly routine investigation, he uncovered what he later described as "a very city of smugglers, and they have all been so closely allied together and the authorities so weak and impotent that nothing could be done with them." His words, published in the *Morning Herald* on January 21, 1876, highlighted the extent to which smuggling had embedded itself in Lewes' economy, even as the town continued to thrive in its many legal industries.

"Lewes, though not a large town, is fruitful in smugglers," observed the *Middletown Transcript* in 1876, and indeed, smuggling had long flourished along the Delaware coastline. A January 30, 1816, article in the *Delaware Gazette* exposed the deep roots of this illicit trade, reporting concerns that pilots colluded with smugglers to bring goods ashore under cover of darkness. The article notably warned that "revenue officers could never secure revenue in the Delaware district if the pilots and smugglers united."

This state of affairs persisted well into the century. For decades, smuggling remained an open secret, an accepted part of life in a town dependent on the sea. But in 1874, federal and state officials suddenly cracked down. Authorities made swift arrests, followed by trials, as smugglers who once operated with impunity now faced heavy fines and prison time. What had shifted?

Economic pressures, which reshaped trade patterns and law enforcement priorities, played a key role in the new offensive. The Panic of 1873 had thrown the United States into one of the worst financial crises of the nineteenth century. The collapse of Jay Cooke & Company, a banking powerhouse heavily involved in railroad financing, sent shockwaves through the economy. Bank failures, layoffs, and a severe contraction of credit left both businesses and state governments scrambling for revenue. Delaware, a small state with limited industry, felt the squeeze.

With the federal government losing tariff revenues from decreased imports, and Delaware itself facing declining tax revenues, pursuing smugglers suddenly became an attractive proposition. Every pound of sugar, every cask of alcohol, and every shipment of cigars that entered Lewes without customs payments represented money that should have gone into government coffers. Smugglers weren't just violating trade laws; they were depriving state and federal officials of desperately needed funds. Fining them—or better yet, confiscating their goods—became an easy way to recoup losses.

U.S. Marshal John M. Dunn, a Republican appointee of President Ulysses S. Grant, marched into Lewes in 1874 with grand ambition. Determined to "exterminate the entire gang of Lewes smugglers and forever banish them from the shadow of the Breakwater," as The Daily Gazette put it, he organized an expedition with twenty-five to thirty deputies and two newspaper reporters to document his success.

While this public show of force drew attention, Treasury Agent J.S. Chalker and Major James B. Morris worked behind the scenes, gathering intelligence on smuggling networks. Morris, stationed in Lewes, stayed at a boarding house run by Miss Mary E. Wells. She accidentally revealed too much, saying, "others were guilty of smuggling as well as Joshua Ellegood, whom authorities had arrested," before her brother abruptly silenced her.

The July 8, 1874 Wilmington Daily Gazette reported on a dramatic raid that had taken place in April, with Dunn's team descending on Lewes under cover of night via the revenue cutter Hamilton. They arrested seven men, including Joshua H. Ellegood, William Crosby, and Andrew Baker, all of whom were deeply involved in smuggling operations. Testimony about chinaware smuggled from the barque Chili in March 1874 revealed the intimate and personal mechanics of smuggling.

W.H. Ellegood described how the steward and crew members first brought two cases of china ashore in the barque's own long boat, seeking $18 for their contraband. When they arrived at his father's house offering their wares, the Ellegoods declined to buy.

From his vantage point a mile away, the younger Ellegood watched as the sailors rowed their boat downstream, eventually stopping at Andrew Baker's house. W.A. Schofield, who was present at Baker's when the sailors arrived with their casks of china, testified to the casual nature of such transactions: "We promised to look at them if they would bring them ashore."

The sailors obliged, but Schofield "refused to buy, and I went away leaving the sailors there." Such scenes played out regularly along the Delaware shore, with contraband moving from ship to shore to buyer through a web of personal connections and quiet negotiations.

The *Wilmington Morning Herald* (January 21, 1876) revealed that Treasury Agent Chalker had carefully built his case over months of surveillance. What he discovered wasn't just a small ring of professional smugglers, but rather a community where smuggling had become a common practice, with townspeople routinely collaborating to bring in untaxed sugar, coffee, and other goods for their own use.

The enforcement of smuggling laws didn't just serve the cause of justice—it served the interests of those in power. Marshal Dunn stood to gain political capital from the raids, reinforcing his position as a tough-on-crime federal officer. For Republicans in Delaware, still trying to solidify their post-Civil War influence in a traditionally Democratic state, proving that they could enforce federal law effectively was a valuable political tool.

When Marshal Dunn arrived in Lewes, "the town was violently agitated and the people suspecting something of the kind flocked upon the streets in crowds." The panic extended beyond common citizens. "Some of the parties arrested are very respectably connected," observed the Gazette. "William Ellegood, Jr., was formerly a wealthy citizen of Sussex County. He is a cousin to the State Auditor." "Nearly half the men in Lewes are frightened over these arrests, and each one fears that it is his turn next," noted the *Smyrna Times*. "They clan together there, it is said, and try to smuggle in sugar, coffee, etc., and thus get their groceries cheap, right from the vessels." The widespread fear and unrest underscored how deeply smuggling had permeated every level of Lewes society.

Local merchants also stood to gain from the roundups. The presence of smugglers undercut legitimate businesses that paid duties on their goods. Those operating legally may have quietly supported the government's actions, recognizing that removing smuggled goods from the market meant higher prices for their own products.

Even the press played a role. *The Philadelphia Ledger*, commenting on the events of 1874, framed smuggling as an outdated relic, writing, "It reminds one of the scenes described in some of the old-time English novels... but down at Lewes they have restored the old romantic style, except they have been caught and are in jail." By casting smuggling as an antiquated and improper practice, newspapers helped shape public opinion in favor of the crackdowns.

Despite the high-profile arrests of 1874, smuggling in Lewes continued. In fall 1875, officials sent Major James B. Morris back to Lewes on other business, and his efforts led to the removal of Captain Lyons as Inspector of Customs. While there, Morris uncovered new evidence of smuggling activities.

Morris' methods proved controversial—in early 1876, after he seized goods from the barque Antoinette, the Treasury Department condemned his "mode of seizures" and directed officials to return the goods to their claimants upon payment of duties and expenses.

A political shift began on August 29, 1876, when the Every Evening reported that new legislation would cut the number of special agents in the customs service from 53 to 20. Officials initially retained Morris as the only agent in the Philadelphia district, but less than two weeks later, he left Lewes. The Dover Sentinel correspondent quipped that if the Breakwater Light, the local Lewes newspaper, had truly reflected the prevailing sentiment of most citizens, "it would have uttered a malediction instead of a benediction at his departure."

The case of Levin A. Jenkins illustrated how thoroughly smuggling had infiltrated even official positions in Lewes. The Lighthouse Board appointed Jenkins as keeper of the Breakwater lighthouse in 1873, and within three years, he entangled himself in the illicit trade.

Major Morris urged officials to dismiss Jenkins, accusing him of several offenses. According to Morris, "the most serious offense was smuggling, the proof of which he [Morris] claims to have," the Wilmington Daily Commercial reported in July 1876.

Rather than face official dismissal, Jenkins chose to step down. The Smyrna Times noted Jenkins's official September 1877 exit with a terse notice: "Purnell B. Norman has been appointed principal keeper of the Breakwater lighthouse at Lewes in place of Levin A. Jenkins, resigned."

While Major Morris had left, Marshal Dunn continued operating along Delaware's coast, though he never returned to Lewes. He seized two schooners, the Nelson and *Sarah Ann*, at Mahon's Creek over a dispute about repairs, said the *Smyrna Times* in January 1878. However, Dunn's own position soon collapsed.

The Senate refused to reappoint him as U.S. Marshal that spring. Senator Thomas Bayard delivered a damning indictment, charging that Dunn participated in the "importation of repeaters from Philadelphia to influence Delaware elections."

The practice of "repeating" involved voter fraud, with individuals casting multiple ballots at different polling places—in this case, allegedly using voters Philadelphia operatives had transported. Bayard concluded that Dunn "was not a man who was fit for the office of United States marshal in any respect."

By 1883, the Customs Service effectively withdrew from Lewes, allowing smugglers to resume openly peddling contraband. "It is a trite interrogation in Lewes," smirked the *Milford Chronicle*, "to say 'have a smuggled cigar,' or 'have a drink of smuggled rum,'" confirming that authorities had ended enforcement efforts. The government briefly disrupted operations, but failed to eradicate them. Economic forces kept smuggling profitable—the high cost of legally imported goods, the ease of maritime transport, and the complicity of local officials persisted.

In the end, the federal crackdown of 1874-1876 remained a brief episode rather than creating lasting change. Post-Panic revenue needs largely drove the government's intense focus on Lewes, and as those pressures eased, enforcement efforts waned.

Though federal attention shifted elsewhere, Lewes remained a working port for a number of decades, where pilots guided ships through treacherous waters, fishing fleets hauled in daily catches, and merchants conducted legal trade alongside the lingering shadow of smuggling. Some residents openly acknowledged the practice, but the town treated it as only one current in the larger flow of daily life.

7

RAIL HERO WANNABE

A desperate railway stunt intended to reclaim an old job.

Harley G. Brown sat before the New Castle Court of Oyer and Terminer in December 1878, on trial for causing the deaths of four men. The question weighing on the packed courtroom was not whether he had placed the obstruction that derailed the passenger train—he had already confessed to that. The real mystery was why this former railroad man would not face the gallows for first-degree murder. "Neatly dressed in a black suit," reported the *Delaware Gazette*, Brown "walked firmly and without hesitancy or nervousness" to take his seat. Yet there were subtle signs of inner turmoil: "a slight contraction of the eyebrows, a tremor of the lips, and a nervous twisting of his pocket handkerchief around his fingers."

The events that had brought Brown to trial had begun less than six months earlier, on the night of June 29. Edwin M. Lossing, station agent at Claymont, had just returned from Wilmington at ten o'clock when he heard the thundering approach of the southbound express. Moments later, the night erupted in the sounds of tearing metal and splintering wood as the locomotive struck an obstruction and toppled from the tracks "like a toy." Flames began licking at the wreckage.

Behind the derailed engine sat two express cars, a baggage car, two passenger cars and two sleeping cars—mercifully, all still on the rails. If they had also derailed, fire might have consumed the wooden carriages, creating an even greater catastrophe. Instead, the crash killed four men: engineer George Babe, his son George Jr., who had been firing the locomotive, and two men who had been stealing a ride between cars.

Witness Cornelius L. Cook vividly described the true horror of the scene: "The engineer was lying between the locomotive and tender badly crushed and completely disemboweled." Among the seventy other passengers aboard, several sustained injuries, though none life-threatening.

Conductor Samuel Phillips organized rescue efforts and sent men with lanterns to warn approaching trains. A peculiar encounter unfolded in the darkness. A man approached Phillips, tapped him on the shoulder, and asked if the wreck was bad. Then, gesturing toward the wreckage, the stranger added, "I did all in my power to stop her." Phillips, startled, asked if the man had been aboard the train. The man—who identified himself as Harley Brown—explained that he had seen a railroad tie on the track, tried but failed to remove it, and attempted to wave down the train with a handkerchief. Phillips, a veteran of sixteen years on the railroad, immediately grew suspicious. "A man ought to be almost able to get anything off a railroad track under such circumstances." Brown disappeared "as mysteriously as he had come" before Phillips could question him further.

Brown's own confessions slowly unraveled the mystery of his actions that night, revealing a plan so misguided it bordered on the fantastical. Brown, who had worked for the Philadelphia, Wilmington & Baltimore Railroad for over a decade before leaving in 1875, had grown desperate to regain his old position.

One evening, sitting alone in his home, Brown conceived what to him was a brilliant idea. He would make himself a hero in the eyes of the railroad company, leading to commendation and the offer of either his former position or a better one. He spent days analyzing his plan: "He tore his plan apart to see if it had any defects, and assembled it again," said the *Journal-Every Evening* of February 16, 1934. "It was fool proof, he thought." He devised a plan to wedge a railroad tie across the tracks near Claymont station—tight enough that even he wouldn't be able to dislodge it. Then he would wait for the Philadelphia accommodation train (i.e. a local train) to stop at the station, run to meet it waving his arms frantically, and relate a story of finding the obstruction.

"The idea first came to my mind," Brown later testified, "that placing a cross tie on the track, and then going back, and warning the train of danger, I might get a situation."

On the warm, quiet night of June 29, Brown set his plan in motion, walking the tracks near Claymont station under cover of darkness. He chose a spot opposite the farmhouse of J. Edward Addicks, just beyond a culvert, and began searching for a suitable tie among the discarded remnants beside the rail bed. He found an old tie in a ditch and wedged it carefully across the rails.

But Brown made a fatal error. He had no idea that a fast express train ran between the scheduled local services. When he heard an unexpected whistle pierce the night, "Brown's mystification changed to horror," reported the *Journal-Every Evening*. "His plan was not fool proof after all. He had miscalculated." Brown confessed, "I had no idea there was an intervening train between the 9:45 and the 11:30 train from

Philadelphia." The express hurtled forward at fifty miles per hour—far too fast to stop even if the crew spotted his frantic attempts to signal them with a waving handkerchief.

What followed was pure tragedy born of delusion. "I had no intention of doing harm to anyone, either to the railroad property or to its employees," Brown insisted. Yet instead of the gratitude and job offers he had imagined, his actions killed four innocent men and led to his indictment for first-degree murder.

Brown's former colleagues and acquaintances painted a portrait of a man who had once been a model employee but whose mind had gradually unraveled. The *Smyrna Times* reported that during his decade-plus with the railroad, Brown had been "regarded as a faithful and efficient officer, prompt and willing in the performance of his duties, and an exemplary man in all respects."

But something had changed during his time away. Witnesses described a man plagued by melancholy and strange behavior. His neighbor William Brannon testified that Brown had become "flighty" and "a man not possessing good common sense." Joseph W. Vandegrift of the coroner's jury observed that Brown acted "like a ten-year-old boy" and believed "his mental condition was very much impaired."

The defense built its case around these observations of Brown's deteriorating mental state, citing a series of head injuries: a severe accident in 1868 while he worked on the railroad, a near-fatal sunstroke, and most recently, a falling tree limb in Maine that knocked him unconscious and left blood oozing from his ear.

When the jury finally retired to consider their verdict, they faced a complex moral and legal calculation. Brown's actions had unquestionably caused four deaths. Yet his confused testimony, childlike demeanor, and history of mental instability suggested someone who, in the words of one witness, was "not capable of distinguishing right from wrong."

After an hour and twenty minutes of deliberation, they weighed three possibilities: murder, manslaughter, or a complete acquittal based on insanity. Chief Justice Comegys carefully instructed the jury on this last option, explaining that "insanity is inability to distinguish between right and wrong in reference to the act itself, and the want of power in the actor to choose whether he will do it or not." He urged them to weigh the evidence of Brown's mental state carefully, noting that mere "low spirits" did not excuse criminal responsibility.

"I had no intention of doing harm to anyone, either to the railroad property or to its employees."

HARLEY BROWN

The jury wrestled with conflicting evidence. Multiple witnesses, including members of the coroner's jury, testified to Brown's unstable behavior. Juror John Traphagan had stated definitively that he "didn't think he was in his right mind." But Brown's detailed planning of the obstruction and his attempts to pose as a hero afterward suggested some degree of rational thought.

Years earlier, growing frustration with the railroad set Brown on the path to that dark night. His cousin Adolphus Brown, who worked in the freight department, testified that "he often consulted me as to his chances for a better position; talked as if he was not doing well enough; seemed discouraged and dejected and talked as though his friends did not consult him enough to do anything for him." Despite Brown's exemplary conduct, promotions remained elusive. "As time passed," Adolphus continued, "I noticed this dejection growing on him; sometimes when he came to me I would put him off; would tell him to come again; did not feel like treating him as a business man."

In 1875, Brown left the railroad for what he hoped would be a fresh start in his native Maine. There, he joined his father and brother Silas in a farming and forestry partnership. But this new venture turned out to be more challenging than he expected. Silas testified that while cutting trees together, he noticed his brother "standing in a peculiar way," and later, when harrowing, "he sat down with his head resting upon his hand; he said his head felt bad."

The dangers of forestry work became clear when, as Silas recounted, "the branch of a tree fell upon him, knocking him senseless; shortly after this blood oozed from his right ear; he was senseless ten or fifteen minutes." Afterward, his mood darkened, and he remained deeply melancholy until he left Maine.

Brown likely decided to return to Delaware and seek reinstatement with the railroad because of his head injury and the precarious nature of forestry work. Despite its risks, railroad work promised steady employment and a familiar routine.

But when he arrived in Wilmington, he found that his years of faithful service and spotless conduct carried no weight. Someone had taken his old position, and P.W. & B. refused to offer him another job. Stillman A. Hodgman, a master machinist, recalled Brown's humiliated appeals: "He asked me for a job as fireman, and if I couldn't give him that give him anything we had to do." Hodgman found Brown "rather down-hearted" and "in an embarrassed condition," noting bluntly that he considered Brown "not a man of good common sense when he applied to me for a job." The rejection was absolute—P.W. & B. refused to offer even entry-level work to this former veteran of the rails.

Just a year before his crime, the Great Railroad Strike of 1877 erupted across the country as workers protested wage cuts imposed by major railroads. Workers blocked trains and clashed with militia forces, while federal troops killed dozens of strikers in cities like Pittsburgh and Baltimore. The public increasingly viewed railroads as ruthless monopolies that discarded even their most loyal workers.

Brown's case struck a nerve precisely because he embodied this dysfunction. During his decade-plus with the railroad, he remained "strictly temperate in his habits, avoiding both liquor and tobacco," and even when he resigned, he gave proper notice and trained his replacement. Yet when he returned seeking work, his sterling record meant nothing.

"There is a great amount of sympathy expressed for Harley G. Brown," noted *The*

Daily Gazette on July 3. This sentiment reflected both pity for his mental state and the public's deep-seated anger at a system that drove even its most dedicated employees to desperation. In Brown, they saw the human cost of the railroads' callous disregard for worker loyalty.

The jury's verdict split the difference: not guilty of murder, but guilty of manslaughter. The decision suggested they believed Brown's mental state had impaired his judgment without completely absolving him of responsibility. He served five years in New Castle jail instead of facing the gallows.

Brown left prison in 1883 and moved to Mount Holly, New Jersey. The *Delaware Gazette and State Journal* reported on January 31, 1884, that he was "finishing his new house on his father-in-law's farm," where he planned to "engage in agricultural pursuits"—finding in farming the stability that railroading and forestry had denied him. He remained there, living quietly until he died in 1912.

Harley G. Brown's tragedy stemmed not from malice but from the collision of a disturbed mind and a ruthless industry—his last-ditch attempt to reclaim a place in a system that had already discarded him. His actions cost four innocent men their lives and forever marked him as the hero that never was.

8

PROSTITUTION AND THE BROTHEL ERA

An insider's view of Wilmington's vice district.

The girls would not let them in. They said they were looking for a woman, but were still refused admittance and burst in the inner hall door," Ada Winters recounted to an *Every Evening* reporter on the morning of May 21, 1891. The previous night's events had begun around 10:15 at her Wilmington "maison de joie" at 718 Shipley Street. What followed resembled a Keystone Cops routine more than a professional police raid.

After breaking in, the officers "lit all the gas, called for beer, and said they wanted the landlady," Winters told the reporter. They had effectively taken control of her house in her absence, creating such a commotion that concerned neighbors suggested they ought to have a warrant for such behavior. Mayor Robert Harrington and Walter Hayes, who had heard about the disturbance while eating supper at Ainscow's, arrived to investigate. Rather than restore order, their presence sparked a wild melee in the yard involving the mayor, Hayes, Constables Neutz and Brown, and several others. A crowd gathered to watch the spectacle, and for a time, according to *Every Evening*, "it seemed as if pandemonium had been let loose." In the height of the chaos, Constable Brown somehow ended up with his fingers "entwined around Mayor Harrington's windpipe," showing remarkably little regard for Wilmington's chief executive.

When Winters finally returned home around 6:30 the next morning, having spent the night conducting business elsewhere, she found her girls "all crying and very much worried over their threats." The morning brought no peace —shortly after her return, three men climbed over her back gate, claiming to have a warrant. They said they would read it, but only if she agreed to accompany them quietly to the squire's office, plead guilty to keeping a house of ill fame, and settle the matter.

When reporters questioned Brown about choking the mayor, he offered a matter-of-fact response to *Every Evening*: "Yes, I grabbed him by the throat, but he grabbed me first." The constables, clearly embarrassed by the entire fiasco, tried desperately to keep the story out of the papers. "Why can't you suppress it as the *Morning News* did?" they pleaded with the *Journal* reporter. "That isn't what I was sent out for," he responded flatly.

Winters' establishment did not stand as an isolated case of bungled raids; years earlier, similar theatrics played out elsewhere in Wilmington. The *Delaware Gazette and State Journal* noted in December 1880 that while "some of the men upon Mayor Allmond's police force are excellent officers," others were "entirely unfit for their position" and could be found "loafing about brothels and saloons. Even when raids occurred, they followed a peculiar choreography that seemed designed more for show than effectiveness."

Sergeant Whelan demonstrated a typical raid from this era in October 1875 when he led an operation against establishments in Marsh Lane, using an impressive show of force. *Every Evening* reported that ten officers descended upon two adjacent houses—one run by Dan Bantum as a gambling establishment, and another operated by Francis Simmons as a brothel. The raid led to sixteen arrests, but as was common for the period, officials merely fined the defendants "50 cents and costs," most of which were paid before the night was over.

Police arrested Amanda Archer in 1867 for keeping a house of ill fame, and the *Delaware Gazette and State Journal* reported that officials fined her $80 plus costs—a more substantial sum, but hardly a deterrent given the profitability of such establishments. "The law in relation to the suppression of vice and crime is always the same," the *Smyrna Times* observed in an April 1879 editorial, "but its execution is lax or direct as the public sentiment in regard to vice is weak or strong."

This inconsistent enforcement created an environment where brothel operators knew to expect periodic raids but faced few serious consequences. When authorities raided Kate Mackey's "notorious house of ill fame" at 410 Madison Street in 1874, the *Wilmington Daily Commercial* reported that they simply "put her under bonds to keep the peace and ordered her to vacate the premises immediately." These orders to leave often proved temporary, as proprietors reopened establishments once public attention shifted elsewhere.

In this context, the bumbling raid on Ada Winters' establishment was less an aberration than a particularly visible example of the city's confused approach to vice enforcement. The jurisdictional clash that night on Shipley Street between county constables and city authorities exposed the dysfunction that usually stayed hidden behind closed doors.

Clashes like the one at Ada Winters' establishment occurred frequently. Her Shipley Street house operated within a web of similar establishments that had taken root throughout central Wilmington. By 1891, certain streets had gained notoriety for housing what newspapers labeled "dens of degradation." The intersection of Fourth and Orange streets became particularly infamous. In August 1874, the *Wilmington Daily Commercial* reported a violent scene where three or four men attacked another man in front of a reputed house of ill fame. One assailant fired two pistol shots—one toward the victim lying on the pavement, another into the air toward Chamberlain's Leather Manufactory. The assailants fled, some carrying away the wounded man, whose path could be traced the next morning by blood drops on the pavements.

Brothels clustering reflected a shift from earlier patterns. While houses of ill fame had long existed in Wilmington, they had previously been more scattered. The emerging geography of vice reflected clear class distinctions: while "bawdy houses" served laborers in areas like Marsh Lane on "the other side of the Harlan & Hollingsworth Company's works," the so-called "disorderly houses" of central Wilmington catered to a more affluent clientele.

Chick Foy's "Green House" at Front and King streets ranked among the city's more notorious establishments. The *Morning Herald* reported in December 1875 that Foy's operation was substantial enough to accommodate entire crews from visiting naval vessels like the Powhattan. His house maintained a dedicated bar room in what had once served as the kitchen, employed multiple women, and handled the inevitable rowdiness that came with serving sailors on shore leave. During one especially raucous evening, Foy himself had to emerge from behind his bar with a club to restore order after his patrons began breaking chairs over each other's heads.

These various operations—from Ada Winters' Shipley Street house to Chick Foy's wild Green House—didn't cluster in central Wilmington by accident. Multiple factors drove this consolidation. Wilmington's rapid industrialization in the 1870s and 1880s drew an influx of single male workers to the city, increasing demand for such establishments and fostering public resignation to their existence.

Newspaper coverage from as early as 1867, when the *Delaware Gazette and State Journal* reported Amanda Archer's $80 fine for keeping a house of ill fame, suggests that authorities already viewed these places less as criminal enterprises than as enterprises to be regulated. Over time, madams and local officials systematized their arrangements.

Even when authorities ordered proprietors to vacate properties, they often treated the directives as temporary. Selective enforcement stabilized conditions, allowing certain operations to flourish. Most significantly, the relationship between brothel keepers and city authorities evolved into an informal system of tolerance.

While Wilmington's brothel district was the most infamous, vice was not limited to the city. Across Delaware, prostitution functioned on a spectrum—some women entered the trade by choice or necessity, while traffickers coerced, exploited, or outright forced others into it. Cases beyond Wilmington revealed the darker extremes of this world, where desperation, deception, and violence played a far greater role.

Every Evening reported on August 3, 1888, that Agent Stout of the Society for Prevention of Cruelty to Children uncovered what the paper termed a "hidden den of vice" in North Milford. There, a woman named Annie Ricketts operated "a low brothel, a rendezvous for whites and blacks" that was "foul, filthy and squalid almost beyond description."

Most disturbing was the presence of Ricketts' own children - Joseph, aged 4, and Mamie, aged 7 - in these deplorable surroundings. After a hearing before Squire Fowler, Ricketts failed to post the $200 bail for keeping a disorderly house, so authorities sent her to Dover jail. Agent Stout removed her children to the Home for Friendless and Destitute Children. The case horrified the public but revealed an ugly truth—poverty and desperation often led to parents exploiting their own daughters.

A cautionary tale published by the *Seaford Citizen* on February 28, 1874, starkly illustrated the horrors of sex trafficking. The paper recounted the tragic fate of Clara Williams, a 17-year-old from Virginia's Eastern Shore—"indeed a beautiful being" before her corruption. A sewing machine agent named Hopkins had set his sights on her, courting her under false pretenses until her father intervened and banned him from the farm. Undeterred, Hopkins maintained secret contact, convincing

Clara to elope.

One night, she packed a trunk and slipped away. Hopkins took her by train to Philadelphia, where he led her into a brothel under the lie that its occupants were his relatives. The madam posed as his aunt, and in this deception, "the scoundrel succeeded in effecting her ruin." He stole her jewelry and $30,000 before vanishing.

Her father, Henry Williams, refused to give up. He spent nearly four months searching before finding Clara in the Philadelphia brothel. The Citizen captured their heartbreaking reunion: "It was impossible to imagine his feelings when I saw the white-haired old man brought face to face with his only child in this den of vice—a faded, crushed, and drooping flower, torn from the parent stem, and surrounded by the shriveled and faded leaves of virtue." When Clara "pleaded for mercy," her father shepherded her home to Virginia.

The Seaford Citizen framed the story as a warning—one rooted in a rural community's fear that such a fate could befall any of their daughters. Beneath its sermonizing lay an undeniable truth: in a world where deception thrived, a determined predator could turn innocence into tragedy in just a few short months.

The anguish of fathers confronting their daughters' exploitation echoed across decades. Sixty-two years after Henry Williams rescued Clara from that Philadelphia brothel, the Journal-Every Evening of July 30, 1936, reported a Wilmington father standing outside Edna Powell's notorious establishment at 811 Tatnall Street, firing his gun into the windows as he demanded the release of his daughter. In both cases—separated by two generations but united by the same parental torment—fathers confronted the brutal reality that the vice trade had swallowed their daughters. While Clara Williams' story had unfolded in the gaslit world of Victorian Philadelphia, by 1936 the business operated through sophisticated urban brothels protected by police payoffs, as Powell's later testimony would reveal. Yet the fundamental heartbreak of fathers losing daughters remained unchanged.

Not all women entered prostitution through abduction or deception. The Daily Republican of May 24, 1866, detailed divorce proceedings that revealed how domestic abuse and economic abandonment could drive women into the trade. In the case of Woods vs. Woods, testimony painted a picture of Maggie H. Woods, a woman who chose what she saw as the lesser evil when faced with an impossible situation on a farm in St. Georges Hundred.

According to court testimony, John F. Woods had maintained a relationship with his housekeeper, Mary Verables, even before his marriage to Maggie. Multiple witnesses testified that Woods and Verables "lived like man and wife," with one servant reporting she had "frequently seen him and Mary Verables together in bed." After his marriage to Maggie, Woods continued to keep Verables in the house, telling Maggie that Verables "had a better right to be there" than his own spouse. When Maggie objected to this arrangement, Woods told her "she might live at his house if she would live in the garret and cook for herself."

Unable to tolerate these conditions, Maggie fled to Philadelphia. On June 10, 1865, Woods and his brother tracked her down in the city. They confronted her at a house on Wood Street, triggering a clash in which they found her in bed with a client. The *Daily Republican* reported the altercation: "Maggie, you might as well uncover your head; I know you," Woods said. Her response cut to the heart of her circumstances: "Why don't you support me then like a man?"

Multiple witnesses at the divorce trial testified that Maggie had declared she would "rather whore for a living than live there" in the country with her unfaithful husband. Another witness, Nathaniel Fry, testified that Maggie had said "she would rather drown herself or live a life of lewdness than stay with her husband." Her stark choice—between degradation in her husband's house or degradation in the brothels—illustrated how limited women's options could be when abandoned by their husbands in the 1860s.

Authorities often turned a blind eye to vice, regulating it loosely rather than eliminating it. That same laxity extended to laws meant to protect young girls. Delaware's legal codes made it abundantly clear where the state's priorities lay. State legislators lowered Delaware's age of consent in 1871 from ten to seven years old—the lowest in the nation—while neighboring southern states kept theirs at ten.

This unconscionable situation persisted despite public outcry. In February 1889, the Woman's Christian Temperance Union presented a petition to the Delaware General Assembly demanding the age be raised, with ten yards of signatures from Delaware residents. Astonishingly, Delaware lawmakers left this seven-year-old age of consent unchanged until they overhauled the state's legal codes in 1972.

Wilmington entered the 20th century with an established red-light district rivaling those of larger cities. Just as San Francisco had its "Barbary Coast," Wilmington maintained a cluster of well-established houses operating with tacit police approval. By the 1920s and 30s, these establishments built clear hierarchies and reputations. "Some of the most upstanding men in town were regulars in the district," reported Bill Frank in the Evening Journal on July 5, 1973, "well aware that as long as they followed the rules—pay their money, keep quiet, and leave when told—there was no risk of exposure."

At the top of this hierarchy stood Mom Grimes' establishment at 602 French Street. Frank described it as "the most dignified of all," with Mom Grimes herself as "a matronly type" who claimed to have "known two generations of customers and liked them all." She furnished her house like a middle-class Victorian home, complete with overstuffed chairs and plush accoutrements. She employed more mature women and catered primarily to an older, wealthy clientele. Though the establishment had an emergency exit on East 6th Street through an alley, there's no record of it ever being raided. When Mom Grimes died in the early 1940s, Frank noted that "some thought she deserved a civic funeral for services rendered."

Sadie Miller's operation at 502 Orange Street stood in stark contrast. Her establishment ran on a brisk business model with high worker turnover, bringing in fresh young women every two or three weeks. Miller maintained strict rules: no obviously drunken customers and no military men were allowed entry. "Sadie's place was all business," Bill Frank observed. "Little or no hanging around and talking. She was serving only one commodity: sex."

Madams carefully vetted newcomers for police or informants. The Morning News reported on March 3, 1919 that they maintained arrangements with corrupt officers who alerted them to suspicious inquiries. Some operations took evasion even further. *Every Evening* reported on June 18, 1925, that one house installed a false wall to conceal clients during raids.

Edna Powell dominated Wilmington's vice trade from her establishment at 811 Tatnall Street, operating under a sophisticated system of police protection. She testified to paying Captain George A. Black $25 regularly, often meeting him on West Street or Tatnall Street near her home. The protection system operated with elaborate methods—the *Journal-Every Evening* of July 30, 1936, reported that "one member of the bureau signaled by dialing her telephone three times, and if there was no response from the sending end, then it was understood that raiders were coming to the house."

Harold Witsil, who helped Powell gather her payoffs, testified and revealed the scale of corruption. The December 5, 1936 *Journal-Every Evening* reported that "At Christmas time, he would prepare from 30 to 40 Christmas money envelopes for distribution among the policemen." The rates were fixed: "Patrolmen, he said, rated $5; sergeants, $10; captains, $20. Captain Black received $25."

Powell testified that even after a mysterious death at her establishment temporarily closed it, the protection system continued. She met Captain Black at Ninth and Orange Streets to discuss reopening. "Mrs. Powell stated Captain Black told her if she did not receive a telephone message from him, everything would be all right for her to reopen," reported the *Journal-Every Evening*. "When Captain Black's message failed to arrive, she resumed business."

But Powell's empire crumbled in 1936 when the court sentenced her to multiple terms: six months for illegal liquor sales and a year for running a disorderly house. Rather than go quietly, she retaliated by exposing the entire system of police corruption through detailed testimony to Attorney General Percy Warren Green. Her revelations created "a big stir around the public building and among persons uptown," stated the *Journal-Every Evening* of July 30, 1936. This explosive testimony prompted a complete overhaul of the police department and effectively ended Wilmington's organized brothel system.

With Prohibition's 1933 repeal, vice adapted. Call girls returned to bars, seedy hotels replaced once-grand brothels, and streetwalkers became more common. Wilmington's red-light district faded into memory, but Powell stayed in business—just in a different form.

After she served time for her brothel operations and gained release in 1939, Edna Powell remained undeterred. By 1941, she had simply shifted her enterprise to bookmaking.

On October 3, 1941, the *Morning News* reported that authorities had arrested her again. When detectives raided her operation, "she threw her arms around Detective Berry in an effort to prevent seizure of the evidence."

This desperate embrace marked a fitting coda to her defiant life—an attempt to outmaneuver the law before they closed in for good. After that last arrest, Powell's name vanished from the papers, her era effectively over.

9

MUTILATED BODY SPARKS TOWN INVESTIGATION

A sensational murder haunted Delaware City.

On the morning of December 26, 1891, William H. Steele reported once more to his post along the Chesapeake and Delaware Canal in Delaware City, where he had served as lock-tender for nearly a quarter century. About twenty feet from the wharf, something caught his eye in the basin. "I got in a skiff and held the arm up while a man by the name of Cook put a rope around it and we made it fast," Steele later testified.

The body they hauled to shore horrified and haunted Delaware City for decades. Where the head should have been, there was only a ragged neck stump. The corpse wore nothing except a single piece of cloth binding one ankle. Thomas Vail, a local veterinary surgeon who helped retrieve the body, had a long history with the victim: "I had known Benson for about twenty-five years." He recognized features he had known in life: "He had very peculiar hands. They were very long and thin, and he had salt rheum upon them." Though the face was gone, Vail was certain about the victim's identity. "I remarked that if Noah Benson was missing, I would be qualified that it was his body."

Police launched an immediate investigation after the discovery. Steele's expertise as lock-tender proved crucial to determining how the body ended up in the canal. He explained that leakage from the locks created a constant current flowing eastward toward the Delaware Bay. This meant Benson's body couldn't have drifted into the canal from the bay. The current would have prevented it. Someone must have thrown the body in the water somewhere within the canal itself.

Within days, investigators suspected George Henry Hutt, his wife Julia, and James Johnson. "Detectives McVey and Witsil are doing good work in Delaware City towards bringing to justice the murderers of Noah Benson," reported the *Daily Republican* on January 4, 1892. "They have had George Henry Hutt, James Johnson, and Julia Hutt arrested on suspicion of being concerned in the murder if not the real murderers. The evidence against them is very damaging."

Daniel Miller, a fourth suspect, had already fled. He disappeared from Delaware City the Saturday after Thanksgiving, just days after locals last saw tha Black man alive. Detectives tracked him to Media, Pennsylvania, but there they lost his trail. Then, remarkably, in March 1892, Officer Lucas spotted Miller walking brazenly on Front Street in Delaware City— he had lived back in town for nearly a month. When officers arrested Miller, he appeared nervous, and denied any knowledge of or connection to Benson's murder, though investigators believed he "knew more about the killing of Benson than any other person in Delaware City."

The web of suspicion extended beyond these four. Edward Williams, a local farmhand, had been among the first to view Benson's body in the canal. During the trial, Williams appeared as a witness, described by observers as "black, backward, and perspiring copiously" as he testified. Though he claimed he "could not swear that it was him," referring to the body's identity, Williams admitted he "had it in my mind that it was his body." His testimony revealed that authorities had initially arrested him as a suspect, though they later released him. This detail took on new significance years later.

Locals last saw Benson alive on Thanksgiving night, exactly one month before William Steele found his body. That evening, he drank with a group of men including Hutt, Johnson, and Miller. Philip Borgher, a Delaware City clothier, witnessed an exchange from about fifty feet away. Standing by his store, he saw Benson with Hutt and another man he didn't recognize. "Hutt wanted to take Benson home," Borgher testified, "but Benson said he was afraid they would throw him into the canal." He identified Hutt by his white shirt and face when Hutt passed near the streetlights.

John G. Borgher, a Delaware City flour dealer, provided additional testimony about that final night: "I saw Benson, Hutt, Miller, and Johnson together on Thanksgiving night. Benson was drunk and swearing. Hutt told Johnson that if Johnson did not handle Benson, Hutt would take care of it himself. Johnson replied, 'He's all right; we will attend to him.'" They stumbled to the next corner. There were two women, one of them Ella King, a local woman who would later figure prominently in the investigation. "One of the women said, 'Hello, Benson!' I think that the other woman said, 'Hello, Miller!'" Here was a glimpse of Benson in motion—loud, unruly, but known to those around him.

Townspeople and authorities widely believed that this drunken encounter turned violent. Investigators believed Hutt and Johnson mortally wounded Benson with knives. To cover their crime, they took him to the Hutt house on Washington Street, less than 500 feet from where William Steele would later find his body in the canal. There, they decapitated him before disposing of both body and head in the water. No one ever found the head.

After that Thanksgiving encounter, Benson vanished. And now, a month later, his mutilated body had surfaced, launching Delaware City into its most sensational murder investigation—a case that would span decades, see multiple convictions, and leave lingering doubts about whether justice was truly served.

Noah Benson had lived in Delaware City for years, working for local farmer William Beck. Though he was considered a fixture of the town, he was not an invisible man—he had his ways, his habits, and his moods. Some remembered him as a steady laborer; others recalled a man who could turn rowdy when drink was in him.

Benson's history included a notorious incident from a decade earlier. On August 1, 1882, while intoxicated, he had attempted to shoot his wife during a domestic dispute but accidentally shot himself instead. Leonard G. Vandegrift, a Delaware City resident who had employed Benson some ten years before the murder, testified about the incident. "He woke me up at midnight to get me to help him," Vandegrift later testified. The bullet remained lodged in Benson's left hand between his fingers, creating a distinctive identifying feature that would later prove crucial in confirming the identity of his mutilated remains. This glimpse into Benson's past revealed a troubled relationship with alcohol and a capacity for violence that occasionally surfaced.

Suspicion fell first on George Henry Hutt, his wife Julia Hutt, and James Johnson. Detectives McVey and Witsil found blood-stained clothing in the Hutts' house on Washington Street, drawing both husband and wife into the investigation. Johnson had been seen near the docks on the night of Benson's disappearance, his demeanor unusually nervous. Hutt was known for a violent streak.

The medical evidence suggested a far more brutal scenario than a simple murder. Benson's body bore signs of horrific, sustained violence, attested Dr. W. J. Jacobs. "There was a fracture on the left leg near the knee, and the back was broken," Jacobs reported. He noted that "the condition of the interlapped bones showed that the body had been bent double," suggesting the victim had been violently contorted. These wounds went far beyond the initial knife attack, indicating the perpetrators had likely kicked and stomped on Benson with savage fury.

The murder of Noah Benson bore the marks of deeply personal violence—broken bones, a severed head, and a body so battered it had been bent double. That level of brutality suggested rage, not opportunism. Benson had shown interest in Ella King, a local woman known to those involved, and witnesses placed both Benson and King on the street with Hutt, Johnson, and Miller on Thanksgiving night.

In such a volatile mix of liquor, reputation, and unspoken rivalries, jealousy becomes a plausible motive—perhaps even the motive. Yet the investigation never assigned that motive to a single man. Instead, prosecutors cast a wide net, charging all three men with full responsibility for the killing. Whether they acted together or whether one killed and the others covered for him remains unclear. But the physical evidence pointed to a crime of passion—committed not in silence, but in a violent outburst.

Ella (or Ellen) King's involvement exposed deep social fault lines. James H. Dilworth, editor of the *Delaware City News*, and William H. Walker, a reporter for *Every Evening*, hid in a jail cell next to James Johnson's and secretly listened as he spoke to his cellmate. In his testimony, Dilworth reported that Johnson "wondered why Ella King had not been arrested." The January 8, 1892 *Morning News* article hinted that King would have "lots to tell," noting she was the woman "to whom Noah was paying attention." Dilworth also testified that Johnson said, "If we can only keep that Hutt woman's mouth shut until after court, we are all right."

Julia Hutt's case proved distinct from the others. While Investigators found blood-stained items in her house—a pillowcase and towel—she maintained consistently that these came from carrying hog meat during a butchering that took place two or three days before Christmas. Her mother, Deborah Moody, and a woman named Maria Johnson both testified in support of her account. Maria specifically recalled that James Johnson had helped with the butchering and that witnesses saw him coming from the yard with a bloody butcher knife.

However, Dr. Henry E. Formad, who had conducted over fifteen thousand post-mortems and served as examiner and instructor in microscopy and pathology at the University of Pennsylvania since 1874, delivered devastating expert testimony. His detailed scientific analysis proved the blood could not have come from hogs, showing instead that the blood corpuscles matched those of humans or other large mammals.

The shared blood evidence in the Hutt house helped convict Julia's husband. Despite the belief that the decapitation occurred in their shared home, the jury acquitted Julia but found George guilty of the murder.

With Julia Hutt acquitted, prosecutors focused their case on the three men. While Maria Johnson testified she had seen blood on Johnson's sleeve from the hog butchering days before Christmas, she could not positively identify the bloody shirt presented at trial as the same one he had worn that day.

George Hutt's and James Johnson's alibis frayed under scrutiny. Though Hutt claimed he was home all evening with his wife and had company until 9 o'clock, his purported witnesses contradicted each other. Annie Davis, Hutt's sister, testified that only George and Julia Hutt were at the house that night. But Mary Wright claimed she was there with George Smith and Lewis Taylor. Mary Davis ("Long Jane") gave yet another version, saying she was present along with Wright, Smith, Taylor, and the Hutts. When Smith took the stand, he offered a fourth variation, testifying he was there with Taylor, Jane Davis, and Wright but left at 7:30. These wildly conflicting accounts about who was present and when they left undermined Hutt's claim of having reliable witnesses to his whereabouts.

Johnson's alibis proved equally inconsistent. He first claimed he left Hutt's house during an argument and stayed at Ann Hinkelman's until the early morning hours. Later, he said he had been nursing a sick child that night. At trial, Annie and Elias Hickman stated Johnson had actually spent the entire night drunk in their bed. Like Hutt's, Johnson's shifting accounts of his whereabouts only served to heighten suspicion.

The investigation revealed not only conflicting alibis but also a community reluctant to speak against the accused. George Burgher, a key witness who saw Benson with the suspects on Thanksgiving night, initially withheld crucial information. He later admitted he "was afraid of the crowd of bad negroes, of which they are a part, and because he did not wish to go to court and testify against them." When pressed on the witness stand about his hesitation, witness John G. Borgher explained his reluctance bluntly: "Well, when a man gets in jail once and gets out, he is not responsible." This atmosphere of intimidation cast a shadow over the proceedings, revealing deep social tensions that complicated the pursuit of justice in the tight-knit community.

The physical evidence proved even more damaging. In Hutt's house, detectives found trousers with blood stains that matched a vest Benson had left at his employer's farm. Both were part of a new suit Benson had purchased shortly before his death.

Miller's case relied more on circumstantial evidence than those of his co-defendants. While John G. Borgher had placed Miller in the group with Benson on Thanksgiving night, and his flight from Delaware City the following Saturday counted against him, the key testimony came from Sarah Fields, described in court records as "an infirm and aged colored woman with very bad sight." She testified that Miller appeared at her house in Poketown the day after Thanksgiving wearing only a "gauze shirt." She claimed he admitted "I wuz in a mob and got my shirt bloody" and later declared "I cut de n— to death."

Multiple alibi witnesses challenged this testimony. Hattie Harris testified that Miller visited her restaurant several times that day. William H. Hudson saw him at Institute Hall around 7 p.m., and Jennie and William Brown swore he spent the entire night at their house. The jury delivered its verdict: "We find George Henry Hutt, James Johnson, and Daniel Miller guilty as murderers and Julia Hutt not guilty of murder." On June 15, Judge Grubb sentenced each man to life imprisonment, along with fines of $1,000 and court costs. When Miller heard he'd been convicted of second-degree rather than first-degree murder, he "cut a pigeon wing" and "seemed to be very happy that he was not on his way to have his neck stretched."

The Daily Republican later questioned the legitimacy of these convictions: "If their skins were white, they would never have been convicted. It would have been impossible from the evidence." Miller's flight from Delaware City the Saturday after Thanksgiving likely counted heavily against him in jurors' minds, despite the weak evidence tying him directly to the crime.

The three men landed in New Castle jail together, but they soon went separate

---

> ## "She has the bloody shirt that he wore when he done it. He took it to her to be washed after we was convicted."

JAMES JOHNSON

---

ways. Johnson kept to himself, working in the kitchen, reading the Bible. According to the *Evening Journal* on September 11, 1893, jail time took an unexpected turn when Edward Williams—the same man who had testified at the trial and had himself once been arrested as a suspect—was brought to New Castle jail on charges of chicken theft.

Upon seeing Williams enter, Johnson caused a stir by pointing at him and declaring, "The man has come in here now who killed Noah Benson." Johnson claimed that George Hutt's wife still possessed damning evidence: "She has the bloody shirt that he wore when he done it. He took it to her to be washed after we was convicted and sent here. She kept it and has it now. Noah Benson's blood is on the sleeve." Williams denied any involvement, and no further investigation appears to have followed up on Johnson's accusation. The incident added another layer of uncertainty to a case already clouded by doubt.

In 1901, the governor pardoned Jim Johnson after a decade of good behavior, and Johnson later moved to Virginia (*Delaware Gazette and State Journal*, May 23, 1901). The governor also pardoned Hutt, but he plunged straight back into crime. Police arrested him in 1908 after a brawl in Chester, Pennsylvania. He called himself the "King of Bethel Court," but a mob beat him and chased him out of town.

Miller, meanwhile, had been a trusted prisoner, working in the kitchen and even managing the jail's medicine chest. When the Board of Pardons approved Hutt's and Johnson's release in May 1901 but delayed action on his own case, Miller grew restless.

Though officials had restricted his movements after his companions' release, on June 4, they allowed him outside for errands—his first time in several days. He seized the opportunity, slipping away around 2:30 in the afternoon, still wearing his jail stripes.

No one noticed his escape for several hours. The practice of allowing prisoners to move freely through New Castle's streets had long been controversial. "Occasionally one makes up his mind and grants his own pardon. He is seldom captured," the *Delaware Gazette and State Journal* observed (June 6, 1901). True to this pattern, Miller disappeared completely—authorities never found a trace of him.

10

INSIDER VANISHES WITH BANK'S FORTUNE

A high-profile theft redefined financial scandal.

The teller's window at the First National Bank of Dover sat empty on the morning of May 29, 1897. William N. Boggs, a man once hailed as a model bank employee, had vanished. On July 14 bank directors finally confirmed the staggering truth. Boggs had stolen $107,000, driving them to reduce the bank's capital stock from $100,000 to $50,000. *Every Evening* dubbed it "the crime of the century."

The theft sent shockwaves through Delaware society. "Boggs was regarded as one of the most remarkable young men in Delaware—and he was. His system of carrying along balances and deficits without ever getting into a tangle, his cool head and quick judgment under the most trying circumstances, and his unerring judgment of human nature were wonderful," marveled *Every Evening* on January 18, 1902. Yet beneath that carefully cultivated exterior lay a web of deception so intricate that it would take investigators months to unravel. Even more shocking, the investigation would eventually implicate some of Delaware's most prominent citizens, including a sitting United States Senator.

The day after Boggs' disappearance, panic gripped Dover. Depositors, hearing rumors of the bank's possible insolvency, began withdrawing their funds. A full-scale bank run seemed imminent until Harry A. Richardson, the bank's president, took extraordinary action. Richardson posted a notice declaring that he would "be personally responsible for the deposits in case the bank was unable to pay the depositors," reported the *Morning News* on January 15, 1907. "Knowing his standing in the community, the depositors took his word. There was no run on the bank and within a short time it had been restored to its old reputation of being one of the soundest financial institutions in the state."

The mystery of Boggs' escape deepened when investigators discovered he had not acted alone. Colonel Ezekiel T. Cooper, a prominent Dover attorney and lobbyist known as "Colonel Zeke," had purchased the railroad ticket that carried Boggs to safety. Cooper "not only aided and abetted Mr. Boggs in the robbery of the First National Bank of Dover, Delaware, by means of worthless checks," reported *The Baltimore Sun* on February 19, 1898, "but actually bought the ticket that carried the fleeing teller from the scene of his downfall." Cooper secured the ticket at Philadelphia's Broad Street Station for passage to New Orleans.

Behind Cooper's involvement lay an even more sordid tale. Through the New York firm of E.B. Cuthbert & Co., Cooper had funneled over $20,000 of stolen bank funds into stock speculation between January 1896 and June 1897. The Sun's investigation revealed that Cooper's large checks were regularly honored by the bank. "Not a few of these large checks," the paper noted, "were drawn by him and credited to him when his balance on the books of the First National Bank of Dover, Delaware, was exactly twenty-six cents."

Mrs. Lizzie Boggs received an anonymous letter urging secrecy on June 3, 1897, the day her husband's embezzlement became public. "Don't you write or wire to your husband," it warned. "Tell no man where he is, if you know. Shut your teeth together. Be brave. Guard his secret as you would your life and honor." The letter came from Frederick E. Bach, a former clerk for Senator Anthony Higgins with powerful ties in government, especially in Cuba. Bach initially denied authorship but admitted his role after investigators confronted him with evidence comparing his handwriting to another letter. Every Evening published the incriminating missive.

Bach scrambled to contain the fallout. "I spent much time at Dover during the first half of the year 1897, reporting the proceedings of the constitutional convention, and thus came to know Mr. and Mrs. Boggs... My first and only thought was of Mrs. Boggs. I knew the ways of the agents of the Secret Service. I knew that they would not hesitate to use any means, legal or illegal, to accomplish their ends, and I foresaw the torture and humiliation to which they would subject her if she so much as opened her mouth."

In response, Every Evening pointedly published the anonymous letter a second time, signaling to readers that Bach's explanation warranted closer scrutiny. The implications were particularly striking given that Bach was the founder and former editor of Every Evening itself, yet even his former paper maintained a conspicuous distance—when Bach died in 1907, they gave their founder only a perfunctory obituary.

His involvement takes on greater significance when considering Boggs' escape route, which reportedly took him through Cuba en route to South America. Just two years later, in 1899, Bach secured a position in Cuba's Office of the Assistant Auditor of Customs Accounts. The timing and Bach's government connections suggest he may have provided Boggs with a network for safe passage, though Bach would never admit to such involvement.

But the most explosive revelation was yet to come. In February 1898, after nearly nine months as a fugitive, William N. Boggs suddenly reappeared. The Sun reported, "The entire credit for Mr. Boggs' voluntary return justly belongs to Mr. Boggs himself and to a noble woman—his wife. He said (through unnamed intermediaries): 'Have Lizzie signify her wishes in the matter; I will be guided entirely by her.' She wrote: 'Come home and stand trial.'"

On the morning of his surrender, Boggs arrived from Philadelphia with Francis Shunk Brown, Esq., and his brother Walter M. Boggs. The group reached Wilmington's B&O station just before 10 o'clock and went directly to District Attorney Lewis C. Vandegrift's office. "Neatly dressed in a brown check suit, a dark blue overcoat, and a brown sombrero," said The Sun, Boggs marched into the Federal Building to turn himself in.

The circumstances of Boggs' return sparked immediate speculation. Vandegrift issued a terse statement: "William N. Boggs positively declines to tell where he has been. This he has decided on after mature consideration, and he will not depart from this determination." Alongside his vow of silence, Boggs offered a broader pledge: "Now that he has voluntarily returned, he will do everything in his power to make reparation for what has been done. He will tell the whole story of the defalcation [embezzlement] and will neither shield nor persecute anyone."

His pledge to reveal where the money flowed sent tremors through Delaware's political establishment, noticeably when investigators began examining the financial dealings of U.S. Senator Richard R. Kenney. The connection between the senator and the absconding teller exploded into what The Sun dubbed "a sensation of national importance."

A portrait emerged of Boggs as far more than a simple embezzler as the investigation expanded. "He was a wonder at figures," noted Every Evening on January 18,

1902. "The fact that he stole more than the entire capital stock of the institution, in just a few years and under the noses of both the directors and the national bank examiner, offered the clearest proof of his ability."

The inquiry quickly expanded far beyond Boggs himself. On February 20, 1898, *The Sun* reported that authorities had arrested four prominent men: Colonel Ezekiel T. Cooper, Thomas S. Clark, ex-Wilmington Sheriff Amos Cole, and Charles H. Butler. Of these, Thomas S. Clark emerged as a key figure in the unfolding drama. A 52-year-old Dover resident, Clark was a prominent real estate broker with a reputation for shrewd land speculations and an exceptional talent for attracting New York investors to Kent County properties. A tall, broad-shouldered man with soft gray hair and a ruddy complexion, he was an influential Democrat deeply embedded in the local power structure.

While Clark would go on to be convicted and serve a full five-year prison sentence, Amos Cole and Charles H. Butler proved to be relatively minor players. Though initially arrested and charged, their involvement faded from the bank scandal's central narrative.

The Sun reported the men's early morning roundup with barely concealed relish: "Didn't we do it slick?" boasted Harry A. Richardson, the bank's president. "Well, I should say we did. There weren't half a dozen people in Dover who knew that Cole, Clark, and Butler were under arrest this morning as they were going to the train."

But the most sensational indictment targeted U.S. Senator Richard R. Kenney. The prosecution painted a picture of intimate financial collusion between the senator and Boggs. The case against Senator Kenney reached its dramatic peak in December 1898. During his closing argument, D.A. Vandegrift laid out the prosecution's central charge: he described how Kenney had "seated himself on the back of this young man, who was then staggering under the load of other men that he was carrying," according to the December 16 *Morning News*. "He jumped on the back of this young man and helped to carry him down."

Kenney's trial became a masterclass in courtroom drama. His defense team included his Senate colleague George Gray, who argued that Kenney was merely careless with his finances, not criminal in his intent. Former Attorney General John Biggs, also defending Kenney, attacked Boggs' credibility in colorful terms. "This man Boggs, this poor little innocent boy, this cherub, the immaculate young man, as the district attorney would have everybody believe," Biggs sniffed sarcastically to the court. "The district attorney's little pet, his little Willie, this little angel without a black thought in his heart."

Levi C. Bird, another defense attorney, went even further in his theatrical denunciation of Boggs: "He comes to the stand through broken oaths," Bird thundered, according to the *Morning News*. "His whole life is a line of broken oaths and vows. He is as tainted as hell. He has come through seas of lies. What would you have us do? Erect a monument? It would be a monument of lies and broken oaths."

The prosecution countered by focusing on Kenney's stock speculation in Bay State Gas, funded partly through his dealings with Boggs. "The inside information didn't do Senator Kenney much good," Bird responded sarcastically. "The inside information cost him $5,000. He was an unlucky man to have inside information."

Prosecutors tried Kenney twice on the charges, but both juries deadlocked. His first trial began on June 11, 1898, with the jury discharged on June 25 after being unable to agree. A second trial commenced on December 5 and ended on December 19 with the jury again being deadlocked. District Attorney William Michael Byrne ultimately decided to drop the prosecution, noting that "despite a careful and adequate presentation of the contentions of the government, a definite result is not likely from a multiplicity of causes to be attained."

While Kenney escaped conviction, others in Boggs' orbit faced harsher fates. Colonel Cooper drew an eighteen-month sentence but died in prison before completing his term. Thomas S. Clark received five years. After serving four years and five days—earning the maximum reduction for good behavior—he expected to walk free on July 5, 1902. But because he couldn't pay his $5,000 fine, authorities kept him in prison for another 25 days. He finally got out after swearing under oath that he couldn't afford to pay.

The most dramatic turn in the case came from an unexpected quarter. In January

1902, Lizzie Boggs made a bold personal appeal to President Theodore Roosevelt. "I touched him on the arm," she explained, "and asked to be allowed to see him." When Roosevelt heard her story, he responded characteristically: "I do not generally believe in pardoning embezzlers, but you are a plucky woman, and I will consider the case." At the time, the White House maintained a level of public accessibility unthinkable today—citizens of sufficient nerve and timing could, quite literally, reach out and touch the President. For a president who prided himself on fighting corruption, Roosevelt's flippant reply stood out.

However, Mrs. Boggs' personal boldness represented only part of her strategy. She had strategically secured assistance from Congressman L.H. Ball (R-Del.) and "several other influential men" beforehand. She methodically interviewed officials at the Department of Justice and obtained the congressman's cooperation, which helped secure her audience with the president. Despite his busy schedule, Roosevelt gave her a patient hearing and personally investigated the matter before determining the sentence reduction was justified. While her direct appeal clearly made an impression on Roosevelt, it formed part of a broader, well-orchestrated campaign that combined both formal channels and personal initiative.

Lizzie Boggs' gambit worked. Roosevelt commuted her husband's sentence to expire on April 25, giving him credit for time served between his guilty plea and sentencing. Every Evening noted on that date that "Delaware never had a greater scandal than the one which grew out of the defalcations of this young man Boggs. It involved a United States Senator... a member of the Delaware State Legislature... and several other prominent citizens of the State."

Boggs demonstrated a remarkable candor about his crimes on his release. Within days of his April 25 release, Boggs spoke to a New York World reporter, offering a stark warning about bank security: "It's not a hard thing to steal from a bank. What I did can be done by any bookkeeper left in charge of the books every day in the week. The banking regulations need to be changed so as to change bookkeepers at irregular intervals and to keep every employee out of the bank for at least forty-eight hours at unannounced periods."

Boggs secured employment as a bookkeeper for the Cartwright Metal Roofing Company in Philadelphia through his brother Walter's connections. "He is in excellent health," the *Smyrna Times* reported, "and to those who knew him intimately, traces of his long confinement are scarcely perceptible." He had even been "permitted to recover his mustache and full growth of hair before leaving the prison."

The scandal's aftermath revealed much about the nature of justice in Gilded Age America. Those with powerful connections, like Senator Kenney, emerged largely unscathed. Although Kenney faced two trials, he ultimately avoided conviction. District Attorney William Michael Byrne formally entered a *nolle prosequi* (a legal term meaning the prosecution would no longer pursue the case), effectively ending the prosecution. Despite the serious allegations, Kenney's political position and legal representation allowed him to escape significant personal consequences from the bank scandal. Others, like Colonel Cooper, died behind bars.

In the years following the trials, several men closely tied to the scandal died—including District Attorney Lewis C. Vandegrift, jury foreman William T. Porter, bank cashier John H. Bateman, and bookkeeper Irving D. Boggs. Their deaths, clustered so soon after the case, lent weight to the perception that the scandal had exacted more than just legal penalties.

Amid this chronicle of personal and professional destruction, one remarkable detail emerged: not a single depositor at the First National Bank of Dover lost a penny. Harry Richardson's personal guarantee protected the bank's holdings. The *Morning News* proclaimed in 1907 that the bank had been "restored to its old reputation of being one of the soundest financial institutions in the state."

The Boggs scandal exposed deep fissures in Delaware society, revealing how powerful men could manipulate the financial system through personal connections and political influence. The case made clear that even in major acts of fraud—what newspapers breathlessly dubbed "the crime of the century"—justice often depended less on the magnitude of the crime than on the accused's status.

Subsequent investigations reshaped Delaware banking, leading to stricter oversight and more rigorous accounting practices. The scandal's most lasting legacy? The realization that a single trusted insider—with enough skill and audacity—could quietly upend an entire institution.

11

OYSTER PIRATES

Illicit harvesting pitted local crews against one another.

Walter Graham, keeper of the Mispillion River Lighthouse, had a clear primary duty: tending the light that guided sailors safely through the river's mouth. But on the night of October 12, 1901, his attention turned sharply to the waters below. He spotted two vessels slipping into the river's mouth behind the steamer *Reis*. One was a two-mast sloop, the other a cat-rigged pungy. Neither vessel displayed the required signal lights, immediately arousing Graham's suspicion, reported *The Sun* on October 17. Launching his yawl, he cautiously approached but discovered the crews had concealed the vessels' names beneath stretched canvas. From a safe distance, Graham observed the crew lowering dredges, and aided by a stiff breeze, raking the river bottom. By morning, the pirates had made off with an estimated 1,500 bushels of oysters, Graham told the *Delaware Gazette and State Journal*.

It could have been someone from Howard Shull's oyster bed bootlegger gang out of Turkey Point, New Jersey, though Shull himself was behind bars in Trenton. It could have been a bay dredger out of Lewes or Woodland Beach, barred by law from river dredging. It could have been a long-prohibited renegade Yankee boat (New Englanders introduced the oyster dredge into Delaware Bay around 1800, seeking seed and market oysters for their private oyster beds. Delaware responded in 1812 by enacting its first shellfish law, restricting oystering to Delaware-owned vessels.)

The next day, R. P. Small, a local advocate for Mispillion River oystermen, telegraphed Attorney-General Herbert Ward to request urgent action. Ward vowed to send State Detective John Ratledge to investigate the matter. Meanwhile, oystermen gathered in Milford, their frustrations boiling over. "License-taker Albert Archer was besieged by them to do something looking to the arrest of the pirates," said the *Delaware Gazette and State Journal*.

Detective Ratledge arrived in Milford late on Tuesday evening and began organizing his investigation. By Wednesday morning, he had sworn in R. P. Small as a special officer to assist. They met first with Walter Graham, who recounted the events of October 12 in vivid detail, describing the vessels and their maneuvers. Armed with this intelligence, including Graham's crucial observation of the word "Little Creek" faintly visible on one of the boats, Ratledge and Small expanded their search. Starting in Milford, they followed the lead to Little Creek, then moved on to Mahon's Ditch.

There, they located a sloop and a bugeye matching Graham's description. "Writs were obtained from Magistrate John B. Hutton, and arrests were made," reported the Delaware Gazette and State Journal on October 24.

One might assume that the captains of Delaware's oyster boats, operating in close quarters and often familiar with one another, formed a tight knit "band of brothers." However, the events of October 1901 revealed a starkly different reality. "There was a sensation when Detective Ratledge brought before Magistrate Hutton James Munsey and Isaac Burris...on three charges connecting them with the piratical act," gasped the Smyrna Times on October 23. Munsey and Burris, considered pillars of the oyster community, stood accused of piracy!

But rather than express shame for their actions, Munsey and Burris doubled down, boldly hiring former U.S. Senator Richard Rolland Kenney, a high-powered and high-profile attorney, to defend them against the charges. Ultimately, the court fined them $95—a sum that paled in comparison to the estimated 1,500 bushels of oysters they had illicitly harvested. In a striking display of leniency, the court charged them merely with "taking from State protected beds of more than twelve bushels," conveniently ignoring evidence that they had hauled in more than 125 times the legal limit from protected waters.

Despite their transgressions, Munsey and Burris faced no lasting repercussions within the oystering community. Their peers neither ostracized them nor barred them from the industry. This leniency rendered their punishment a mere slap on the wrist—a nominal cost of doing business.

The 1901 case of Munsey and Burris represented a relatively tame episode of oyster piracy, one resolved through the normal channels of law enforcement and the courts. This incident paled in comparison to the bloody conflicts that had raged in Delaware Bay during the 1880s. Those earlier "oyster wars" painted a far grimmer picture of violence on the water.

Both Munsey and Burris had reestablished themselves as respected figures within the industry by 1907. They joined a group of oyster captains in petitioning the state for better protection of their oyster beds. Their requests included increased enforcement against illegal dredging (!) and enhanced measures to preserve the oyster population.

Representative Herman Taylor emphasized the severity of the situation. "The oyster laws have been flagrantly violated for two years. This is due probably to the leniency of the officers of the State guard boat," he said.

"The oyster beds are so exposed to pirates that the planters, in self-defense, have been compelled to secure private watch boats, which patrol the bay throughout the night." Ah, the complex dynamics within the oystering community, where past offenses were seemingly overlooked in pursuit of shared economic interests.

"Horny-handed veteran oystermen operating out of Murderkill River on the bay south of Dover talked of incidents of the bay strife, handed down from father to son," reminisced the *Milford Chronicle* in 1959. These conflicts, springing from very different fishing methods, frequently erupted between dredge boat oystermen and tongers. Tongers harvested oysters by hand, using long wooden shafts with rakes at the ends to pull shellfish from the bay floor—an arduous, skill-based technique that left the beds relatively undisturbed. Dredge boat operators, by contrast, dragged heavy metal scoops across the bottom, scraping up large quantities in a single pass. Tongers, many of whom relied on these same beds year after year, saw dredgers as outsiders who stripped the grounds bare and threatened the future of the harvest.

One extremely harrowing encounter, known as the "Blood Point Battle," erupted when a massive fleet of dredgers engaged in hours-long combat with tongers while police vessels attempted unsuccessfully to intervene.

The violence sometimes extended beyond the water. Reports indicated that oyster pirates "shanghaied" crews directly off the streets or from shady drinking spots in Baltimore, and even along Wilmington's "coast" section. But perhaps the most chilling sign of the era's brutality came in the form of a grisly discovery, described in the Chronicle: "The bay net came in with oysters out of the mud, plus the remains of two human skeletons. Investigators found the victims' necks chained together with anchor wire. The skulls had been crushed by repeated blows from some blunt instrument."

Captain "Pungy Joe" from Blackbird Hundred earned a reputation as a fearless dredge captain and leader of men among the legendary figures of this violent period. His name became synonymous with one of the most infamous confrontations on the bay—a massive battle involving forty oyster dredge boats against police vessels that resulted in seven ships being sunk, along with numerous casualties.

The violent clashes between tongers and dredgers stemmed from a crucial moment in oystering technology. In 1865, Baltimorean Edward Fairbanks patented improvements to the mechanical oyster dredge that revolutionized harvesting capabilities. His design, featuring iron teeth and a rope mesh bag, proved devastatingly efficient. Maryland immediately embraced the innovation, allowing Chesapeake Bay dredging that same year. This technological watershed created instant winners and losers on Delaware Bay, where by 1888 some 1,400 vessels and 2,300 men competed for the precious bivalves.

The new dredge's efficiency masked its destructive nature. While dredging boats could harvest vastly larger quantities in less time, they damaged the beds faster than nature could replenish them. Tongers, using patent tongs invented in 1887 that could reach deeper waters than traditional tonging methods, still found their more selective approach vastly outpaced by mechanical dredging. They looked on in anger as dredgers ravaged their traditional grounds.

"The state's great oyster treasuries are the natural rock, from which the seed oysters are taken," explained Little Creek fleet owner John W. Fennimore Jr. in the Morning News on April 18, 1906. He decried how dredgers "take all they can dig up, throw back nothing and dump it all upon their grounds for 'bottom,' as they claim," rather than returning smaller oysters to breed. [By "bottom," Fennimore referred to the practice of using immature oysters and shell debris to harden the substrate of private oyster grounds instead of allowing these young oysters to replenish public waters.]

The conflict also reflected a stark economic divide. Patent tongers typically ran small, family operations using inexpensive craft like skiffs, sharpies, tuckups, and tongys—later switching to modest powered workboats. In contrast, mechanical dredging required substantial capital investment in larger vessels like skipjacks and bugeyes, which later gave way to motorized buyboats. These bigger boats demanded larger crews to service and maintain, creating intense pressure to maximize short-term profits through intensive harvesting. This approach clashed fundamentally with the tongers' smaller-scale, sustainability-minded operations. One side treated the oysters as a shared resource. The other treated them as a short-term yield. They were not just competitors; they were antagonists in a philosophical war over what it meant to fish, earn, and belong. "The people of Delaware are growing poorer," Fennimore observed, "while others and non-residents are growing rich over Delaware's oyster deposits."

The oyster piracy era drew to a close through a combination of technological advancement and biological calamity. State governments steadily tightened their grip on the industry, deploying armed patrols and motorized enforcement vessels that could effectively chase down poachers. Delaware and New Jersey strengthened their cooperation, creating a unified system of licenses and patrols that made it harder for pirates to exploit state-line jurisdictional gaps.

But perhaps the most devastating blow to oyster piracy came from nature itself. In the late 1950s, a microscopic parasite called *Haplosporidium nelsoni*, known as MSX, began ravaging Delaware Bay's oyster populations. Another pathogen, *Perkinsus marinus*—commonly called Dermo—compounded the devastation.

The combination of aggressive law enforcement and collapsing oyster stocks had rendered large-scale piracy economically futile by the 1960s. The remaining oystermen largely abandoned illicit ways, turning instead to regulated cultivation. The waters that had once witnessed such brutal conflicts between tongers and dredgers grew quieter, though the oyster beds they had fought so viciously over would never fully recover their former abundance.

12

DOUBLE LIVES
EXPOSED

Bigamy and legal loopholes unraveled marriages.

The last thing Rev. Irvin B. Taylor expected was for his brother to show up unannounced at his parsonage in Mt. Pleasant, Iowa. Taylor had built a new life there, gaining the admiration of his congregation with stirring sermons and tireless evangelistic work. He had the respect of his peers, the sponsorship of a university president, and a wife—the daughter of a wealthy Martinsburg man—who believed she had married an upstanding minister. But when Taylor's brother arrived from Delaware and knocked on the door, he found more than a respected clergyman; he found a bigamist.

The woman who greeted the visitor introduced herself as Florence Graves Taylor, the minister's wife. That was the moment the secret unraveled. Taylor's brother knew another Mrs. Taylor—Agnes Maser Taylor—waiting in Wilmington with their two children, abandoned and struggling to make ends meet. At first, the brother considered keeping quiet, perhaps out of shock or loyalty. But by the time he returned to Delaware, he'd decided. He told their father. He told Agnes. And before long, Wilmington authorities were preparing to act. The response came quickly. On November 21, 1903, the *Morning News* reported that Taylor, now back in Delaware, had been arrested. The charge was not bigamy—Delaware law required both marriages to have taken place within the state—but desertion and failure to support his first wife, Agnes Maser Taylor. The court ordered him to pay her $25 a month and post a $2,000 bond to ensure compliance. He failed to meet the court's terms, so authorities sent him to the New Castle County Workhouse.

News of Taylor's double life made its way to Iowa, where the law posed no such obstacle. The Keokuk County grand jury indicted him for bigamy, and on January 15, 1904, Sheriff John Beatty arrived in Wilmington with extradition papers. Delaware officials approved the extradition and sent Taylor to Iowa for trial.

During the proceedings, evidence made clear that Taylor had lived as a respected minister in Iowa for more than two years while maintaining his first marriage in Delaware. His deception had been complete—his new father-in-law had used his influence to secure Taylor a position at Iowa Wesleyan University, and his congregation in Martinsburg had seen him as a rising star in the church. Even Florence

Graves, Wife No. 2, had no idea she had married a man with an existing family. The court confronted her with the truth, but she refused to abandon him. Pregnant with their second child, she vowed to wait for his release so they could be legally wed.

The jury convicted Taylor, and on April 25, 1904, the judge sentenced him to four years in an Iowa prison. He remained defiant to the end. Taylor reportedly smiled as the sheriff took him into custody and said quietly, "I'm glad it's all over. Let's go."

His first wife, Agnes, had no such luxury. With no other option, she worked in a factory to support their two children. Florence, despite the outrage of her wealthy family, opened a dressmaking business to sustain herself. The case highlighted a legal gap that lawmakers in Delaware later worked to close. But at its heart, the scandal exposed something more universal: the ease with which a man entrusted with moral and spiritual leadership could live a lie in plain sight.

While Taylor's betrayal of trust played out in pulpits and parsonages, others sworn to serve the public good found themselves tangled in similar scandals. Law enforcement officers, expected to enforce the rules, proved just as susceptible to the lure of deception. Three cases spanning decades—William F. Long in the 1940s, Julian J. Brown in 1960, and Wilbur F. Justice Jr. in 2013—each revealed how figures in uniform, bound by duty, could breach the very laws they were sworn to uphold.

Long, a former city policeman who had served for 25 years, faced a bigamy conviction after marrying his second wife, Myrtle R. Barry, just 13 days after obtaining a questionable divorce from his first wife, Della Schleif. Long claimed he had met Arkansas' residency requirements, but Delaware courts ruled otherwise. The jury found that he had never truly established a permanent domicile in Arkansas, meaning his divorce from Schleif was invalid—and his new marriage to Barry, illegal. Long's case, however, became more than a simple matter of bigamy; the prosecution exposed systemic issues with interstate divorce recognition.

His attorney, Stephen E. Hamilton Jr., argued that there were approximately 300 similar cases of Delaware residents who had remarried after out-of-state divorces, calling it "a mockery on justice to indict one person for bigamy where it is notoriously known that there are hundreds of comparable cases." In a surprising turn, the

Delaware Supreme Court overturned Long's conviction in April 1949. The justices ruled that the lower court should have considered evidence that Long had consulted an attorney before remarrying and had acted on legal advice. The case ultimately helped highlight the need for clearer divorce recognition laws across state lines.

Two decades later, in January 1960, the Wilmington Police Department dismissed another officer, William J. Brown of the 800 block of Monroe Street, for similar misconduct. The Department of Public Safety's board of directors approved the trial board's recommendation that Brown be terminated after he allegedly married a second wife the previous June without divorcing his first wife, with whom he had two children. The names of Brown's wives were not published in news accounts, a common practice that often rendered women in these cases as anonymous.

"I borrowed $5 from friends and paid my way out of the arranged bondage."

MARTHA LIGHTCAP

Unlike Long's complex legal battle, authorities handled Brown's case swiftly and internally. When his second wife discovered his deception, she initiated annulment proceedings, and the department charged him with violating his oath of office and a moral count. The department dismissed him effective at midnight on January 18, 1960, with little of the legal debate that had surrounded Long's case, suggesting a hardening of attitudes toward such ethical breaches among police officers.

Most recently, in 2013, Wilbur F. Justice Jr., another Wilmington police officer, found himself at the center of a bigamy investigation that revealed the changing nature of such cases in the modern era. Justice, 45, had served on the force for only three years when a routine background check by the Delaware Division of Alcohol and Tobacco Enforcement uncovered a startling oversight: he had married his fourth wife in September 2012, just one month after filing for divorce from his third wife,

Gina, but before that divorce had been finalized.

Adding to his legal troubles, Justice falsely claimed on his marriage application that this was his first marriage. Justice's case appeared rooted less in deception than in carelessness. His attorney called it "sloppiness," explaining that Justice had wrongly assumed his divorce was final. By June 2013, Justice resigned from the department, citing unfair treatment, according to his attorney. He later pleaded guilty to making a false statement, bringing the matter to a close. Superior Court Judge Charles H. Toliver IV showed leniency, suspending even the $1 fine and imposing no probation, indicating that he believed the case should never have been prosecuted. Although prosecutors dropped the bigamy charge, the fallout ended Justice's career—a reminder that even unintentional legal violations can cost a law enforcement officer their job.

Men did not hold a monopoly on bigamy. Delaware women from various walks of life also found themselves involved in bigamous unions. While social contexts and consequences varied by sex, men and women alike shared similar motivations. Some engaged in deliberate deception, others acted out of financial desperation, neglected proper divorce procedures, or sought escape from unhappy marriages. Society and the legal system responded to these actions differently, shaped by the gender expectations of the time.

Martha Lightcap's case combined sensation with tragedy. Arrested in December 1924, Lightcap stood before Magistrate D.W. Stevens in Middletown charged with bigamy—but her testimony exposed a far darker reality.

During the four-hour hearing, Lightcap testified that her second husband, Joseph Huselton of Greenspring, had not only deceived her but had literally gambled her away. Lightcap testified that "on one occasion, Huselton was shooting crap with a negro bootlegger, and, having no more money, put her up against a 'five-dollar fade'." He lost the bet and "she was to be delivered to the negro two days later." The newspaper reported that "in the meantime, she said, she borrowed $5 from friends and paid her way out of the arranged bondage."

But that wasn't the only time she had been treated as property. She testified that "on another occasion, Huselton was pressed for the payment of a $6 store bill and she was sold to the storekeeper to liquidate the bill." She "told the magistrate how she went to live with the storekeeper and was released to Huselton two weeks later," reported the *Morning News*.

"Recently, a longing for her children possessed her, and she left Huselton and returned to her first husband," reported the *Morning News*. "Incensed at this, she declared, Huselton then procured the warrant that resulted in her arrest and the baring of the tale of how she had been used as a commodity to pay Huselton's debts."

The court appeared to recognize the cruelty of her situation. Officers took Huselton himself into custody under $500 bail as a witness, while the magistrate released her on $1,000 bail. When he failed to post the required amount, officials committed him to the Workhouse. Lightcap's first husband and their three children attended the hearing.

Six years after Lightcap's case, authorities arrested Virginia Brittingham Kettner of Summit Bridge for bigamy in October 1930. Unlike other cases, where the accused expressed regret or claimed ignorance, Kettner had no such hesitations. When asked about the charge, she told authorities, "It was worth it."

Kettner had been married to William Kettner since October 11, 1924, in a ceremony performed by the Rev. George F. Bounds, and had two children with him, ages three and four. But six months before her arrest, she left her husband and, without obtaining a divorce, married James P. Husfelt on April 21, 1930, with the Rev. Henry S. Dulany officiating. When her first husband discovered the second marriage, he complained to authorities, prompting them to arrest her along with Husfelt.

Authorities struggled to find the couple. Constable Leroy F. Campbell searched for several hours before discovering them at their residence, which sat deep in the countryside near Summit Bridge, far from main roads and difficult to reach. Once in custody, Husfelt claimed he had no idea Kettner was already married. Initially, Magistrate Haley set bail at $2,500 each for Kettner and Husfelt for the Court of General Sessions. He later reopened the case and dismissed the charge against Husfelt, accepting his claim of ignorance about Kettner's previous marriage. Kettner, however, stayed in custody, clearly unrepentant about her bigamous union.

Three decades later, in October 1960, authorities charged another Wilmington woman with bigamy—not due to a deliberate investigation, but because of a domestic dispute. Joan Beech, 25, had married John Waller Jr., a sailor, earlier that year in North Carolina. Waller didn't know that Beech had failed to divorce her first husband, John Beech, whom she had married in 1955.

Her marital status might have gone undiscovered, but after an argument with Waller, she called the police to report him for disorderly conduct. As officers investigated the case, they discovered that Beech had two husbands. Instead of pursuing only the initial charge, they arrested both Beech and Waller on suspicion of bigamy.

Christine L. Orengo's 2002 case represented a more modern entanglement of failed relationships and legal oversights, unlike earlier cases of deliberately hidden second marriages.

Orengo married her first husband in 1986. At some point, they separated but never legally divorced. By April 2000, she had moved on and married another man. For two years, she lived as though her second marriage was legitimate, until authorities discovered the legal contradiction. Authorities arrested Orengo on a felony charge of bigamous marriage contracted outside the state. She was later released on $2,000 bail.

Unlike their male counterparts, these women often faced social scandal beyond the legal charges. In Lightcap's case, she became more a victim than a perpetrator, trapped in a situation that the legal system barely knew how to address. Kettner, on the other hand, seemed unrepentant, seeing her crime as worthwhile. Police uncovered Beech's case almost by accident, while Orengo's seemed more like an unfortunate bureaucratic mistake than a deliberate deception.

Public scrutiny united all four cases. The law classified bigamy as a felony, yet the social consequences often burdened women more than the legal penalties. Their stories, though different, each show how deeply personal betrayals could become public scandals. They also reveal how marriage, law, and morality did not always follow rigid boundaries.

By 1988, Delaware viewed bigamy as a less sensationalized charge. When the *Evening Journal* reported that a New Castle County grand jury indicted Boyd Paul Reeves for bigamy that year, the newspaper's phrasing—"a rare charge of bigamy"—highlighted a shift in how officialdom perceived and prosecuted such cases. While bigamy still occurred, legal reforms reshaped how authorities addressed marital irregularities.

One of the most significant changes came from within the Catholic Church. For much of the twentieth century, Catholic law offered few legal options for those seeking to remarry after a failed marriage. Divorce was a civil process, but within the Church, remarriage was only possible if the first union was annulled—effectively declared to have never been a valid marriage in the first place.

Until the 1970s, annulments remained rare and expensive, requiring proof of extreme circumstances such as deception, insanity, or bigamy. But new guidelines allowed the Church to simplify the process. A 1982 *Evening Journal* article noted that Catholic annulments were no longer limited to the wealthy or well-connected. This shift enabled many divorced Catholics to remarry without fearing excommunication from their religious community. The change also reduced the incentive for clandestine second marriages.

At the same time, Delaware's civil divorce laws were undergoing a major transformation. Divorce once demanded proof of wrongdoing—adultery, abuse, desertion, or extreme cruelty. This burden often triggered drawn-out legal battles and, in some cases, drove spouses to fabricate evidence or allege bigamy to speed up the process. But in 1974, Delaware adopted "no-fault" divorce, removing the need to assign blame. The only legal threshold now became "irretrievable breakdown of the marriage relationship." The *Morning News* reported in 1975 that the new law caused a surge in divorce filings as the process became more accessible. This shift offered couples a more straightforward path to ending their marriages without the need to engage in public, adversarial proceedings.

Beyond no-fault divorce and Catholic annulments, Delaware also addressed the issue of out-of-state divorces, another legal gray area that had previously contributed to bigamy cases. Before 1945, Delaware law refused to automatically recognize divorces granted in other states, meaning that authorities could technically charge someone with bigamy for divorcing in, for example, Las Vegas, and remarrying in Delaware. That year, lawmakers passed a divorce recognition law requiring courts to honor properly obtained out-of-state divorces.

But the law did not resolve every ambiguity. In 1947, the conviction of former Wilmington police officer William F. Long highlighted how questions over residency requirements could still render an out-of-state divorce invalid—and leave a second marriage open to bigamy charges.

Before modern legal mechanisms and communication networks, geography and personal reinvention often facilitated bigamy. Emerson Wilson's January 6, 1973 *Morning News* column recalled the saga of Cornelius Barnhart, a young baker whose audacious bigamy attempt revealed the legal vulnerabilities of 19th-century America.

In 1849, Barnhart, a 25-year-old with "very black hair and a black goatee," arrived in Wilmington and quickly wove a web of deceit. He applied for lodging at the Bewley boarding house and soon met Mary Shannon, a 16-year-old cotton factory worker. With the Bewley owners' help, the two quickly married.

Barnhart's past resurfaced when Bewley received a letter from Antoinette Barnhart of New York City, who claimed to be his wife and the mother of his two children. After Bewley informed the police, officers arrested Barnhart on a bigamy charge. Barnhart's trial took place before Judge J. T. Robertson, who dismissed the charge for lack of evidence, stating he would only hold Barnhart if Antoinette appeared in person.

After his release, Barnhart and Mary fled Wilmington without a trace. In Philadelphia, Barnhart took a job as a baker but soon disappeared again, leaving Mary penniless and owing two weeks' room rent. Nearly a year later, rumors circulated that he had resurfaced in Baltimore and married yet again. He reportedly told friends he planned to head to California to make his fortune in the gold fields.

Columnist Wilson noted that criminals often used "going to California" as a ruse to escape capture, since crossing state lines typically provided safety from prosecution unless they faced a capital crime indictment.

Bigamists in Barnhart's era often found disappearing to be the easiest solution. A new town meant a clean slate. The law relied on firsthand testimony, and without rapid communication across jurisdictions, an accused man could simply cross a state line and vanish.

Routine checks and bureaucratic records eventually made that escape impossible. Modern bigamists often expose themselves through oversights—a misfiled divorce, an unfinalized separation, or a careless background check. The law no longer needs a deserted spouse to arrive in person; digital records, mandatory reporting, and cross-checking make it increasingly difficult to maintain multiple marriages.

Though bigamy never disappears entirely, it transforms. For the bigamists of old, disappearance was an art. For their modern counterparts, navigating bureaucratic loopholes is the art.

13

MOONSHINERS

The indelible mark of Prohibition-era bootlegging.

" B eat it! The officers are here!"

The sharp cry cut through the Sussex County woods as a barefoot girl of about seventeen leapt from the underbrush. Federal prohibition agents, who had been tracking across open country toward a patch of woods along Dupont Boulevard, froze in their tracks.

The girl, her long blonde hair streaming in the wind, raced ahead with surprising speed, always keeping about one hundred feet ahead of the pursuing officers. In the distance, men in blue shirts and slouch hats scattered into the dense forest. By the time agents reached the site, all they found was a copper 35-gallon still and "a laugh and scorn from the girl just before she disappeared in the thick woods." The Smyrna Times of November 2, 1927, reported that neither Prohibition Director George A. Hill nor his agents would reveal the location of the camp, as they were "still looking for the girl and the moonshiners."

This was the reality of Prohibition enforcement in Delaware's remote areas—a constant game of cat and mouse played out in some of the state's most challenging terrain. "The place is fifteen miles from the nearest railroad," explained Federal Prohibition Director Robert B. Elliott in May 1922, "roads are almost impassable in dry weather because of sand and in wet weather because of mud. In the swamp itself, our men were obliged to wade about knee-deep in water in an endeavor to follow hidden trails."

These swamplands provided perfect cover for Delaware's moonshiners. Between Lewes and Rehoboth stretched a dense swamp measuring about one mile long and three-quarters of a mile wide. In August 1922, agents found themselves "wading through the dense thickets, and finding it necessary at times to cut away the undergrowth which blocked their path" to reach stills set up deep within. Even when they knew where to look, the physical challenge of the pursuit gave moonshiners a critical advantage.

Sophisticated intelligence networks made the chase even more difficult, keeping moonshiners one step ahead of law enforcement. "The moonshiners have an elaborate spy system," reported the *Smyrna Times* of July 13, 1927. "They are tipped off when Federal men make their approach, and if anybody is found at the camp, he is usually some irresponsible watchman hired by the real moonshiner. While operating their stills, they are fully armed but when surprised by Federal agents, they do not shoot unless the Federal men open fire first. The moonshiners would rather trust to their knowledge of the swamp and woodland trails for escape or with their fate in the courts than to be hunted for murder or manslaughter." The barefoot girl who warned the moonshiners of approaching agents was the perfect example of this system in action—just one link in a network of lookouts that helped operations vanish into the landscape when danger approached.

Moonshiners found an additional tactical edge in Delaware's southern swamplands along the Maryland state border. Charles Savage, operating near Delmar, exploited the lack of cross-border arrest authority by placing his still directly on the state line. At the time, Delaware and Maryland law enforcement held no power to make arrests across state boundaries.

If Delaware officers closed in, Savage could simply step into Maryland and evade them. If Maryland authorities gave chase, he could slip back into Delaware. Without formal extradition or coordination—rare in routine Prohibition enforcement—local police had little recourse. The *Wilmington Daily Commercial*, clearly exasperated, commented that pursuing Savage required a "flying squadron" of federal agents capable of coordinating across state lines.

While many moonshiners operated alone or with family, Prohibition also gave rise to several organized gangs, each with their own colorful methods and reputations. Delaware's newspapers reported on these outlaw enterprises with a mix of alarm and amusement.

Perhaps none were more flamboyant than the self-styled "Gentlemen Moonshiners" who operated between Lewes and Rehoboth in the summer of 1922. Dressed in white flannels, white sport shirts, and yachting caps, these young men in their early twenties looked more like they belonged at a country club than in the dense swampland where they had established their operation.

When Federal Agent Edwards and State Detective Ottie Donoway finally tracked them down, the young men maintained their aristocratic pretense even as officers arrested them. One of them, with an elegant bow to the agents, announced, "And I am Dan Schimer, known as Gentleman Dan."

Their moonshine operation matched their sophisticated attire. They scattered and hid four fifteen-gallon stills throughout the swamp, ensuring that if authorities found one, the others would remain concealed. A single large coil served all four stills, ensuring that at least one still was always in operation. The *Evening Journal* reported that the young men had "an exclusive trade, for which they supplied a high-grade corn whisky" to the fashionable summer resorts.

When caught, Schimer tried to flee. Agent Edwards fired a single shot—the bullet sent Schimer's yachting cap flying from his head. He stopped and surrendered. The Gentlemen Moonshiners' refined appearance may have been unusual, but their fate—arrested and held under $1,000 bail each—was typical of moonshiners who weren't quick enough to escape into the woods.

If the Gentlemen Moonshiners represented moonshining's stylish face, Bryan Lynch and his brothers embodied the trade's industrial scale. Based in the remote swamplands near Roxana in Baltimore District, Lynch operated what federal officials described as "the largest manufacturer of illicit liquor in this State, his plant equaling any of those in the mountains of Virginia or Southern moonshine States."

Lynch's moonshine operation had become notorious by the spring of 1922. That May, federal agents captured a 100-gallon still—nicknamed the "Old Lunch Burner"— hidden deep in the swamps between Roxana and Fenwick Island. The rig produced a gallon of whiskey every fifteen minutes. Although Lynch escaped during the raid, Director Robert B. Elliott himself joined the manhunt, underscoring the seriousness of the case. The liquor from that still was reputed to be the best in Delaware, tinted with added coloring to mimic aged whiskey.

Lynch remained at large until December 1924, when authorities arrested him during a raid on his farm. There, they found another fully equipped 100-gallon still, ten barrels of mash buried beneath the earth, and about forty gallons of finished whiskey.

His operation reportedly netted $40,000 in 1925—more than half a million dollars today—through the production of rye whiskey and peach brandy.

Even after Bryan Lynch's arrest, the family name continued to surface in moonshine investigations. In December 1925, agents raided the woods behind Clarence Lynch's home and found another still, smaller in size but buried with the same care. Whether Clarence was directly involved or simply unlucky in proximity, the surname had by then become shorthand for liquor-making in Sussex County.

Perhaps the most surprising moonshine ring operated under the leadership of a man of the cloth—or at least someone who claimed to be. In October 1921, federal agents arrested the Reverend A. H. Pierce, a Black preacher who "claimed supernatural powers," in Seaford. Pierce "exercise[d] great influence over a certain element of the Negro population," using his status to organize an extensive moonshine network.

Prohibition officers considered his arrest "the most important yet made in Lower Delaware." During the raid, agents discovered "a complete moonshine distilling outfit, with three barrels of sour mash and a quantity of distilled corn whisky" in an abandoned house Pierce had rented. His followers revered him, a devotion that made the operation especially effective—and, in the eyes of authorities, especially dangerous.

Near Felton, prohibition agents uncovered a moonshine ring structured more like a cooperative than a typical illicit outfit. In July 1931, they discovered seven separate stills scattered throughout patches of woods within a two-mile radius of Sipple's general store, rather than a single large still.

Deputy Prohibition Administrator Harold D. Wilson concluded that the woods had "the appearance of liquor operation being worked on shares, each member operating a still on a production basis, and all members pooling their results." This shared-risk strategy distributed the risk while maximizing production capacity.

The collective's operations were extensive, with agents seizing "three 500-gallon mash vats, five 10-gallon pressure tanks, condensers, and five gallons of liquor" at just one location. Nearby they found "five stills, three of 25-gallon capacity and two of 50-gallon capacity."

The Felton setup's distributed arrangement ensured its durability. The collective could keep running even if authorities discovered one still. They also maintained an early warning system. During each raid, agents found evidence of recent activity but no operators—gang members running the stills likely learned of the agents' approach through a posted guard and fled. Despite a sophisticated organization, this crew eventually collapsed under increasing pressure from prohibition agents who made "dozens of visits to woods in the lower part of the State."

Public sentiment during Prohibition wavered between moral condemnation and quiet resignation. In 1922, the *Smyrna Times* insisted that Delaware's courts stop tolerating liquor offenses and impose harsher penalties. "The class of men who make the deadly moonshine whisky," the paper argued, "can offer no excuse, and should pay the full penalty." Others took a more somber view. "It is clear that enforcement has failed to break the trade," observed the *Milford Chronicle* in 1929, reflecting the fatigue of a public that had seen years of raids end with empty stills and missing suspects.

On the ground, enforcement agents trudged through swamps, thickets, and mud-flats in what often felt like a thankless pursuit. During a raid in late 1922, officers descended on a suspected still site in the marshes of Milford Neck, long under surveillance. As they reached the scene, they found the copper apparatus still set up, one of the stills "warm," and liquor "dripping into a pitcher left by the fugitives." The crew had disappeared into the reeds. Similar frustrations unfolded across the state. In 1927, *Smyrna Times* reporters noted that "almost daily" raids produced stills and mash—but rarely people. "The capture of operators is no easy matter," they admitted. "As a rule, the principal moonshiners are farmers... fully armed but trusting instead to their knowledge of the swamp and woodland trails."

Agents sometimes met these frustrations with gallows humor. In 1922, a Washington circular suggested that Delaware's Prohibition Director might deploy bloodhounds to sniff out stills. The idea prompted laughter inside the Wilmington office. "Better get some rumhounds," one agent muttered.

Eventually, the strategy evolved. Raids grew more coordinated, with teams fanning out across multiple locations. In August 1922, officers executed simultaneous strikes across West Dover Hundred, arresting eight men in a single morning. By 1924, agents brought photographers along to document operations in real time. Others pushed farther into swamplands under increasingly dangerous conditions, as in the 1929 Victor Killen raid, when agents advanced under rifle fire and dynamite. Though enforcement seldom yielded dramatic showdowns, it gradually eroded the most entrenched operations—one raid, one missed opportunity, one confiscated barrel at a time.

Local folklore suggested that not all of Delaware's moonshiners were homegrown. In August 1922, the Smyrna Times reported that a gang known as "the North Carolinians" had arrived in the Dover locale two or three years earlier and were rumored to be involved in moonshine production. Their presence spoke to the migration of moonshining expertise from traditional strongholds in the southern Appalachians to new territories ripe for profit.

Records do not make clear whether these outsiders brought special techniques or simply saw opportunity in Delaware's wilds. They stood out enough to earn their own moniker among locals, who credited them with some of the most professional results.

Hardened criminals or experienced distillers did not run all of Delaware's moonshine operations. Ordinary citizens who saw opportunity in Prohibition became some of the most surprising producers. Sixty-nine-year-old Pauline Jevins operated one of "the most up-to-date and largest distilling plants ever uncovered in this State" on her farm eight miles north of Milford.

During the August 1925 raid, officers uncovered a sophisticated distillery setup with hundreds of gallons of mash hidden in barrels sunk into the ground. When officers arrived, Mrs. Jevins attempted to flee, but they captured her after a brief chase.

Economic necessity or medical rationalization often drove small-scale home brewers to turn to moonshining. "My doctor advised me to take a moderate dose of whisky every day," explained W.W. Whittacker when caught with a still in his kitchen in August 1921, "but really Mr. Elliott, it is too high for me to buy. The doctor told me if I wanted to keep on my feet I would have to drink whisky and that is the reason I bought the still."

Some, like James O. Dickerson, openly admitted their motivations. When federal officers arrested him in a swamp west of Redden in September 1927, he confessed that "he had secured the still and intended to make liquor in order to raise sufficient money to hire a lawyer to defend him in the larceny case" for which authorities had previously arrested him. Many farmers viewed distilling as a way to convert surplus grain into cash. "I can sell my rye for two dollars a bushel, or I can turn it into ten dollars' worth of whiskey," one anonymous distiller told the *Smyrna Times* on August 2, 1922.

Prohibition agents understood the dangers of their work. Moonshiners rarely fired first, but when cornered, they could turn confrontations deadly. In January 1929, federal prohibition officers raided the Victor Killen farm twelve miles southwest of Dover and came under siege in one of the state's most violent moonshine confrontations. After discovering three stills hidden in corn fodder shocks, the agents advanced into the nearby woods only to be "greeted with a fusillade of bullets believed to have been fired from rifles, presumably by moonshiners."

The agents initially sought shelter behind trees as approximately "25 shots had been fired," but the situation escalated dramatically when "a stick of dynamite landed about 60 feet from where the officers were standing." Only then did the agents return fire, leading to "an exchange of shots" where "bullets filled the air around them."

Despite the danger, the agents "steadily advanced" and unearthed 150 gallons of liquor. The *Smyrna Times* reported that the battle, which continued for almost an hour, ended with the agents destroying the stills and liquor, but the moonshiners remained "safely screened in the woods with which they are familiar" as darkness fell and "the agents withdrew."

While Prohibition officers slogged through murky waters and nearly impenetrable undergrowth, their targets knew every hidden path and escape route. Director

Elliott and his enforcement team believed that when trapped, moonshiners "either secured a flat-bottomed boat hidden in the swamp and poled their way down one of the numerous shallow ditches leading into the Indian River or waded through the undergrowth to the water's edge and then swam to the opposite shore."

These raids became routine for one side and a calculated risk for the other for thirteen long years. From the marshes of Sussex County to the secluded woodlands of Kent, the pursuit of illicit alcohol seemed never-ending. The *Milford Chronicle* (January 25, 1929) offered a candid assessment of the situation when it lamented, "It is impossible for anyone to know the extent of home-brewing, home winemaking, and the production of 'moonshine' liquors... but it is clear that enforcement has failed to break the trade." For every still agents discovered and destroyed, they suspected many more remained hidden in Delaware's more remote rural landscapes.

Beyond local consumption, Delaware gained a reputation for quality "hootch" that attracted buyers from other states. Federal Investigator Spering testified in court that "Delaware 'moonshiners' make a high grade product, which 'goes over big' with North Jersey bootleggers."

During his testimony in the U.S. case against Elwood Marker of Wyoming, Delaware, Spering went on to tell how he had posed as "a moonshine buyer from Jersey, interested in making regular 'pick-ups' of Delaware Moonshine for the 'boys back near Newark.' I told him Jersey couldn't make good moonshine, and that Delaware moonshine was okay. I also told him that if his moonshine was good, I'd come back and buy about 25 gallons a week,'" Spering testified about his conversation with Marker, according to the *Milford Chronicle* of September 2, 1932.

Federal Investigator Spering's testimony just confirmed "what has been known for some time"—that Delaware moonshine, always considered by chemists unusually fit for human consumption, was getting bought up in bulk by "buyers" who hauled the stuff to Newark and nearby Jersey towns, where they doctored it to taste like imported liquor, bottled it in fancy containers, and sold it as the real thing.

While Federal chemist Harold Tiffany testified to the quality of properly made Delaware spirits, a poorly made batch might turn deadly. Historians Rachel Kipp and

Dan Shortridge documented in their book *Lost Delaware* that one still near Laurel, made from a lead-lined kerosene can, likely fatally poisoned a seventy-six-year-old man. Authorities recognized the dangers. "Casket, hearse, and grave are staring those square on the face who drink of the moonshine now being manufactured," warned Prohibition Director Robert B. Elliott.

Medical experts at the time expressed equal alarm. A Wilmington doctor suggested testing moonshine's potency by soaking a piece of raw beefsteak in it. "The steak probably will have its surface eaten off," he told *Every Evening*. "That is certain proof that the beverage contains a 'kick,' also proof of what it does to the inside of the human body." The doctor warned that homemade wine, "unless scientifically made, turns to vinegar, an acetic-acid compound," and that the "cross between wine and vinegar" might contain acetone, "which lacerates like sulphuric acid."

Federal officials echoed those concerns. Prohibition Director Robert B. Elliott later cautioned that chemical analysis of seized liquor revealed every sample contained fusel oil, which "causes the lips and body to turn blue and removes oxygen from the blood."

By the early 1930s, the tide had turned. Moonshiners, once emboldened by lax enforcement, began deserting their stills. "Dozens of visits to woods in the lower part of the State by prohibition agents has worried moonshiners to such an extent that they are abandoning elaborate distilling plants," noted the *Milford Chronicle* (August 5, 1932). Dismantling and relocating equipment no longer seemed worth the potential profits. Though Prohibition remained in on the books, crackdowns became more symbolic than effective.

As stills sat abandoned and the government's campaign lost momentum, Delaware's moonshining era neared its end. The final blow came in April 1933, when the state legalized 3.2 beer. Within five weeks, the newly established Liquor Commission issued 480 licenses, most of them permanent. "People seem to have turned to beer instead of the moonshine and other concoctions they indulged in before," said Alexander J. Taylor, the commission's executive secretary.

Consumers who once risked poisonous, poorly made moonshine now had access to regulated, standardized beer. This legal alternative crippled the dangerous moonshine trade, offering consumers a more reliable product while also reducing the social and health risks of illicit alcohol production.

For some backwoods brewers, repeal forced them to close up shop for good. But the spirit of resistance ran deep. "Human nature seems to hate prohibition of any kind," reflected *Every Evening* in 1922. "Tell the nation that instantaneous death would result from pulling the lobe of the left ear four times in rapid succession, and the undertakers would do a big business. Thousands could not resist."

Some moonshiners disappeared, some went legitimate, and others devised new ways to stay one step ahead. Delaware's hidden still sites, with their copper coils and whispered wheeling-and-dealing, faded into history. The game of cat and mouse ended—not because the agents won, but because the rules changed.

14

KKK INTIMIDATION FINALLY FAILS

Public displays of hate and organized hate-mongering.

The Ku Klux Klan prepared for one of their signature spectacles along U.S. Route 40 near Newport in 1923. They made their message clear: Delaware belonged to "true" Americans, and they intended to remind Catholics, immigrants, and African Americans of their place.

Word spread about their plans for a cross-burning, and New Castle Catholics weren't going to let it happen without a fight. "Get your guns," came the Klan orders when they heard of the opposition gathering.

The Klan followed a precise ritual for these ceremonies. Three oil-soaked crosses stood at the center, poised for ignition, while automobiles formed a perfect circle around them, their headlights trained inward like floodlights on a stage. When the moment came, Klansmen doused the lights and fired the crosses.

The Klan rode high that summer. "A big thriving affair," one former member would later recall, involving "a lot of young boys" like himself who were "having a lot of fun" burning crosses. But their revelry was about to meet its match that August.

At a farm outside New Castle, hooded guards kept spectators at bay along the edges of a cornfield. But when the crosses erupted in flames, the Catholics surged forward, overwhelming the Klan's defenses. "All hell broke loose," one spectator reported. The night descended into a wild club-swinging, rock-throwing riot. By morning, some fifty people were injured, several with gunshot wounds.

The night reached its breaking point when one Klansman, watching the crowd over-run the Klan's defenses, jumped into his car and barreled straight into the Catholic ranks. Screams rose above the chaos as bodies scattered. That act—desperate, reckless, and almost certainly criminal—shifted the fury of the crowd into something colder. When the Catholics traced the car's owner, they delivered a message with no room for misinterpretation: he was "as good as dead." The man fled town that same night. According to local lore, "nobody ever saw him again."

In the Deep South, the Klan staged spectacles without resistance. In Delaware, they misjudged their strength.

The Klan was no stranger to the First State. As early as 1868, just three years after the organization's founding in Tennessee, mysterious notices appeared throughout the town of Smyrna, bearing ominous messages: "Beware—You are Watched" and "The Avenger is on his Path." Witnesses saw young men in York carriages—the preferred conveyance of the middle and upper classes—posting these warnings under cover of darkness. The Klan's appeal in Delaware extended from the beginning beyond the uneducated masses to include those of means and social standing.

The New Castle violence exposed the Klan's vulnerability, but internal divisions ultimately led to the Klan's downfall. Despite its national claims of moral and racial purity, the Ku Klux Klan in the First State operated more like a pyramid scheme than an ideological movement. "We were sold a bill of goods," an old-timer from Newport would later recall with a laugh, describing the principal organizers as "money-skimming scoundrels."

"They're mean. They're hateful. They shouldn't be allowed to walk around on U.S. soil."

REP. AL O. PLANT

The Newport chapter gained notoriety for corruption. The local den flaunted its reach, claiming three members on the Newport school board and two each on the school boards of Marshallton, Five Points, and Christiana. A den of thieves hid behind the facade of respectability. "It was a money-making scheme. That's all it was," the Newport old-timer admitted. "There would be collections at every meeting. There was a $10 initiation fee and dues of about $3 a year... You bought your regalia from the organization."

But the Newport Klansmen had their own ideas about profit. As the elderly former member recalled with a laugh, "the Newport boys were so damn crooked they never sent the money" to the "Imperial Palace" in Atlanta. When national Klan officials arrived to investigate the missing funds, the local leadership took swift action—they burned their financial records right on Market Street in Wilmington. For this former Klansman, the organization's true nature became clear quickly: "they were nothin' but a bunch of damn bums and I wouldn't walk across the street to have a damn thing to do with 'em." He, like his parents, burned his white robe and hood.

"The Klan continued on in a mild manner in Delaware through 1928 as a weapon against the election of Al Smith, the Democratic candidate for president and a Catholic. After the election and the defeat of Smith, the Klan quietly subsided."

The Klan remained publicly inactive in Delaware until 1954, when the U.S. Supreme Court struck down school segregation in Brown v. Board of Education. Just four months after the ruling, as Delaware grappled with implementation, Milford became ground zero for resistance. The Milford Board of Education enrolled ten Black students in the previously all-white Milford High School, prompting the school to close for a week and causing the entire board to resign.

Bryant Bowles entered this charged atmosphere with his National Association for the Advancement of White People (NAAWP). He presented his organization as a legitimate civil rights group for whites. But when he invited the Ku Klux Klan to organize in Delaware, the Laurel State Register responded with biting sarcasm: "We would like to rescind that invitation, adding our suggestion to the professional hate mongers of the Klan that they stay out of Delaware altogether." The newspaper dismissed Bowles and his allies as "white-robed, white trash representatives of the Ku Klux Klan."

Delaware authorities arrested Bowles and charged him with urging others to violate state school attendance laws and conspiring to break those laws. State Police Detective Allen J. Wentz testified that at a mass meeting at the Harrington Airport on September 26, Bowles acknowledged that Delaware law required school attendance. But he argued that parents had a right to keep their children home to prevent them from being hurt. He added that if children stayed home long enough, something would be done about segregation.

State Detective James Collins testified that Bowles made similar statements at a Gumboro meeting the next day. Corporal Earl Clark reported that at a Lincoln meeting, Bowles urged everyone to keep children home and promised his organization would back them if they got into difficulty.

The State Supreme Court ruled that the Milford board lacked proper authorization because the State Board of Education had not approved its integration plans in advance. In his defense at trial, Bowles testified that Joseph Danes, a local tractor dealership owner, had asked him to come to Milford after seeking him out in Washington.

A dozen parents testified that they chose to keep their children out of school during the crisis of their own accord, not because of Bowles' urging. A Superior Court jury later acquitted Bowles, overturning his initial conviction in the Court of Common Pleas on charges of conspiring to violate school laws, the Morning News reported on December 28, 1955.

Although many condemned the effort to revive organized white supremacy in Delaware, the movement set the stage for the next wave of activity.

The 1960s brought a new chapter in Delaware's Klan history with the emergence of Ralph E. Pryor Jr., a 33-year-old former Wilmington police officer who had resigned from the force in June 1964. As the state's acting grand dragon, Pryor initially portrayed the Delaware Klan as a benign organization focused on fighting communism and corruption through literature distribution. He claimed to devote 16 to 17 hours a day to Klan organizing "because I believe in it."

The Klan returned to public view in Delaware on July 31, 1965, for the first time since 1928, staging a massive rally at the Emil J. Walther farm near Bear. Newsmen counted 791 cars stretched along U.S. 40, with crowd estimates ranging from 2,000 to 5,000. The rally featured Robert M. Shelton Jr., imperial wizard of the United Klans of America, who delivered a 75-minute speech attacking civil rights leaders, government officials, and religious organizations. The evening's spectacle ended with the burning of a 30-foot cross.

Littleton P. Mitchell, head of the State Conference of the NAACP, responded forcefully: "I cannot believe that the intelligent citizens of this state will tolerate this invasion of imbeciles."

Some Delaware officials did more than tolerate the Klan—they defended it. State Representative Glenn W. Busker, (D-Smyrna), publicly supported the organization, telling the *Evening Journal*, "They're only trying to get good government, from what I read in the newspapers... I'm not turning my back on them." The *Morning News* years later cited such "mouthings of prominent townfolk" as key to Smyrna's reputation as a hotbed of racism.

Pryor struggled to maintain stable leadership. He suddenly resigned in August 1965 as grand dragon, claiming that threats over the phone had targeted his estranged wife and children. The Klan chose a new leader at an emergency meeting in Newark, identifying him only as a businessman with five children. But Pryor's exit proved short-lived. Within weeks, he reclaimed his position as grand dragon.

He told the *Morning News* that Klan membership "will hit 1,000 very shortly" and predicted 14 or 15 units by spring. He claimed the organization had already expanded from two units to eight, with active chapters in Wilmington, Claymont, Newark, New Castle, Bear, Middletown, Milford, and Dover.

The Klan sought to turn Delaware into "the seedbed for the spread of its propaganda and membership in this general area," warned an October 22, 1965 *Morning News* editorial, comparing the strategy to "Castro in making Cuba a seedbed for the spread of communism in Latin America." The editorial denounced the organization as "anti-Negro, anti-Jew, anti-Catholic, anti-you-name-it."

Public Klan activities in Delaware would soon decline. In 1966, they attempted two rallies near Millsboro, but state officials thwarted a planned cross-burning by invoking a ban on outdoor burning. After these events, the Klan did not hold any publicly recorded rallies in Delaware for more than a decade.

Racist attitudes that sustained the Klan's presence persisted, particularly in towns like Smyrna. In 1981, the Morning News reported that a "respected Smyrna merchant boasted of using a cattle-prod to chase blacks away from in front of his store." But change was coming. That same year, Smyrna elected Delaware's first Black mayor, prompting local barber Vance Cole to declare, "They always said that Smyrna was prejudiced. They can't say that now."

In March 1982, Rep. Al O. Plant (D-Wilmington) introduced legislation aimed at curtailing Klan activities in Delaware. House Bill 419 would criminalize gatherings of people wearing masks or hoods if they planned to violate someone's civil rights. Lawmakers fiercely debated the measure's impact on constitutional rights and law enforcement practicality.

Plant stated his motivation unequivocally: "Those people should be ashamed of their name and their track record," he told the Evening Journal. "They're mean. They're hateful. They shouldn't be allowed to walk around on U.S. soil."

The Klan fought back. Roger Butler of the United Klans of America called the bill "totally illegal" and threatened to bring robed Klansmen to Legislative Hall in protest. He argued the law would violate "freedom of assembly, freedom of association, or freedom of speech."

Even supporters voiced concerns. Bruce Hudson, the chief House attorney, advised against the bill, arguing that conspiracy laws already addressed such activities, making the bill redundant. "If a person violated such a law, he would be guilty of the much more serious offense of conspiracy," Hudson explained. He also questioned its enforceability: "I don't think you'll get any Klansman to say the reason they gather is to plan a criminal act."

An Evening Journal editorial on June 8 urged caution. "Let's move very deliberately indeed in taking basic rights away from any group, even if the members of any such group happen to be contemptible and cowardly rats who need to cloak their identities under hoods and masks."

The House unanimously approved the bill in March, though several members admitted they voted more out of courtesy to Plant than genuine conviction in its merits. The Senate debated the bill more contentiously. Sen. James T. Vaughn (D-Clayton), a former state trooper, refused to vote, calling the measure "unenforceable."

Despite concerns, the Senate approved the bill 19-0 in June 1982. Sen. Herman M. Holloway (D-Wilmington), a co-sponsor, clarified that the law wouldn't prevent peaceful Klan gatherings: "I'm not trying to put them out of business. I'm just trying to get them to uncover their faces if they're up to some devilment."

On a sweltering Sunday in June 1997, the Ku Klux Klan staged the group's final public stand in Delaware. Pulaski Park sits in Wilmington's working-class Hedgeville neighborhood. Generations of immigrants once filled the modest homes that ring the park. Later waves brought Hispanic and African American residents.

Just six members of the American Knights Ku Klux Klan's Delaware chapter showed up, led by Paul W. Deputy Sr. They claimed "black-on-white violence" plagued the city and said they were there to protest it. Deputy chose this location deliberately—it bordered Browntown, where a white police officer had allegedly been driven out by African American neighbors following accusations of brutality during a traffic stop.

But the Klan's message found little welcome reception. A diverse crowd of about 400 counter-protesters gathered behind fences and police barricades along Maryland Avenue, their chants of "Klan Go Home" drowning out the white supremacists' speeches. Among them was 13-year-old Billy Carrow, who declared simply: "I think they're wrong. They should like all races."

Wilmington Mayor James H. Sills Jr. came to observe after the Klan singled him out in leaflets, accusing him and other African American community leaders of fostering what they falsely claimed was anti-white sentiment in the city.

The mayor dismissed their propaganda, pointing to the day's turnout: "If people were really believing their assessment of racial problems in Wilmington, then why were so few of them accepting their literature?"

One hundred thirteen police officers from various jurisdictions, including mounted units, heavily fortified the scene to maintain order. Local business owners like Lamont Graves, who ran the Ultimate Convenience Store across from the park, took a pragmatic view. "I'm a retailer. I don't care what the occasion is, I've still got to make a buck," Graves said. "I'll even sell to the Klan. I don't like them being here, but I don't discriminate."

Wesley Henry, a 30-year-old African American resident, came not to taunt but to deliver a message: "We all have to live together as one to make this world go around right." The City Council and Browntown Community Association tried to draw attention away from the rally by hosting a neighborhood picnic six blocks away.

Though observers considered the American Knights among the country's most volatile Klan groups, their tiny showing in Wilmington revealed increasing irrelevance. White supremacist group researcher Tawanda Shaw observed that the minimal turnout masked a more volatile reality: "You're dealing with the hard core, the ones who are committed. These people are more dangerous than your larger groups."

The overwhelming response from the community made clear that the Klan's influence in Delaware had withered to almost nothing. The rally ended without violence, closing the afternoon and effectively marking the Klan's final public stand in Delaware. Signs of the group's decline had appeared long before: in 1988, a spokesman for the Anti-Defamation League in Philadelphia, which tracks hate groups in Delaware and eastern Pennsylvania, reported, "there have been no rallies, no meetings, no activities" in the First State for a number of years. And a 2007 study by the League stated the Klan no longer had organized chapters in Maryland or Delaware.

The Klan in Delaware floundered as much as it menaced—scam artists led its early efforts, backlash greeted its mid-century resurgence, and its 1997 rally ended in embarrassment.

But to assume the Klan's downfall marked the end of its ideology would be naive. The white robes and hoods have disappeared, but the hatred and racial resentment that fueled them endures—shifting form, not vanishing.

Delaware rejected the Klan, but the state has never fully shed the attitudes that once empowered the group.

15

KIDNAPPERS TAKE YOUNG HILDA BRODSKY

The harrowing ordeal of a Wilmington home abduction.

Frank Romano, 42, stood before Magistrate Nathan Beifel in the Philadelphia courtroom. His two daughters, Rose, fifteen, and Hattie, eleven, sat watching—they hadn't seen their father in four years. His wife had made the trip from Baltimore, though she and Romano had lived separately. Romano wept openly as he reached for them.

"I just want to go home," he told the judge, according to the *Wilkes-Barre Times Leader*, August 13, 1936. "To see my wife. To be with my daughters."

The Brodskys did not attend. Harry and Rose Brodsky, parents of the girl who accused Romano of kidnapping her, not only refused to appear but also informed authorities they had no interest in prosecuting the case.

Magistrate Beifel tapped his gavel. "Mr. Romano, the state of Delaware declines to pursue charges." With a single stroke, it was over. Why would the parents of a kidnapped child refuse to press charges against her alleged abductor?

Nine-year-old Hilda Brodsky left her house on Monroe Place in Wilmington that morning of April 15, 1932, in her blue chinchilla coat, her mother's careful hand-stitching evident in the hem. The coat fit loosely—she still had room to grow—but she liked the way it swayed when she walked. She had traveled this route to school a hundred times before: out the alley behind the house, east on Twenty-first Street, then north on Baynard Boulevard.

At Twenty-third Street and Baynard Boulevard, a car pulled up beside her. A woman leaned out, someone Hilda recognized from her father's place of business. Her voice was warm, familiar.

"Your father wants you at the store before you go to school, Hilda. We'll bring you right back."

It made sense. Papa sometimes needed errands run in the morning. Hilda climbed into the car, where a man sat behind the wheel. Instead of heading toward her father's store, they drove to a street adjoining No. 30 School. There, they stopped briefly. A man who had been loitering nearby approached the car and got into the back seat beside Hilda.

As they drove up Concord Pike, the man held her arms too tightly. The grip was painful.

"You're hurting me," Hilda said, her voice trembling.

The man's response sent ice through her veins: "One sound out of you and we'll break your neck."

Hilda made no noise after that, except to cry for her parents. She wasn't bound or gagged, but the threat was enough to keep her quiet as they drove toward Philadelphia, away from everything familiar, away from her family, away from safety.

The three kidnappers—the woman she recognized, the driver, and the man who had threatened her—had set their plan in motion. Within hours, her father would receive their ransom demand, and the longest fifty hours of Hilda Brodsky's life would begin.

Years later, police identified Frank Romano as the driver of that car, placing him behind the wheel with two companions that morning. Captain M. Harry Clark of the murder squad recognized him as the man who had driven the kidnapping vehicle through South Philadelphia after the crime. But on that April morning in 1932, Hilda knew nothing of names or identities, only that she was being taken far from home by people who meant her harm.

Harry and Rose Brodsky were not the kind of people who attracted the attention of criminals. At least, that's what Harry wanted people to believe. He ran a successful hosiery manufacturing business, moving product as a jobber for larger firms. They lived in Wilmington's desirable Baynard Boulevard District, an area lined with stately homes and manicured gardens.

The Brodskys were more than just successful business people—they were established members of Wilmington's Jewish community. Harry Brodsky had already demonstrated his leadership through the his involvement in the construction of Congregation Chesed Shel Emeth's Talmud Torah building in 1925-1926. He was an active member of B'nai B'rith and helped establish both the Associated Hebrew School and the Hebrew Free Loan Society, serving on the boards of both organizations. But such prominence could attract unwanted attention. And as some would later suspect, they had enemies.

"I am not wealthy by any means," Harry insisted. "And if the persons who kidnapped my daughter were doing it for gain, they would certainly have selected a more affluent person to make their victim."

A modest claim. A false one.

The family had lived at their Monroe Place address for about seven years, having settled there after moving from 309 French Street, where Mr. Brodsky now maintained his place of business. They were well-known enough that when news of the kidnapping broke, crowds gathered outside their home, requiring police to be stationed there to keep them back. Photographers jockeyed for position as flashbulbs popped, the bursts of light drawing even more onlookers. Eventually, police had to order the crowd to disperse and permit only those with business in the neighborhood to pass.

Delaware authorities, under immense public pressure, pursued an investigation aggressively. Mayor Frank C. Sparks stated that "if the child is not returned to her parents by tomorrow morning, I shall summon a conference of the directors of the Department of Public Safety," reinforcing the state's commitment to punishing the culprits.

The kidnappers kept her at the first house only briefly before transferring her to a second, where she spent most of her captivity. Life in the second house felt strange and frightening. The woman kidnapper, who had three children of her own, let Hilda play with them. But she could hardly sleep. "She said she had slept but two hours each night she was away because her kidnappers would not permit her to sleep in a room by herself," *Every Evening* reported.

On Saturday night, the kidnappers took her to a place Hilda called "not an ordinary restaurant. They called it an automat. "I didn't dare say anything to anybody in the automat because I was afraid the man and the woman who were with me would kill me," she later recounted.

Even there, her religious upbringing guided her choices. "They told me I should eat some beefsteak, but I didn't because I was afraid it wasn't kosher. So, I drank some milk instead." When asked about her overall treatment, Hilda repeated a phrase her brother had taught her, saying it was "not so hot."

An unexpected tragedy ultimately triggered Hilda's release. On Friday night, while Hilda played with one of her captor's children, that child swallowed a small pin. The situation quickly became desperate. Someone rushed the youngster to a Philadelphia hospital, where the child died the following day. Police later theorized that this death had terrified the kidnappers, who realized their location could be traced through hospital records and the child's remains. The parents never claimed the body, likely fearing identification.

The increasingly desperate kidnappers approached Father Joseph Pugliese at Philadelphia's Church of St. Mary Magdalene de Pazzi, seeking his help as an intermediary. They asked him to relay their demands to the Brodsky family: a $50,000 ransom payment and a promise of immunity from prosecution. Dr. Arthur Keegan, a coroner's physician assisting Father Pugliese, described the delicate negotiations: "When he explained the circumstances, I strongly advised that he negotiate, but under no circumstances make any deal or promise immunity."

The kidnappers finally left Hilda at the church rectory on Sunday morning as their plans unraveled and police pressure mounted. While waiting for detectives to arrive, Dr. Keegan found a creative way to calm the frightened child. He gave her a collection basket and had her search through it for 1913 buffalo nickels, keeping her occupied until she could be reunited with her family.

The ordeal lasted exactly fifty hours, but the consequences endured much longer. Hilda remained deeply traumatized in the days following her return. Her mother reported that she became terrified every time a telephone rang, or someone knocked at the door. "They're coming after me," she cried out, and only her mother's reassuring words could comfort her.

By early May, just weeks after her return, anonymous callers began threatening to kidnap her again. These ransom demands, ranging from $5,000 to $50,000, placed "all members of the family in a highly nervous condition." The family hid the threats from Hilda, fearing they might seriously affect "the heart condition from which she suffers." Her mother or one of her sisters now accompanied her each day on her way to and from school.

The public reacted immediately and viscerally to Hilda Brodsky's release. The *Philadelphia Evening Bulletin* described it as "a happy ending to another threatened tragedy," but also declared that the child's return "cannot lessen the horror which the community feels at such crimes and its keen desire for authorities to track down those responsible and deliver them to justice."

Observers inevitably compared the case to the Lindbergh kidnapping that had occurred just weeks earlier in early March 1932. The nationally sensational case—in which the 20-month-old son of famous aviator Charles Lindbergh was abducted from his home and later found dead despite a ransom payment—had horrified the nation and sparked widespread fear among parents. Coming so soon after the Lindbergh tragedy, Hilda's kidnapping intensified public anxiety. Editorials warned against negotiating with criminals and demanded harsher punishments, with many calling for federal legislation to address what seemed to be a growing epidemic of child abductions.

One letter to the editor urged that "when the case is solved, it will reveal amazing angles" and that the kidnappers should be hanged. The abduction gripped Delaware as the first major case of its kind. "No parent in Wilmington felt safe," declared *Every Evening*.

Morris Astrin, an uncle of Hilda, spoke out forcefully, telling reporters that "the family will not show leniency in prosecuting the abductors of the child." His declaration put further pressure on Harry Brodsky. Whether Brodsky personally wanted to let the case drop or not, he could not risk looking weak or complicit in the eyes of the community.

In 1929, law enforcement arrested Benjamin Sherman—Harry Brodsky's brother-in-law—for embezzling funds from Brodsky's hosiery business, where Sherman worked as a salesman. Authorities held him on $2,000 bail, committed him to the workhouse in December, and released him in January 1930. At the time of Hilda's kidnapping, the two were estranged, which led the police to hold Sherman for 24 hours as a potential suspect. However, when Hilda returned, investigators quickly cleared Sherman of involvement, and the men soon reconciled.

Harry Brodsky, if he knew from the start that Sherman had arranged the kidnapping, at this point could not have stepped away from the investigation without exposing himself to public outrage.

The investigation into Hilda's kidnapping yielded frustratingly inconclusive results in the months following her return. Despite intensive efforts by Wilmington and Philadelphia police, the kidnappers had seemingly evaporated. Detectives pursued numerous leads—including a raid on a Chester, Pennsylvania gambling club and surveillance of suspected local criminals—but they failed to make a substantial breakthrough.

Captain Ellwood H. Wilson, who led the initial investigation, approached the case methodically. Shortly after the kidnapping, he distributed wanted fliers to police stations across the country and sent detailed information and fingerprints to the Department of Justice in Washington. These efforts kept the case alive, even as leads grew cold.

By June 1933, more than a year after the kidnapping, investigators finally made a breakthrough. On Saturday, June 24, as New York City detectives William Florence and Mike Edberg patrolled Broadway, they noticed a man acting suspiciously aggressive. They arrested him, and during questioning, they realized they had captured Michael Cohen, a small-time Philadelphia gangster with a known criminal history.

During extensive interrogation, Cohen allegedly admitted his involvement in the Brodsky kidnapping. However, he remained tight-lipped about specific details, refusing to elaborate on his involvement. His silence showed his familiarity with law enforcement. At 31 years old, Cohen frequently encountered police and operated under multiple aliases—including "Jew Moishe" and Albert Saltzman—to evade authorities.

Delaware Superintendent of Public Safety George Black immediately moved to capitalize on this development. New York police sent him a telegram about Cohen's arrest, and he quickly wired back, demanding that they hold Cohen. The next step involved extradition, never a simple matter.

Delaware Attorney General P. Warren Green personally traveled to negotiate the transfer. "The state will not waver in its pursuit of justice," he insisted.

Cohen's extradition process proved complex and protracted. He faced multiple legal hurdles after his New York arrest. On July 14, his lawyer, Ira W. Levitas, successfully obtained a continuance in the West Side Court, claiming he had an important witness to produce.

Cohen's true identity proved more complicated than his arrest suggested. He operated within the intricate world of Philadelphia gangland crime. Newspapers revealed his long criminal record, detailing previous arrests in Philadelphia for various charges, though no convictions had stuck.

Hilda Brodsky initially believed she could identify Cohen, telling reporters she would recognize "Pimple-Faced Mushie" anywhere. But the identification grew problematic after Cohen apparently underwent plastic surgery to alter his appearance. Hilda failed to positively identify him when she first appeared in court, claiming the man before her looked different from her kidnapper.

The brutal realities of gang warfare sealed Cohen's fate before any trial could take place. On February 12, 1934, hitmen executed Cohen—now using the name Albert Paul—inside Charles Gross' Manhattan apartment. Three unidentified assailants entered while Paul watched a pinochle game with Gross and two other men.

Without warning, they shot him twice in the back of the head. Police arrived to find the card players frantically attempting first aid, to no avail. The men claimed to know nothing about the killers. According to the Morning News, it was a typical underworld execution.

The killing seemed to be part of a larger power struggle within Philadelphia's criminal franchises. Police speculated that new gang leaders attempted to "horn in" on various racket territories. Paul and another man named Steigel apparently got caught up in an internal conflict that led to their murders.

Paul's girlfriend, Nancy Caruso, provided police with some insights. She described Paul as the son of a well-to-do, respectable family and noted that he had sent her home earlier that night, saying he planned to go to a Turkish bath—instead, he went to the fatal card game.

Albert Paul/Michael Cohen became just another victim in the city's ongoing gang conflicts, his potential testimony about the Brodsky kidnapping silenced forever by two bullets to the back of the head. With Paul's murder, any hope of prosecuting him for the Brodsky kidnapping vanished.

Four years after Hilda Brodsky's kidnapping, federal agents finally tracked down Frank Romano. Agents captured Romano in a house near Ninth and Wharton Streets in Philadelphia, said the August 7, 1936 Journal-Every Evening, after an extensive search spanning several southern states. Romano "emphatically denied any connection with the kidnaping" when initially questioned.

Harry Brodsky's reaction was notably subdued. When first informed of Romano's arrest, he told reporters, "It's all news to me," and seemed reluctant to pursue the matter. "We felt the case was dead long ago," Brodsky said. He was still hesitant to press charges, stating he would only cooperate if "some real evidence is developed warranting reopening the case."

The investigators never located the woman Romano allegedly associated with—

believed to be a key figure in the kidnapping. Earlier inquiries mentioned the name Marie Costa, but she remained just another unresolved thread in a case that had captivated two cities for years.

The search for Hilda Brodsky's kidnappers, which had consumed so much time and energy, ended not with justice, but with a whimper of judicial indifference.

The lingering question remained: who had orchestrated the kidnapping? Harry Brodsky consistently suggested that "business enemies" were involved, and police repeatedly pointed to a local Wilmington businessman as the true instigator. Throughout the investigation, Harry Brodsky expressed more interest in understanding who planned the kidnapping than in pursuing the actual kidnappers. This unusual focus, combined with his reluctance to press charges against Romano, raised questions. His subdued reaction to developments in the case suggested he might have been protecting someone—or perhaps himself. Benjamin Sherman lingered as a shadowy figure at the edges of the investigation. He represented the most plausible answer to the mystery of who wanted to harm the Brodsky family—and why, though authorities never formally charged him.

On a warm evening in late August 1938, the extended Brodsky family gathered for a surprise buffet supper at Mrs. Sarah Brodsky's home at 1101 West Second Street. The relatives hosted this belated celebration of Harry and Rose Brodsky's 25th wedding anniversary, which they had officially marked on Wednesday, August 17.

The room buzzed with warmth and connection. Telegrams and cards from across the country surrounded the couple—friends and family had sent messages from Canada, New York City, Baltimore, Atlantic City, and Brooklyn. Messages from loved ones reflected the deep bonds the Brodskys had nurtured over the years.

All of Harry and Rose's children attended, except one. Their youngest, Sidney, spent that summer at Camp Saginaw. Frieda, Jeannette, and Hilda filled the room with life. Hilda laughed and helped serve food, surrounded by her clan. For the first time in years, things felt normal.

Then, just over a year later, she was gone.

A streptococcal infection—one of the many that had ravaged children before the advent of antibiotics—claimed her life. On midnight of September 8, 1939, Hilda Brodsky died at Johns Hopkins Hospital in Baltimore after a long illness. She lived only 15 years. The *Baltimore Sun* noted that she had been ill for many months before her family sent her to the hospital. She ultimately succumbed to an infection that, only a few years later, doctors could have treated effectively with the antibiotics that emerged during World War II.

Something far smaller, far quieter, took Hilda Brodsky after she survived a crime that could have stolen her life. And just like that, the story ended—no grand conclusion, no justice. Just a girl who had once been lost, found again, and then lost forever.

16

MOTHERS KILL CHILDREN

Acts of maternal filicide driven by desperation.

Helen Maloney, 54, sealed off her Wilmington apartment and turned on the gas. In the next room, her son Millard, 25, lay sleeping, unaware that his mother had decided they would both die that night. She had spent Sunday with him and his girlfriend, a nurse named Bertha Mackison, who Millard had been discussing marriage with. By Monday morning, another boarder in the house discovered their bodies. The police ruled it a murder-suicide, attributing Helen's actions to a fear of losing her son to marriage, reported the Morning News on August 1, 1933.

Florence Dukes, an elderly mother in Georgetown, took a different approach. She left a note before walking into the woods with her son, Harry Everett Dukes, a 41-year-old man with cognitive challenges. She feared he wouldn't be able to care for himself after she was gone. Using a 12-gauge shotgun, she shot and killed him. Then she attempted to end her own life—first with the shotgun, failing and wounding herself, and then with a pistol, succeeding on the second shot. Before leaving the house that day, she also killed her two pet dogs, unwilling to leave them behind, according to the Journal-Every Evening on February 6, 1960.

These incidents stem from pathological attachment to sons, a belief that no one else could care for them as a mother could. Helen Maloney lived alone with her son in a Wilmington apartment. Florence Dukes lived with her adult son and his wife on the family farm. These mothers had defined themselves solely through caregiving and saw no future where they were not in control. Even the presence of a daughter-in-law did not diminish Florence Dukes' conviction that only she could properly care for her son. These were not acts of rage or despair but of possession.

But these are the exceptions. The more familiar stories of mothers who kill their children come from young, overwhelmed women, often trapped by poverty or isolation, struggling with mental illness.

In 1931, Ida Twaddell stood before a jury in Media, Pennsylvania, not far from Beaver Valley, Delaware, where she had taught Sunday school, to face charges of drowning her two young sons in a bathtub. Assistant District Attorney William B. McClenachan Jr. questioned her, and she responded with chilling directness. "I thought I was doing the right thing," she said, "but I knew it was wrong." When asked if she recalled the events of that night, she replied simply, "I know I did it." She then described how, after drowning the children, she had tied a weight about her own neck and climbed into the bathtub to commit suicide. Her attempt failed, she explained, because she "had no one to hold me down."

Her defense described her condition as puerperal insanity—a term once commonly used to describe extreme postpartum mental distress, reported the *Evening Journal* on March 24, 1931. The jury found her guilty of first-degree murder, and Judge Albert Dutton MacDade immediately sentenced her to life imprisonment. As she trembled on the verge of collapse, Twaddell cried out, "My husband has forgiven me; my father above knows all, and I'm satisfied." Her case marked an era when society framed infanticide as a result of irreversible madness, something that could consume a mother entirely.

By the late 20th century, the terminology shifted. Society no longer attributed these crimes to insanity—a word that implied permanence and hopelessness—but instead to postpartum depression, a treatable, temporary condition. The media began referencing famous cases of postpartum struggles, such as that of actress Brooke Shields, framing the condition as a legitimate, medicalized challenge rather than a personal failure. Yet, even as the language softened, society still viewed women who killed their children as incomprehensible.

Dr. Phillip Resnick of Cleveland's University Hospitals published a study in 1969 that categorized maternal filicide into two types: neonaticide, where mothers kill their infants within 24 hours of birth, and filicide, where a mother kills a child older than one day. The latter far more often stemmed from mental illness, with Resnick finding that two-thirds of filicide cases involved psychotic mothers, reported the *Morning News* on August 22, 1969. This distinction is crucial in understanding how the legal system prosecutes these crimes and how society perceives them.

At 29, Cathleen Hone took her three children into the garage of her Wilmington home, started the car engine, and waited. She had left a note for her husband explaining her despair, writing that she "loved her children so much she wanted to take them with her." When Grant Hone returned home that evening, he noticed something unusual about the garage and panicked.

"He pulled up directly in front of the garage door, saw a curtain draped over the window, ran to the garage door and saw through a small opening his wife and two of the children in the rear of the car.

"He pulled up on the garage door, but the red curtain jammed in the mechanism, giving the appearance of being stuffed in there. He entered the house through the front door, called a relative, explained what he had found, and asked her to call police and the ambulance.

"My husband has forgiven me; my father above knows all, and I'm satisfied."

IDA TWADDELL

"She did, and he ran into the garage through the inside of the house. He got the car's hatchback up and opened the garage door."

By the time emergency responders arrived, they found her and her three children—Grant, 5, Stacey, 4, and Nicholas, 23 months—already dead.

Legal expert Michelle Oberman, a law professor at DePaul University, has examined how different countries handle cases of maternal filicide. In Britain and Canada, laws automatically classify the killing of an infant by a mother as manslaughter rather than murder, recognizing the likelihood of mental illness. In the United States, however, these cases are often treated with more severity, though juries tend to lean toward lesser charges. "If a parent kills a child, prosecutors and juries just look at it differently," Oberman explained to the News Journal on April 21, 1998.

Lita Linzer Schwartz, a professor emeritus of psychology and women's studies at Penn State and co-author of *Endangered Children*, told the Associated Press on August 10, 2001, that "Women need better treatment not only before, but after. They get tormented in prison, when often what they need is psychological care.'"

Edmund D. Lyons Jr., a Wilmington defense attorney, told the *News Journal* on April 21, 1998, that in most cases, prosecutors push for manslaughter over murder, reflecting an understanding that these women do not fit the profile of a typical killer.

This pattern of prosecutorial restraint makes the 2019 child custody case of Laura Connell all the more striking. Unlike many cases with frustratingly opaque details, Connell's story stands apart in its detail. She left behind a long suicide note addressed to judges, attorneys, and family members, explaining her descent into hopelessness.

Her terror centered on Glen Alex Terry, her son Walton's father. A 6-inch scar running down Connell's right jawline bore witness to the violence she allegedly endured. According to her application for a protective order filed in Tarrant County, Texas, Terry had hit her in the face with his fist on September 29, 2016, with enough force to damage her teeth and jawbone. The impact left her needing three surgeries and caused small, noncancerous lumps to form in her jaw.

Terry, who declined multiple interview requests through his Delaware attorney, never faced criminal charges in Delaware or Texas. However, Texas Judge Hennigan wrote in granting Connell's protective order that "family violence has occurred, and that family violence is likely to occur in the future. The court finds that respondent, Glen Alex Terry, has committed family violence." Both Connell and Terry, along with their attorneys, attended court the day the judge issued that order.

Unlike many cases where financial instability plays a role, Terry had significant resources to wage his legal battle. "I understand they have built quite a case, and that's easy when you have the money to spend," Connell wrote in one of her final emails. While she struggled to find legal representation in Delaware, Terry had already accumulated what Connell estimated to be $24,000 in legal fees that she feared she would be ordered to pay.

Her case reveals not just the personal despair that leads to filicide but also how institutional failures enable it. In the weeks before their deaths in her Newport-area apartment, Connell had desperately tried to navigate Delaware's legal system, hauling a worn black suitcase stuffed with court documents through courthouse doorways while managing her toddler's stroller with her other arm.

"Intuition says, and I know this might sound grim," she told a reporter from the *News Journal* two weeks before her death, "I don't think I'm going to get to see my day in court."

Her sister and niece had been helping care for Walton when Connell was filing paperwork or attending doctor's appointments. They noticed how she kept the blinds perpetually drawn in her apartment, living in constant fear. Her niece, McCormick, felt that dread even in the brief periods she watched Walton.

"I was paranoid," McCormick told the *News Journal*. "I can't imagine living my life like that."

Connell's desperation grew with each passing day. "This is why women don't leave," she explained, discussing domestic violence. "At least if you stay, you hope that you take the blows and the children don't, but at least you still get to see them. Because when you do leave, this is what they do. They come after your kids when you leave the abuse."

Connell made preparations as her court date approached. Five days before their deaths, she arranged for Walton's baptism in a private ceremony—something she never mentioned to her sister and niece, though they knew how important her Christian faith was to her. Looking back, they wondered if she had signaled her choice of a different way out.

The final morning, Connell's sister Andi Bender came to drive them to court. When Connell texted "one minute" in response to her knocks, but didn't emerge, Bender retrieved a spare key. Music played inside the darkened apartment. She found Connell dead from a self-inflicted gunshot wound. Bender later recalled through tears that Walton lay in his crib, already gone, "looking like an angel."

In her extensive suicide note, Connell wrote about reaching her final decision: "Abuse doesn't stop when you leave," she wrote. "And you can never be anywhere safe again. There is help. If you get it early enough in the court. Maybe. This was the only way to make this time—stop."

She wrote that Walton had his usual bottle before bed and never woke up. While New Castle County police did not immediately confirm the exact cause of Walton's death, they stated he was not shot.

Recognizing that some would view her actions harshly, Connell wrote in her final message: "I will face a judge and court that know the truth, and I will accept that ruling."

"She did everything she could to not show him the fear she was feeling," Bender told the News Journal. "She was just terrified."

In her final message, Connell acknowledged that some might view her as the villain. The woman, whose apartment walls were covered with crosses, had made her peace with her decision.

Jocelyn Noveck, writing for the Associated Press in 2011, tackled the question that arises in every maternal filicide case: How could she? The answer, Noveck reports, is far more complex than most people realize. These crimes happen with shocking frequency—by conservative estimates, at least once every three days in America, amounting to over 100 cases annually. Yet most go unnoticed by the broader public, which only learns of the most dramatic cases. The patterns of these deaths defy simple categorization. Some women, said Noveck, suffer from severe mental illness, like Andrea Yates, who drowned her five children in a bathtub believing she was saving them from the devil. Others are overwhelmed by abuse or isolation—a factor that links the poor teen mother who kills her baby in a bathroom with an older, wealthier mother who takes her children's lives in a suburban home. "These women almost always feel alone, with a total lack of emotional support," explains

Schwartz, the Penn State professor.

Some mothers believe they are actually saving their children, which experts describe as a twisted extension of maternal protection. "We see cases where the mother thinks the child would be better off in heaven than on this miserable earth," Schwartz notes, adding that this often occurs in situations involving abusive partners. "They think it's a good deed, a blessing."

What connects these cases, according to Oberman, the law professor, is that "almost all these women are not in their right minds" when they commit these acts. The line between mental illness and criminal responsibility remains blurry. "The debate is whether they're sick enough to be called insane," Oberman explains.

Control and possession ruled the Maloney and Dukes cases, placing them at one extreme. But the rest—the overwhelmed mothers, the desperate ones, those who saw death as the only escape—remind us that maternal filicide is not just a crime of rage. These acts are more often than not crimes of despair that still affect Delaware today.

In the end, the question is not just "how could she?" but also "who failed her before she reached that point?"

HAMMOND'S FAMILY BURDEN

A destructive legacy that spanned decades & generations.

The judge barely had time to get the words out: "second-degree arson"—and then, as if on cue, the fire siren blared. The courtroom in Georgetown fell momentarily into farce as the piercing wail drowned out the indictment. A few chuckles rippled through the assembled, the timing too perfect to ignore. But at the center of it all, Robert John Hammond Sr. remained stone-faced, unimpressed by the cosmic joke at his expense. Authorities accused him of burning down a building that belonged to Joseph Gray, just south of Lincoln on Route 113. He wielded fire as just another tool in his long repertoire of destruction.

Hammond had been burning things down long, metaphorically speaking, before he was officially charged with it. He had been burning bridges, burning relationships, burning his own future from the moment he came of age. The roots of his ruin ran deep, back to his childhood in a household where violence was a language spoken fluently. Police dragged his father, Alonzo Hammond, before a magistrate in 1932 on charges of wife-beating. His mother, Mary, pressed the charges, and police initially held Alonzo under $500 bail at the Greenwood jail. But the charges didn't stick—prosecutors never presented a bill of indictment to the grand jury. Maybe fear silenced her, maybe Alonzo convinced her to withdraw the charges, or maybe the community simply accepted such behavior as normal. Regardless, Alonzo walked free.

He was back in court soon enough, this time with his son beside him, both men charged in the theft of a sedan belonging to Thomas F. Salmons of Milford. The judge saw through their act—Alonzo Hammond tried to take all the blame, insisting his son had no part in the theft. But under questioning, he admitted that his son participated in taking the stolen car to Norfolk, Virginia, where authorities finally captured them. The court sentenced both to eleven months in jail and ordered them to pay $250 in restitution.

Trouble had started even earlier for Robert. Before he was old enough to drive, court officials sent him to Ferris Industrial School for "incorrigibility." Delaware established Ferris in 1885 as its answer to a growing reform movement that sought to rehabilitate rather than merely punish young offenders. But for Hammond, as for many others, this experiment in reformation failed. He spent four years there before running away.

If he had any illusions about escaping his father's legacy, they didn't last. By 1939, at twenty-three, he was shooting at police officers and escaping manhunts. In one particularly violent encounter, he fired four shots at Officer Andrew Kosci while resisting arrest in Milford. A posse of thirty officers and deputized citizens hunted him through the town before Officer James Holleger finally captured him. The court sentenced him to five years in the Kent County Jail and fined him $500.

But Hammond refused to serve his time quietly. That same year, he stabbed guard Norris Garrison during an unsuccessful jailbreak. Two years later, on January 9, 1941, he orchestrated an even more dramatic escape. Along with inmates Hansel Marvel of Houston and Layton Conway of Laurel, Hammond sawed through the window bars of Kent County jail and made a run for it. Marvel had cunningly smuggled in the tools for their getaway. He later confessed that he had hidden saw blades between the soles and inner soles of his shoes when police arrested him on a bad check charge, just two days after completing a term for a similar offense. Marvel sprained his foot while jumping the fence during their flight, but he kept going.

With cash in their pockets, the three stole a car belonging to Joseph F. Coleman of Wyoming and tore off on a wild journey through southern Delaware, Maryland, and Virginia. The escapees' luck ran out at 7:30 p.m. on January 12, when State Trooper Leon McCauley spotted their car crossing Route 13 without lights on. That oversight cost them their freedom. McCauley gave chase along the Harrington-Denton Road. Following a brief but speedy pursuit, he overtook them. Hammond and Marvel surrendered without resistance. They admitted they'd split from Conway in Cambridge, Maryland, leaving him with $20.

Despite all the drama—sawing through window bars, jumping fences, stealing cars, and leading police on a multi-state chase—their stated reason for the elaborate prison break bordered on the ridiculous. When questioned, they didn't mention yearning for freedom or fear of lengthy sentences. Instead, with straight faces, they claimed they were simply "tired of the food there and wanted to get a good meal." As if they'd merely stepped out for dinner rather than committed multiple felonies during their days on the run.

While Hammond's string of crimes continued into the 1940s, his family had already been marked by tragedy. Years before the jailbreak, events unfolded that didn't involve Robert directly but hovered over his life like omens. In 1937, his stepmother, Lillian Taylor Hammond, drowned in the Nanticoke River alongside her 15-month-old son, William Albert. Somehow, she backed her car off the Woodland ferry into the water, trapping them inside. Rescuers later pulled their bodies from the river, and mourners laid mother and child to rest in the same casket at Woodland M.E. Church. Alonzo had lost a wife and son in a single moment, but whatever grief he felt, it didn't soften him. If anything, the savagery in the Hammond household seemed to fester. And Robert, shaped by it, carried that violence into adulthood.

By the 1960s, Delaware's crime reports regularly featured his name. He had added arson to his skill set, torching the Joseph Gray property near Lincoln. The violence escalated with a shotgun incident in 1973, when he fired two blasts into his own son's home at 500 McCauley Street in Milford. No one suffered injuries, but authorities sent him to Beebe Hospital in Lewes for psychiatric evaluation. The justice system had long since given up expecting him to turn a corner. He waged perpetual war— against the law, against himself, against anyone unlucky enough to enter his orbit.

And then came Myrtle.

Hammond had argued with his wife plenty before, loudly enough for neighbors to remember. Police had arrested him for drunkenness, for carrying weapons, for firing shots into homes, and still, he remained free. Then in September 1975, Myrtle Mae Hammond, age 46, failed to show up for her shift at the L.D. Caulk Co. in Milford. The neighbors reported hearing arguments at their home at 412 Charles Street. Both Myrtle and Robert had vanished.

Police issued a thirteen-state alarm and sent messages to Washington, D.C. and the Clearwater, Florida area, where Hammond had relatives. The search took a confusing turn when officers in Pinellas County, Florida actually stopped and questioned Hammond. When a municipal policeman ran a "10-29" check through the FBI's National Crime Information Center computer, the system failed because programmers had temporarily shut down the network for maintenance (a "10-29" check is a routine police query for warrants or stolen property). Hammond slipped away.

Then, on the morning of October 2, a farm worker made a grim discovery on the Sharp Farm, about ten miles northeast of Milford: Myrtle's nude, partially decomposed body lay in a cornfield. Someone had strangled her.

The manhunt finally ended at a Rehoboth Beach bus station. Why he returned, no one knows. Hammond had taken a bus from Washington, D.C., and upon arrival, drunk and belligerent, he refused to leave his seat. Police dragged him off and realized who he was; he was too intoxicated for them even to arraign him.

Myrtle left behind her son, Robert Joseph of Dover; daughter, Beverly Letterman of Lincoln; mother, Mrs. Joseph Gray of Milford; brothers, Lester Gray of Concord, Pennsylvania, and Hartley Gray of Smyrna; sister, Elizabeth Marvel of Houston; and one grandchild. Though Elizabeth Marvel shared a surname with Hansel Marvel, no known connection tied them beyond that. Hansel, one of Hammond's accomplices in the 1941 Kent County jailbreak, had died just months before Myrtle's murder. By then, Hammond's violent end seemed inevitable. If it hadn't been Myrtle, it would have been someone else. Hammond had established this pattern long before. A boy watches his father beat his mother and learns the lesson well. He grows up, his name surfacing in ever darker corners of the newspaper—larceny, assault, escape, arson, attempted murder. He aims a gun at his son. And then, finally, he turns his hands on his wife.

Hammond died in 1991 at the age of 75 in Smyrna. He served his final sixteen years at the Delaware Correctional Center, the state's main maximum-security prison. For over half a century, Robert J. Hammond's name filled Delaware crime reports—first as a reform school inmate, then through escalating violence, and finally, his ultimate crime. The cycle that began in that Greenwood household in the 1930s ended behind prison walls. His life embodied the harsh logic of generational violence, where brutality breeds brutality, and some men never escape the shadows of their origins.

18

RATION COUPON COUNTERFEITERS

WWII fraud schemes exploited Delaware's rationing.

On January 13, 1944, in a Wilmington courtroom, Judge Paul Leahy found himself presiding over a case that had descended into comic absurdity. Before him stood Andrew A. August and William Jones, both accused of trafficking in counterfeit gasoline ration coupons—fraudulent copies of those issued by the government during World War II to limit civilian fuel consumption. The issue at hand was not their guilt—both had pleaded guilty—but rather the degree of their involvement. Who was the seller, and who was the buyer? The answer seemed to depend entirely on which attorney spoke last.

Assistant District Attorney W. Thomas Knowles informed the court that August was the dealer, the one responsible for distributing counterfeit ration stamps to motorists. August, given the chance to respond, immediately objected, claiming Knowles had it backward—Jones was the dealer, and he, August, was merely a customer. The back-and-forth continued as an attorney from the Office of Price Administration (OPA) joined in, first confirming that August had indeed been the distributor, only to later reverse himself, insisting that Jones had been the one selling the illegal stamps. As confusion mounted, Francis A. Reardon, former OPA enforcement attorney, could take no more. Rising from his seat, he declared, "I cannot stand by and see the doubt continued." He stated unequivocally that August had received the coupons from Jones.

Judge Leahy, exasperated by the conflicting accounts, ended the discussion. "I've had enough," he declared, instructing a probation officer to conduct an independent investigation. This farcical legal debate, while momentarily entertaining, highlighted a much larger and more serious problem: the black market in wartime rationing coupons, which was siphoning off millions of gallons of gasoline and tons of foodstuffs meant for the war effort.

During World War II, the federal government implemented a strict rationing system to manage scarce resources. The OPA oversaw the distribution of ration books containing coupons required to purchase essential goods, including sugar, meat, dairy products, canned goods, gasoline, and rubber. The goal was to ensure that both civilians and military personnel had fair access to these limited supplies.

However, the system quickly attracted criminals who saw an opportunity to profit by counterfeiting and illegally distributing ration coupons.

The system operated through a complex network of "ration banks." Just as regular banks handled money, these specialized institutions processed ration coupons. Retailers like grocers and gas stations collected coupons from customers making purchases, then deposited these coupons in their ration bank accounts. The deposited coupons allowed them to obtain new stock from their suppliers—a butcher shop's deposit of meat coupons, for instance, entitled it to order more meat from whole-salers. The government structured this banking system to ensure that businesses received new supplies in direct proportion to their legitimate sales.

Of all the rationed commodities, gasoline was the most heavily targeted by coun-terfeiters. The OPA estimated that black marketeers drained 2.5 million gallons of gasoline per day from the civilian allotment.

Criminal enterprises operated through sophisticated distribution chains. In gasoline fraud, racketeers would acquire counterfeit coupons and sell them to both motorists and complicit gas station owners. When stations accepted these fake coupons, they could claim more fuel from suppliers than they were legally entitled to receive, profiting from the difference.

While the largest counterfeiting operations concentrated in major metropolitan areas like New York, Chicago, and Philadelphia, Wilmington's position just twenty miles south of Philadelphia made it a natural market for fraudulent coupons. In September 1943, Wilmington police arrested Andrew August, John Burke, and William Jones after finding them in possession of more than 1,200 counterfeit gasoline ration coupons. [Remember August and Jones, whose case became the courtroom farce that opened this chapter?]

For example, in May 1944, Wilmington authorities arrested six men in a 24-hour period for possessing or transferring large quantities of counterfeit coupons. They charged Lawrence E. Wadman with possessing stamps worth 1,600 gallons of gasoline, David Bradburn with 800 gallons, and Edward Papes of Camden with transferring 2,400 gallons' worth of counterfeit coupons in Wilmington.

Much of the gasoline ration fraud in Delaware traced back to a single source, Dennis A. Hill. Hill, a Philadelphia print shop operator, ran one of the most extensive counterfeiting operations in the region. In October 1943, OPA agents raided his small Philadelphia printing plant and uncovered counterfeit coupons redeemable for ten million gallons of gasoline. Investigators confirmed that Hill's presses had produced many of the fake stamps circulating in Wilmington. In December, a judge sentenced him to three and a half years in prison for his role in the conspiracy.

Law enforcement continued to uncover the extent of Hill's operation. In one of the more dramatic turns in the investigation, OPA officials revealed that Hill had printed the counterfeit coupons at the request of an associate, Robert P. Douglas. Described in court as an Indian, Douglas died by suicide shortly after federal agents questioned him. His death closed off a key lead, and left investigators with little chance to probe deeper into the network's upper tier.

Despite Hill's arrest, black market operators continued circulating counterfeit coupons, proving how deeply they had infiltrated the rationing system. While Wilmington was the epicenter of Delaware's ration coupon fraud, criminal activity extended throughout the state. The OPA, for example, cited five service station operators in Kent and Sussex counties for suspicious coupon activities in October 1943, charging that they possessed unauthorized gasoline rationing coupons representing 4,226 gallons of fuel.

In February 1945, investigators arrested Goldey Collins of Freeport, Long Island. They caught him using counterfeit coupons while delivering used cars through downstate Delaware for resale. However, these cases occurred less frequently than the concentrated criminal networks operating in and around Wilmington, where war plants and urban density created more opportunities for large-scale distribution of forged ration stamps.

The OPA ramped up its efforts to dismantle rationing fraud networks in 1944. Enforcement agents raided gas stations, arrested dealers, and held hearings to revoke the rationing privileges of complicit businesses. Col. John P. LeFevre, the chief OPA enforcement officer for Delaware, led the charge in Wilmington against illicit operations. He conducted suspension hearings for numerous gasoline dealers accused of accepting counterfeit ration stamps.

Law enforcement effectively curtailed gasoline counterfeiting by early 1945, forcing criminals to shift toward more lucrative food ration fraud. Sugar schemes proved especially attractive. Criminals employed multiple angles: counterfeiting ration coupons, establishing fake soft-drink companies to obtain bulk sugar purchases, and diverting supplies to illegal liquor manufacturers. Moonshiners drove up demand for sugar in the Southeast, making fraud especially prevalent in that region. By early 1945, the OPA identified counterfeit ration coupons as "the No. 1 problem in controlling illegal transactions in sugar."

The meat racket operated with equal complexity. Slaughterers sold to wholesalers at official OPA prices on paper but demanded additional unreported cash payments. The wholesalers passed this scam down the chain to retailers, who made up their extra costs by shorting customers on weight or charging them for better grades of meat than they actually received.

Prosecutors pursued rationing violations well into the postwar period. They charged Ross Cardinale and Samuel Kornblum, for example, with transferring 138,040 points worth of counterfeit meat ration coupons through their Baltimore Market on King Street in Wilmington in September 1945. A judge sentenced Kornblum to six months in prison and fined him $600, while Cardinale received a two-month sentence and the same fine. Sugar violations persisted into 1946, when officials barred Peter Vassello, a Wilmington grocer, from dealing in sugar after charging him with transferring 1,000 pounds worth of counterfeit coupons. That same month, authorities discovered that the Central Restaurant on Market Street had overdrawn its sugar ration by 5,000 pounds, and suspended George T. Tobin's meat market in New Castle for a 659-pound sugar overdraft.

The Delaware OPA cut its workforce from 123 employees to just 40 by January

1947, leaving only seven staff members to handle sugar rationing as wartime economic controls eased. The agency planned to transfer all Delaware sugar rationing operations to Baltimore by February 15, 1947. The federal government officially abolished the OPA on May 29, transferring some of its functions to successor agencies, such as the Sugar Rationing Administration within the Department of Agriculture, which took over sugar and sugar product distribution. Thus ended an unprecedented chapter in American economic history. While the government had briefly experimented with rationing during World War I, never before or since had it imposed such a sweeping nationwide coupon system.

Wartime necessity blurred the line between petty crime and economic sabotage, turning counterfeit paper into a commodity as prized as gold.

19

LONELY HEARTS

Tragic family confessions revealed personal despair.

Sweeping cultural changes rolled across mid 20th-century American society. Women had won the right to vote. Prohibition had upended social drinking habits. Technology, too, was shrinking distances, allowing people to forge connections in new ways. Among these changes emerged an unusual avenue for romance: the lonely-hearts club.

These weren't social gatherings, but rather classified advertisements—the mid 20th-century's answer to dating apps—where singles laid bare their attributes and aspirations in newsprint. For most, these ads represented hope. For Delaware's Inez Gertrude Brennan, they were bait for a deadly trap.

The spring of 1949 brought an unexpected discovery when Charles and Mrs. Wende made a detour on their journey from Florida to New Hampshire. They planned a friendly visit to Hugo Schulz, who had enthusiastically told them about his new bride Inez back in December 1948. The newlyweds had settled in Dover, or so the Wendes thought.

Arriving at the Brennan farm, the visitors encountered an icy demeanor from Inez instead of hospitality. The 45-year-old woman flatly denied knowing Schulz. Only when the Wendes pressed her did she reluctantly admit, "He stopped here briefly"—four words that would begin to unravel a web of deception and murder.

Troubled, the Wendes took their concerns to Dover State Police, unknowingly connecting two sinister threads. Sheriff Claude Ruff of Bedford County, Virginia had been searching for Wade Wooldridge, a 70-year-old carpenter who had vanished after setting off to meet his mail-order bride—one Mrs. Brennan of Dover, Delaware.

Public records revealed that Inez Gertrude Brennan had a checkered domestic past. Born on September 22, 1903, in New Florence, Pennsylvania, she married twice. Her first husband, William Pribram, whom she married on June 6, 1922, in West Chester, Pennsylvania, died of yellow fever in Baranquilla, Colombia, South America, while serving in the U.S. Army in 1929. Pribram fathered a son, Raymond. She married George A. Dether in 1929 at Norristown, Pennsylvania, but left him around 1935. A Philadelphia court finalized their divorce in August 1948. After the divorce, she resumed using her maiden name, Brennan.

The divorcée's household presented a picture of normalcy with 16-year-old Robert and 23-year-old Raymond living at home, along with a boarder named Dolly T. Dean. Absent were 18-year-old son George, stationed at Lackland Air Force Base in Texas, and her 26-year-old daughter Catherine Hatchett, who lived in Port Arthur, Texas. Behind the façade of this seemingly ordinary family lurked a ruthless operation.

Dr. John L. Halderman, superintendent of Dover schools, described sophomore Robert as "an average student who impressed his teachers as being quiet and well-mannered." He avoided athletics and other extracurricular activities and showed strong signs of his mother's influence. Classmates told the *Milford Chronicle* (April 22, 1949) that Robert constantly referred to his mother, filling his conversations with phrases like "Mom said * * *" and "Mom and I * * *."

Morrell L. Behslage, principal, said some of the teachers regarded Robert as a very trustworthy lad. Mrs. Hiram Everett, who lived across the road from the Brennans, told reporters that "Robert cried like a baby" when the Brennans' cow died the previous fall—a startling contrast to his callousness toward human life.

On April 14, 1949, investigators descended on the Brennan property, shovels in hand. As Major James Turner broke soil in the pigpen, young Robert blurted what became the case's first confession: "There's no sense digging there. The bodies were removed and taken to the city dump!"

Police systematically searched the entire property as standard procedure, not due to any newly discovered evidence of additional victims. Colonel Herbert E. Barnes, superintendent of the Delaware State Police, later explained they "want to make sure there are no more bodies there." The digging yielded no evidence, but police kept searching the old barn. Young Robert confessed to killing Wooldridge there with a 12-gauge shotgun.

The investigation expanded beyond the farm. Police found a truck that Hugo Schulz had previously owned. The Brennans had used it to transport his body from New

Hampshire to Dover and left it on Irving Moor's farm near Little Creek. Moor told police he had "bought it from Mrs. Brennan on April 9 for $175" after seeing an advertisement in a Dover newspaper.

While Inez and Raymond remained silent at the State Police barracks, Robert, true to form, cracked under the dim interrogation room lights. He revealed that on October 10th of the previous year, Wooldridge arrived at their farm just as his brother George left for Air Force duty.

"Mother said, 'Nobody will miss him if somebody puts something through his head,'" Robert testified. "She said he had a considerable sum of money on him, and we could use that."

The teenager's confession continued with chilling detail: "About 4:45 pm on October 10th I decided to get rid of Mr. Wooldridge. So, I took my 12-gauge shotgun to the barn and put it in the loft. Then we all had supper.

"After supper Mr. Wooldridge wanted to see the outside buildings. I took him straight to the barn. While he was looking around, I went to the loft. I shot him in the back of the head as he came up. He rolled to the floor."

"The blast failed to kill Wooldridge," added Colonel Barnes, who led the investigation. Mrs. Brennan then "sent Robert back to the barn to finish the job. The boy shot the victim a second time through the head," Barnes told the *Journal-Every Evening* (April 20, 1949).

Reporters learned from the Virginia Sheriff Ruff that Wooldridge, a widower, had lived with his son-in-law, Romie Ayers, at Stone Mountain in that state. He said that Wooldridge shipped his carpenter tools to Dover on October 8, and that a grandson, Richard Ayers, drove Wooldridge to Roanoke, Virginia two days later to catch a bus for Dover. Sheriff Ruff believed Wooldridge had between $1,500 and $2,000 on him when he left Roanoke, though Colonel Barnes later reported finding only $136. The family split Wooldridge's possessions among themselves and buried his body in the pigpen—a makeshift grave that soon held another victim.

Robert and Inez traveled by train to Concord, New Hampshire, on December 27th, where Hugo Schulz welcomed them warmly to his farm. After enjoying his hospitality for several days, Inez asked Schulz for $1,000 to pay a note on her farm. When they visited a New Hampshire bank together, the bank refused their request. According to Robert's confession, Mrs. Brennan became furious and "accused Schultz of not having the money he had said he had." His inability or unwillingness to help her financially signed his death warrant.

"Mother said, 'Nobody will miss him if somebody puts something through his head.'"

ROBERT BRENNAN

Inez first tried to poison him with five sleeping pills. Schulz survived. When that failed, she increased the dose to seventeen pills. When even that massive dose failed, she turned to arsenic. Remarkably, Schulz survived all three poisoning attempts. Captain Frederick K. Lamb of the State Police reported additional details from his two-hour interrogation with Robert. According to Robert's statement, the heaviest dose of poison only managed to render Schulz "unconscious for about five hours" before he recovered.

Frustrated when her poisoning attempts failed but still maintaining her pretense of romantic interest, Inez pressed forward with her deadly plan. She secured a marriage license with Schulz on January 8th, a cruel irony that marked him as both husband-to-be and victim. With the poisonings proving unsuccessful, Inez decided she needed to take more direct action.

Robert later confessed that she then devised a new angle. "His mother," Lamb stated, "told him she and Schultz were going to town again. Robert said he was to have remained at home with a loaded shotgun and when his mother and the farmer returned, to shoot Schultz." But when the moment came, Robert told Captain Lamb "he lost his nerve. Mrs. Brennan, on her return, took the gun from Robert, went to the barn where Schultz was putting the truck, and fired the two rounds that killed the farmer."

Mother and son stuffed the body into a 50-gallon oil drum and summoned Raymond from Delaware. After they sold Schulz's chickens and farm equipment, they loaded the drum and furniture onto a truck and drove south. By March, the Brennans had buried Schulz alongside Wooldridge in the pigpen corral—Delaware's grimmest two-for-one special.

Meanwhile, Brennan boarder Dolly Dean had seen enough to fear for her life. She fled. The police described her as a material witness and revealed on April 22, 1949, that they "had been hiding her until her release" but did not disclose anything further. Her testimony later proved devastating to the Brennans' defense.

Police investigation revealed Inez's concerning history with acquaintances who either disappeared or died under suspicious circumstances across multiple states.

Fred W. Schub, a well-to-do farmer in his sixties who grew chickens near Melson, Maryland, had financial dealings with Mrs. Brennan that left him poorer but initially alive. Sheriff Jesse M. Pollit of Wicomico County told reporters that Schub had contacted him in the fall of 1947, "to see what he could do to get back $805 he had given Mrs. Brennan to buy a farm near Gettysburg, Pennsylvania. He said he had corresponded with the woman for some time, and that they made plans to marry and settle down on the Pennsylvania farm."

Sheriff Pollit said Schub told him that after he sent the money, he never heard from Mrs. Brennan again. To help the sheriff in his investigation, Schub turned over 15 letters and postcards written to him by Mrs. Brennan. The sheriff said the letters "are typically lonely-hearts stuff." The last one, sent from Laurel Springs, New Jersey, on September 2, 1947, read: "Writing this on the moving van going to the new farm. Wait for the kids to come for you. It will be at least a week. It's a long journey. (Signed) I. B."

From the day Schub left the sheriff's office, until 1949, there had been no trace of him. Sheriff Pollit told reporters he would question Schub's former neighbors near Melson to see if they could provide any information. "There might not be anything to this at all," the sheriff cautioned, "but we can't afford to let it go by without looking into it." Despite extensive investigations, authorities never located Schub or his remains. His disappearance remains unresolved, and he is presumed dead.

Investigators also questioned the Brennans about another suspicious death—that of Mrs. Nettie Henderson Phillips, a 72-year-old widowed pensioner who drowned in a pond near Laurel Springs, New Jersey, in March 1947. The Brennans had been neighbors of Mrs. Phillips at the time, and Robert and George Brennan reported finding her body. Though officials ruled her death a suicide, Detective L. Eugene Droffner of the New Jersey State Police traveled to Dover specifically to question the Brennans about the elderly woman's death. According to later testimony from George Brennan, "mother probably drowned Mrs. Phillips."

New Jersey authorities also sought information about Harvey Dromheller, a man missing from Laurel Springs who reportedly had known Mrs. Brennan from late 1945 until early 1947, and who had been missing for about two years. This growing pattern of mysterious deaths and disappearances surrounding the Brennan family painted a disturbing picture for investigators.

When officers brought George back from Texas for questioning, he confirmed the October 10th events: "Mother told me Mr. Wooldridge had been shot. She said I'd have to get up early the next morning to help bury him."

George gave a "bizarre version of the Wooldridge killing—done by Robert, he said, while Mrs. Brennan, Raymond, and Dolly Dean sat in the living room." He told police that "he picked up Wooldridge at the Dover railroad station on October 10, the day of the slaying. He said he drove Wooldridge to the farm, dropped him off, then returned to Dover on another errand." When he came back, "Robert hurried up to him and said, 'Wooldridge is dead—try to act normal.' He added that 'company was expected soon' and warned George not to say anything that might sound suspicious." According to Colonel Barnes, George said that "relatives of Dolly Dean arrived a short while later, and while the body of Wooldridge sprawled in the hay near the barn, the group chatted in the living room."

Colonel Barnes also learned from George that Mrs. Brennan "is a very smart woman" and that "she really knows how to convince you." He added that George told him "Mrs. Brennan had very strong persuasive powers over him and Raymond and could 'get Robert to do almost anything'."

The case so horrified Delawareans that on April 28, the state's House of Representatives passed a concurrent resolution urging Congress to make "lonely hearts" advertising a federal offense. The resolution referred to the case that had "shocked the state of Delaware and brought chagrin to a people who not only are generally law-abiding but who resent the notoriety brought on by the publicity regarding the murders."

Rep. Noble S. Warren (R-Dover) introduced the resolution, declaring, "It is time we take some action to end this evil practice at its source." On May 18, Senator John J. Williams presented this resolution to the U.S. Senate, which referred it to committee for consideration. Congress, however, never enacted any federal legislation criminalizing "lonely hearts" advertising.

As the case progressed to the Kent County Court of Oyer and Terminer (today's Court of Common Pleas), Robert testified that they had later dug up both bodies and cremated them when Inez decided to sell the farm. The ashes, dumped in cans at the Dover landfill, became state's evidence.

FBI technicians later identified bone fragments among the remains as part of a human hand or hands, but did not indicate whether they belonged to one or two persons. The laboratories also returned a report on their findings in studies of stains found on wreckage of a wooden ladder recovered on the Brennan farm, confirming they were made by human blood.

The prosecution's case strengthened when Richard Ayers identified several items found at the Delaware farm as belonging to his grandfather, Wooldridge. Mrs. Bessie J. Ayers, Wooldridge's daughter, confirmed that various articles had belonged to her father, "including a watch, chain, pliers, tie clasp, a saw, a double-barrel shotgun, a set of false teeth, a padlock, trunk lock, a pig ring, and a shirt."

Dolly Dean's testimony proved devastating: she had heard the shot and Robert's boast, "I shot the old man." When Wooldridge's screams continued, she overheard Inez saying, "We can't have him hollering like that," followed by another shot and Robert's declaration: "I finished off the old man. I shot off half his face."

Though Robert tried to change his story on the stand—claiming Wooldridge had gotten "fresh" with Dolly and pulled a knife when confronted—the testimony had already sealed his fate. The court charged Robert with murder and Inez as an accomplice, with George and Raymond named as accessories.

In a dramatic trial that began September 12, 1949, and lasted more than two weeks, the jury found Robert and his mother guilty, though they recommended mercy for the son. On November 28, 1949, both received life sentences, as Delaware law prevented giving an accomplice a more severe term than the perpetrator. Raymond and George received lighter sentences after pleading guilty as accessories.

Judge Caleb R. Layton III, who handed down the sentences, called the slaying "one of the most brutal crimes in Delaware's history" and said the court believed all persons connected with it should be punished. The court sentenced Raymond Brennan, 24, to two years imprisonment in the Kent County jail, and his 18-year-old half-brother, George Brennan, to one year. In passing the longer sentence upon Raymond, the judge said that as elder of the two, "this defendant should have known better than to conceal knowledge of the crime from the authorities."

New Hampshire's Merrimack County Superior Court indicted both Inez and Robert for Hugo Schulz's murder in September 1949, but the case stalled. On October 3, the Concord Monitor reported, "New Hampshire will have to wait at least 15 years before it can try Mrs. Inez Brennan... She cannot apply for a commutation of her

[Delaware] sentence until she has served 15 years."

Robert Brennan became a model prisoner during his imprisonment and earned the respect of both inmates and officials. In recognition of his conduct, Delaware Governor J. Caleb Boggs commuted his sentence to 15 years in July 1958. The parole board released him in 1959. Although the court had tried and convicted him as Robert Brennan, he later adopted his father's surname, Dether, after his release.

After his release, Dether settled in Middletown, where he found work in a barber shop. He worked hard, made fast friends and became a respected member of the community. He married, and his wife had a child. In his spare time, he built—mostly with his own hands—a house valued at about $40,000.

But in 1970, at age 37, a conviction for third-degree burglary, stemming from a gun shop break-in, called his rehabilitation into question. Judge John J. McNeilly sentenced him to three years in prison. "Mr. Dether," McNeilly asked during the hearing, "just who are you? Are you a Dr. Jekyll and Mr. Hyde?" He added that he had "agonized" over the case.

Inez Brennan served her full sentence, then remained on parole until 1976, when authorities finally released her from supervision. After 15 years in prison, on February 5, 1965, she "walked out of the New Castle Correctional Institution" and was "picked up at the prison by her son, Raymond P. Brennan of Riverside, N.J., with whom she will live. She will be under parole supervision by New Jersey authorities for the rest of her life."

New Hampshire authorities dropped their pending charges against Brennan for the Schulz murder, claiming "so much evidence has disappeared in the 15 years that no prosecution was possible." They had previously taken a similar approach with her son Robert, abandoning the New Hampshire charges against him "after he had served his time for the Wooldridge murder." Inez Gertrude Brennan died in 1984 at age 80, a free woman, her husband-killing spree just another dark chapter in Delaware's criminal history.

In the lonely-hearts clubs of the mid-twentieth century, where newspaper columns offered a lifeline to isolated souls, Inez Brennan weaponized human vulnerability. She crafted meticulously written letters designed to lure the unsuspecting. Desperate individuals seeking connection fell victim to her. They encountered a manipulator who feigned compassion through an elaborate charade. Wade Wooldridge and Hugo Schulz carried their modest fortunes and fragile hopes to Delaware, only to be buried in a pigpen and incinerated, their worldly possessions divided among their killers.

Their stories faded from headlines, but the chilling truth remains. Between loneliness and hope lies danger: the most lethal predator is the one who offers love. Though the Brennan case is now Delaware history, the warning echoes—a longing heart often mistakes the hunter for haven.

20

CLARENCE WELCH STEALS COMPANY MILLIONS

A high-profile financial scandal and disappearance.

Milford Mayor Edward Evans struggled to find the right words as he spoke to a reporter from the *Morning News* on November 16, 1953, trying to explain the inexplicable disappearance of one of his city's most prominent businessmen. "There is very little that anyone knows about this. It was a complete bombshell. He's a very good friend of mine. A successful, well-liked individual with a wide circle of friends, and active in civic enterprises? Yes, I'll buy every bit of that. He was an active Rotarian and a 32nd-degree Mason."

His words echoed the confusion felt throughout the small Delaware town of 5,200, where, as Evans told the newspaper, "Everyone knows his next-door neighbor and the fellow around the corner, too. And none of us know what to make of it."

Clarence M. Welch, Jr., 42, had vanished. He served as president of the recently renamed Welch Manufacturing Company, the nation's leading manufacturer of wooden ice cream spoons and sticks. Welch had left his home on Lakeview Avenue on October 30, 1953, and simply not returned. His wife, Hilda, received a telegram from him the following day from Chicago, saying he would be home the next night. Then, silence.

For more than two weeks, his family kept his disappearance private. But on November 16, the story broke in newspapers across Delaware, revealing that police in thirteen eastern states were searching for the missing executive. Authorities distributed a description of Welch via police teletype: "Six feet, 200 pounds, dark gray hair, heavy build, dark complexion, brown eyes." They believed he was en route to New York City, driving a 1951 light green Cadillac four-door sedan with Delaware Registration No. 6509.

The news stunned Milford. Welch was no ordinary businessman— his presence anchored the rhythms of daily life in the town. One friend painted the picture of a self-made success story: "Welch went to work for Harry H. Mulholland, Sr., — former state senator and president pro tempore of the senate in 1945—when he was still in high school. That was in the summer of 1928.

"He was valedictorian of his class, and after graduation, he went to work for Mulholland full time. Finally, he became president of the Welch Manufacturing Company," the friend continued. "I always knew him as a generous man where charities are concerned. In World War II, he was co-chairman of war bond sales for Sussex County and was a Chamber of Commerce director."

Welch's civic contributions only deepened the mystery of his disappearance. He had served on the Milford City Council with Mayor Evans. The company he led, formerly the John H. Mulholland Company, had been a fixture in Milford for more than thirty years, employing some 200 workers.

While police publicly downplayed the possibility of foul play, Welch's family harbored darker fears. His elderly father, Clarence Welch Sr., told reporters: "We are afraid he must be hurt. He never would have stayed away unless there is something awfully wrong. He has always been a good family man."

Hilda Welch, left with their two children—Stephen Richard, 16, and Martha Lorraine, 10—seemed genuinely bewildered by her husband's sudden absence. "When he left, I had no idea he wasn't coming back," she told the press. "He didn't tell me anything or give me any reason to believe there were any business troubles. After all, I'm an officer in the firm myself (vice president). He never stayed away like this before. Perhaps he has suffered amnesia or met with foul play."

Milford Police Chief Samuel G. Powell was more circumspect in his statements, hinting that there might be more to the story: "His car is missing and never has been located. Several reports have been made to my department, and we've made every investigation we know how. He has just vanished. We have no reason to suspect foul play. No, I can't talk about any other aspect of the case."

Even as the search for Welch continued, events at his company took a dramatic turn. Four days after news of his vanishing made headlines, on November 20, 1953, the Farmers Bank of the State of Delaware took over the entire stock of the Welch Manufacturing Company for $175,000 at a public auction. The sheriff's sale, held in the company auditorium, took just ten minutes. No potential buyers submitted competing offers, and no representatives of Welch's management team attended.

Observers quickly recognized the connection between Welch's sudden departure and the bank's action. Just one month before he dropped out of sight, Welch had borrowed approximately $150,000 from Farmers Bank to purchase controlling interest in what was then the John H. Mulholland Company, worth millions. Upon gaining control, he had promptly renamed it Welch Manufacturing. Now, with Welch missing, the bank had recalled the loan and seized the company.

The Delaware business community buzzed with speculation. How could a man described by Mayor Evans as a "solid citizen" abandon both his family and his newly acquired business? Had Welch simply cracked under the pressure of his rapid business expansion? Or was there something more sinister at play?

The mystery grew more perplexing toward November's end. Welch had been missing for 21 days, and his family, friends, and community were no closer to answers.

Then, on November 23, the truth emerged in a manner that shocked even those who had suspected the worst.

A maid working her shift at the Bretton Hall Hotel on 86th Street and Broadway in New York City entered room 512 during routine cleaning rounds. Hotel staff had certainly seen their share of unusual guest behavior over the years, but the note taped to the desk made this young woman's blood run cold: "Don't go into the bathroom—suicide. Call the police." She ran screaming into the hallway, attracting the attention of a nearby bellboy, who rushed into the room and found a man hanging from a bathroom pipe. He cut him down just in time.

The man was Clarence M. Welch Jr.

He had stayed at the hotel since November 18, using the alias "Carl Winters of Cambridge, Md." New York police found additional notes in the room, including one asking them to notify Major W. Sockrider of Milford—Welch's brother-in-law. From that note, police pieced together Welch's identity and alerted his family.

Emergency responders rushed Welch to Bellevue Hospital for psychiatric evaluation. Robert Tunnell, his attorney from Georgetown, Delaware, told reporters that

Welch appeared to be in good physical condition but was "mentally upset." Welch stayed at Bellevue for several days. Hospital staff described his condition as fair.

The revelation that Welch had attempted suicide transformed the narrative from a mystery to a tragedy. But the question remained: What had driven this respected businessman, family man, and community leader to such desperation?

His tangled financial dealings triggered his retreat—transactions that surfaced only after his suicide attempt.

Welch's rise at J.H. Mulholland Company had been nothing short of meteoric. Starting as an office boy in 1928 while still in high school, he had worked his way up through the ranks of the company. By 1942, he had become Treasurer and General Manager. By 1948, he was Executive Vice-President, effectively running day-to-day operations. Mulholland's success rested on a simple premise: single-use wooden spoons for an America embracing throwaway ease.

But Welch was more than just an executive. He was the company's largest individual stockholder, wielding enormous influence and near-total control over financial decisions. By 1951, directors' meetings had become rare, and Welch operated with minimal oversight, holding borrowing privileges at two banks and moving money freely between corporate and personal accounts.

The first signs of trouble appeared in March 1953, when John Mulholland discovered that Welch had withdrawn over $35,000 from the corporate account without authorization. Mulholland imposed new restrictions on Welch's authority to prevent further mismanagement. But Welch bypassed these controls, withdrawing an additional $9,500 in July.

That summer, Welch's financial maneuvers accelerated. Howard W. Black, a company salesman and one of Welch's closest associates, had known Welch since his early days at Mulholland. Black admired Welch's business instincts and, over the years, had lent him money on multiple occasions. In June, Welch called Black, requesting a substantial loan. Welch explained that he needed funds to buy company stock and pay off debts, Black later testified in court. They agreed on a $25,000 loan, with a corporate note as guarantee. Welch promptly deposited the check in the corporate account but credited it to his personal ledger.

In August, when Black met with Welch to discuss repayment of the $25,000 loan, Welch proposed a new arrangement: Black would buy part of the stock in a new company Welch was forming—Welch Manufacturing. The existing corporate note covered most of the purchase price. Convinced by Welch's persuasive pitch, Black sent an additional $8,000 to seal the deal.

The following month, Welch made his boldest move. He secured a $150,000 loan from Farmers Bank, purchased the remaining company stock, renamed the business Welch Manufacturing, and claimed undisputed ownership. For a brief moment, Welch felt victorious. He had outmaneuvered Mulholland and seized control of the company he had served for over three decades.

But the triumph was short-lived. As October drew to a close, the pressure from his financial house of cards overwhelmed him. Farmers Bank, growing increasingly nervous about its $150,000 loan, recalled the debt. Unable to repay, Welch's control over Welch Manufacturing unraveled in an instant.

On November 16, Howard Black, realizing he had been left in financial jeopardy, took Welch to court and won a judgment for the $25,000 loan. Four days later, Farmers Bank moved to protect its interests, repossessing Welch Manufacturing in a sheriff's sale for $175,000.

Once celebrated as a business genius and community leader, Welch now had nothing—no company, no position, and no standing in the business community. His only escape, it seemed to him, was to take his life in a New York hotel room.

Clarence Welch's story did not conclude in that bathroom at the Bretton Hall Hotel.

On December 9, the *Journal-Every Evening* reported that Bellevue Hospital had released Welch, who was recuperating at his home in Milford. Robert Tunnell, Welch's Georgetown attorney, told the newspaper that his client was "still under the care of a physician but seemed to be recovering." Meanwhile, Farmers Bank took control and supervised operations at the former Welch Manufacturing.

For a year, Welch remained out of the public eye. Then, in December 1954, he incorporated a new company in Milford: Mulco Products, Inc. His focus? Wooden spoons— the same product on which he had built his reputation at Mulholland.

Mulco employed 39 employees by April 1955. Welch fought to rebuild his standing, though legal troubles persisted. Howard Black, still awaiting repayment of his $25,000, faced another setback in 1956 when the Delaware Supreme Court upheld a lower court's decision against him. The court ruled that Black's loan had been made to the now-defunct Mulholland Corporation rather than to Welch personally.

This distinction created a trap that left Black with no recourse. The Mulholland Corporation no longer existed to repay the debt, and Welch himself had no personal obligation to cover it, leaving Black without a path to recover his substantial investment.

In September 1957, perhaps fearing further legal action, Welch transferred ownership of his Cedar Creek Hundred home to his attorneys, Robert W. Tunnell and James M. Tunnel Jr., through a trust arrangement.

Mulco Products continued operating under the "Bentwood" brand name into the 1970s. Welch sold the company to the Simon family of Dover in 1963 and changed course. That same year, he founded Mohawk Electrical Systems, originally named Mohawk Electronic Corporation, to manufacture cable assemblies for the U.S. Army. He built it into a thriving business and led Mohawk until he died in 1998 at age 85.

Clarence Welch's obituary in the Milford Chronicle offered only a brief mention, stating that he "co-founded Mohawk Electrical Systems, Inc., Milford, in 1963, where he currently served as chairman of the executive committee."

The obituary omitted any mention of Welch Manufacturing, Mulco Products, or those tumultuous days in November 1953 when his disappearance captivated the state. Perhaps the newspaper left it out intentionally—a quiet acknowledgment that some chapters of a life should remain untold.

F. Scott Fitzgerald once pronounced, "There are no second acts in American lives," suggesting that failures in business or love permanently define a person's career or life. But Clarence Welch proved Fitzgerald wrong. In the end, he built a second act in his American life—one that lasted longer and remained more stable than his first.

The young office boy rose to become a company president, lost everything in a spiral of financial mismanagement, and then found his way back. He did not regain the heights of his previous ambition. Instead, he found something perhaps more valuable: a life he could manage in a community that, remarkably, forgave if it did not forget his very public fall from grace.

BOOKIES

The evolution of underground gambling.

When Bill Frank spoke, Wilmington listened.

For decades, his newspaper column ran in the Morning News, shaping public opinion with a mix of wry humor and blunt assessments of city life. He became a fixture in Delaware journalism, as much a part of the state's daily rhythm as the first sip of morning coffee. His words carried weight, and when he took aim at hypocrisy, people noticed.

So, when he sat at lunch one day in 1950 with a group of local professionals and heard one of them refer to "my bookie" with something akin to affection, he paid attention.

The warmth in the man's voice struck Frank as telling. The law considered a bookie a criminal. But to the men around this lunch table, he was something else—a trusted fixture, a man who handled business as routinely as a bank teller or butcher.

"There ought to be a popular song along that theme," Frank quipped: "'My Bookie'." He recognized the contradiction. Delaware outlawed bookmaking, yet it thrived in plain sight. "I think that as long as so many respectable and otherwise law-abiding citizens patronize the bookies, all the law's men and all the law's snoopers are never going to curb gambling," Frank wrote in his column.

Frank had seen this paradox before. The country had only recently shaken off Prohibition, a failed attempt to legislate morality that had done little more than push liquor into the shadows. He saw the same dynamic at play with gambling. "Patronizing a bookie is no different in principle from patronizing a bootlegger," he observed in the Morning News.

The state cracked down when it had to—police raids made headlines from time to time—but officials handed down laughable punishments. That same year, Municipal Court records revealed that officials had collected only $400 in fines from bookmaking cases in the entire first three months of 1950. For all its laws against gambling, the state seemed more interested in maintaining appearances than actually stopping the practice. Law enforcement's efforts looked more like stagecraft than strategy—meant to reassure the public, not to end the practice.

This casual, small-time bookmaking scene would not last forever.

Police stopped seeing Delaware's bookies as harmless operators of a tolerated vice by the 1960s and 1970s. A new reality emerged—one where bookmaking no longer operated just as a backroom affair among friends. The small-time neighborhood bookie, the man a customer might trust with an easy handshake, found himself answering to a new kind of authority.

By 1960, organized crime moved in. The old neighborhood bookie, once a fixture of cigar shops and luncheonettes, learned that he now had to operate in secrecy, or pay protection. Some, like James Edmund Spring, took that lesson to the extreme.

Spring, 41, ran his bookmaking operation out of his home in the Wilmington suburbs. Unlike the bookies Bill Frank's luncheon companions spoke of in warm tones, Spring had no storefront, no casual exchanges over coffee. Instead, he built himself a bunker.

When state police arrived at Spring's home with a search warrant on August 24, 1960, they found the house empty. Or so they thought.

The smell of burning paper filled the air. The stench led officers to a six-foot-by-six-foot dugout beneath the wooden floor of his home. A trapdoor concealed the entrance, but when police pried it open, they saw movement.

"Come out," an officer ordered.

Silence.

Then they sent in King, a police dog. The snarling German shepherd ended the standoff. Spring emerged, his clothing covered in dust and the ash of betting slips he had tried to destroy. State police found all the markings of a professional operation—bookie phones, a radio for race results, and wiretapping equipment. Spring had a history. His court record stretched back to 1948, with mounting fines and jail terms over the years:

- February 20, 1948 — Fined $100 for bookmaking.

- January 13, 1956 — Fined $500 and sentenced to six months in jail.

- February 4, 1956 — Fined $100 and given 30 days in jail.

The pattern was clear: Spring kept working, and the state kept fining him. But this time, he had adapted. He had taken bookmaking underground—literally.

It was a sign of things to come.

Wilmington Police Chief John T. McCool made a public admission that rattled city officials on August 14, 1971. Six recent armed robberies had targeted bookies and numbers writers—but not one of the victims had reported what happened. That fear of coming forward told investigators something revealing.

"In other words," McCool told reporters, "organized crime, if it has local connections to any degree, is getting income in one pocket from the drug users who, by robbery and other criminal offenses, are taking it out of another pocket."

This wasn't just speculation. McCool and other officials, including U.S. Attorney F. L. Peter Stone, believed that the same crime syndicates controlling the drug trade also controlled gambling. Stone, along with Delaware's chief medical examiner, Dr. Ali Z. Hameli, had already warned that the Bruno crime family in Philadelphia controlled heroin distribution in the region. Now, police suspected that the same organization was running local bookmaking operations and using them as a source of revenue to finance narcotics trafficking.

The situation created a grim irony: local drug addicts, desperate for cash, robbed bookies who likely paid protection money to the very same organizations that got them hooked in the first place.

McCool recognized that these crimes would continue as long as drug addiction remained rampant in the city. "There is a need for a long-range effort, with focus on stamping out the illegal drug traffic," he said. "This is an absolute necessity if, in fact, we are to bring our soaring crime rate under control."

McCool didn't say it outright, but the truth became increasingly clear. This wasn't just about narcotics. Organized crime syndicates had turned bookmaking into something much larger, and far more dangerous.

An occasional police raid might have worried a bookie before the 1960s. By the 1970s, a bigger concern loomed. Who collected the debts and what happened if those debts went unpaid?

Some bookies saw the writing on the wall.

"If a guy wanted to open a bookie joint right next door to me, I'd say go ahead, good luck to him," one Wilmington bookmaker explained. "But if a syndicate moved in, this guy would have to get permission to operate in my territory and he'd have to make the big payoff to get started at all."

The new reality took hold. Syndicates squeezed Wilmington's independent bookies for a cut or forced them out entirely. They no longer just took bets.

Another bookie, with two prior convictions, admitted that authorities strictly enforcing new anti-crime laws would leave small-time operators like him without a chance. "I only take down about $200 a week. I've already got two convictions on gambling charges. I couldn't afford to risk that five years in the cooler for no $200 a week."

And yet, those who expected a crackdown to eliminate bookmaking entirely fooled themselves. Another bookmaker warned that shutting down independent operations would have consequences:

"Wilmington's a wide-open town now, and as a result, there's no syndicate, no payoffs, and little violent crime. But close up all the small potatoes, and the syndicate would move in here so fast it would make your head swim.

The powerful criminal networks had numbered the days of independent gambling, and those who stayed in the business would soon work for someone else.

Some bookies adapted, carving out space within the new order. Others weren't so lucky.

"No bookie is loved by horse players. I'm the guy who takes their money when they lose. I'm the one they're out to beat..."

BOYD THE BOOK

White bookmakers dominated Wilmington's illegal numbers racket for years. They controlled the money, the operations, and the networks of runners who took bets across the city. That balance shifted by 1974.

The change began after the 1968 riots, when fires burned major sections of Wilmington's Black neighborhoods, closures shuttered businesses, and neglect weakened community institutions. Federal wiretaps in 1971 exposed and dismantled some of the city's largest white-run numbers banks, creating a power vacuum. A new generation of Black operators stepped into that void, seizing control of a business that had long profited off their own neighborhoods.

One of the most recognizable names in this new order was Roosevelt "Hooker" Harris. Operating from the affluent Graylyn Crest suburbs well outside downtown Wilmington, Harris built a numbers operation that extended across the city, pulling in thousands of dollars a day.

He wasn't alone. Van Smothers, operating out of the East Side, was another major figure in the new landscape. Clifton Wise ran a numbers house at 600 West 9th Street. Others opened shop at Moore's Grocery on 3rd and Franklin, and in the 9th and Poplar area, a location frequented by none other than State Senator Herman M. Holloway.

The shift didn't push out white bookies entirely. Jimmy Brady and Jimmy Perillo still controlled pieces of the operation, running a highly profitable numbers bank, but the days when they and their ilk dominated Wilmington's Black neighborhoods were over.

Street-level bookies—whether old-guard operators or newer figures like Harris—made money, but real power remained elsewhere. With the Bruno crime family in Philadelphia playing an ever-growing role, many of these bookies were answering to organized crime interests from Philadelphia, New Jersey, and Baltimore. Crime syndicates provided protection as long as bookies paid their cut. If they didn't, the syndicates shut them down, one way or another.

Boyd the Book now lived in this world. The police didn't worry him. The men who never called the cops did. Boyd ran a careful, disciplined operation in 1975.

"Just because what he does is illegal," the Morning News noted, "doesn't make him any less a businessman. All it does is make him a more-cautious-than-ordinary businessman."

Boyd the Book took over his operation from his brother, who had spent years in the business. His brother acted recklessly and made mistakes. Boyd observed the consequences of a careless bookie and adjusted accordingly: "Unless a bookie is cautious, he doesn't get to be a businessman very long."

His office, a small but steady hub of activity, catered to a regular clientele. Gamblers like Harry the Horse, Telegraph, and Foul Mouth spent their days trying to beat the system and their nights blaming Boyd when they didn't.

Every hustler who walked through Boyd's door had a mission. They might joke with him, gripe about their luck, or pretend they played just for fun, but Boyd knew better.

"No bookie is loved by horse players," Boyd said. "I'm the guy who takes their money when they lose. I'm the one they're out to beat—the adversary, the enemy."

But Boyd didn't worry. Over time, the odds always favored him. "The house odds, the percentages, are with the bookie."

If his clients arrived dreaming of a big score, convinced they had cracked the code of the races, Boyd recognized the reality. "Over the long haul, the horse players always lose."

The system handled payouts straightforwardly, with track prices and Exacta payouts capped at $62. That's why Boyd kept three, sometimes four radios running at once, each tuned to a different station, each giving him the latest results from the tracks. He had a portable TV as well, catching the Saturday feature races as soon as they aired. If results didn't arrive immediately, Boyd delayed payouts until the next morning's papers printed the numbers.

It wasn't a business for the impatient.

"This leaves maybe $20,000 at the end of a year," he explained. Boyd's not getting rich. He's "comfortable, but not running around in a Caddy or Lincoln." Drugs and prostitution brought in the big money, not bookmaking. "For rich and for Caddies and Lincolns, he says, you have to look at the pimps and pushers."

Yet, for all his control over the business, Boyd held no illusions. His clients, the men who walked into his office day after day, weren't there to make money. They were there to lose it.

"They nickel-and-dime Boyd to death," the Morning News observed. "Even if they win, they lose. Horse players don't stop when they have a winner. They hand the money back to Boyd, playing to win still more."

Boyd had seen it happen too many times. The same faces, the same routines, the same cycle of hope and disappointment.

His brother had made the mistake of being too generous with credit. He had loaned out money to bettors who swore they would pay him back, only to vanish when the losses piled up. Boyd had studied those books carefully when he took over the operation. One number stood out: $5,000 in uncollected bets.

Boyd didn't make the same mistake. "If clients are going to lose money," he told the Morning News, "it's going to be their money. Not mine."

That philosophy kept him in business. He ran a cash-only operation. No credit, no advances. If a player ran out of money, tough luck for him.

Even in his record-keeping, Boyd exercised caution. He identified his clients by code numbers or initials. He never kept his own books at the office. In fact, Boyd didn't even know where they were. His "sheet man"—the bookmaker's record-keeper, responsible for tracking bets and balances—was just a voice on the telephone.

A police raid could come at any time, though he doubted the vice squad would find much. "The cops are always welcome because they won't find any real evidence of his business except for some guys sitting around and a batch of racing forms. And that isn't much in the way of evidence."

If they had a warrant, they would arrest Boyd. They would leave his clients alone— that was part of the price of doing business.

And still, Boyd knew that his biggest threats didn't come from the police.

The real danger came from the men who weren't part of his regular clientele, the ones who didn't come in with a racing form tucked under their arm. That's why he had Norris at the door.

Norris wasn't there to keep out the cops. He was there to keep out anyone Boyd didn't know.

"To be accepted, a potential has to be brought in and introduced by an established client. Nobody else gets by Norris." That caution paid off.

Boyd kept the business running, taking bets day after day, managing the same love-hate relationship every bookie had with his customers. And at the end of each night, after locking up his office and heading home, he popped aspirin to deal with the stress.

Government-backed gambling, not crime, delivered the final blow to the old way of doing business. Bookies had always operated on the edge of legitimacy, taking advantage of the fact that gamblers had few legal alternatives. But in 1976, Delaware's Lottery Commission introduced parlay sports betting, a move that pulled casual bettors away from underground books and into government-approved wagering. It wasn't a full takeover—parlay bets were limited, and horse racing remained a staple of bookmaking—but it was a sign of what was to come.

Delaware approved slot machines in 1994 at its three racetracks—one in each county—to support the struggling racing industry. Dover Downs opened its casino on December 29, 1995, and Harrington Raceway's Midway Slots and Racebook followed on August 20, 1996. The expansion of legal gambling further undercut the old bookies. Gamblers who once relied on bookies like Boyd now had a legal alternative.

Boyd had disappeared from the scene. Whether he left the business on his own terms or someone forced him out, Delaware's gambling landscape no longer had room for men like him. By the time legal sportsbooks opened their doors, the neighborhood bookie was already a relic, remembered more in anecdotes than indictments.

In 2018, the U.S. Supreme Court struck down the Professional and Amateur Sports Protection Act in Murphy v. NCAA, giving states the authority to legalize full-scale sports betting. Delaware, having already dipped its toe with 1976 parlay bets, became the first state outside Nevada to accept legal wagers.

A new era of bookmaking began—not in backrooms, but in casinos, on smartphones, and through state-regulated sportsbooks. Gamblers placed the same hopes on the outcomes of games and races. The old bookmaker, with his codebooks, cash-only rules, and first-name clients, was gone.

But the bets? The bets are on.

22

SERIAL RAPIST
UNMASKED

A predatory figure who challenged notions of rehabilitation.

Aesop tells a fable of a farmer who, one winter's day, trudged through the snow-covered fields and came across a viper, half-frozen and near death. Pitying the creature, he lifted it from the ground and placed it inside his coat to warm it. When the viper revived, it sank its fangs into the farmer's chest. As the venom spread and the man collapsed to the frozen earth, he managed only to gasp, "I saved you—why would you do this?" The viper, retreating into the brush, hissed its reply: "You knew what I was when you picked me up."

On February 2, 1969, burglars shot and killed Joseph B. Larkin, a 69-year-old gardener. The night before, he had retired after fifteen years at the Westover Hills estate of George P. Edmonds, in an affluent neighborhood west of Wilmington. Worried the new gardener had not yet arrived, Larkin returned that day to water the plants he had long tended.

Later that evening, Wilmington police stopped a car for running a red light and arrested three men inside: Edward Pritchett, 28, Charles Carpenter, 26, and Aubrey McKay, 22. A search of the vehicle revealed two loaded guns. Police later identified one as the murder weapon. Wilmington police charged McKay with Larkin's killing. At the time, authorities in Union, New Jersey, also wanted him for burglarizing a home and raping a 13-year-old girl—a crime that had prompted the FBI to issue a warrant for his arrest on charges of murder and unlawful flight.

The next day, a grand jury swiftly indicted all three men for second-degree murder, kidnapping, robbery, burglary, and conspiracy. In 1970, McKay pleaded guilty to manslaughter and received the maximum 30-year sentence in a plea deal that halted his extradition to New Jersey.

A new factor in the spring of 1977 caused catastrophe. A federal court ordered the Delaware Correctional Center near Smyrna to reduce its population, ruling that the facility was unconstitutionally overcrowded. U.S. District Court Judge Murray M. Schwartz had ordered the prison population kept to 92 percent of capacity, or approximately 605 inmates. Confronted with this mandate and limited options, prison officials substantially expanded their furlough program.

"With the court order hanging over the state and no new prison in sight," Prison

Commissioner James T. Vaughn said in the July 6, 1977 *Morning News*, "we have no choice but to continue the furlough system."

Milton B. Horton, Delaware's chief of adult corrections, later acknowledged the pressure this created: "In recent months, we've had to step up the furlough program to keep down the Smyrna prison's population. But we don't have sufficient staff to keep a close tab on furloughed inmates."

Delaware officials appeared convinced that they had rehabilitated Aubrey McKay. Between 1970 and 1977, he built a reputation as a model inmate: collecting toys for needy children as part of the Greenbank Jaycees, leading the prison's New Hope Gospel Chorus, and earning his GED while taking numerous vocational courses. His behavior was so commendable that between 1974 and 1977, he was granted fourteen different furloughs.

Aubrey McKay's carefully constructed facade concealed a far darker reality. Even as prison officials praised his efforts, reports of sexual violence followed him from the beginning of his incarceration. Within his first year behind bars, McKay's predatory nature was already surfacing.

In October 1969, while he still awaited sentencing, a grand jury indicted McKay for sodomizing an 18-year-old who had been jailed for 10 days for hitchhiking. Prosecutors later dropped the charge after McKay received his 30-year sentence, arguing that a second conviction was unnecessary given his lengthy prison term.

The pattern continued. In March 1970, just months after he began his sentence, prison officials charged McKay with a second sexual assault — this time on another 18-year-old inmate serving a 10-day sentence for contempt of court. McKay lured the youth into a recreation room where he "had no business being."

The *Morning News* reported on March 25, 1970 that despite the previous sodomy accusation, McKay "had been returned to his regular janitorial and clerking duties at the prison" and that he "wrote himself out a pass which allowed him to get into the first-floor recreation room, which was being cleaned by some other inmates, including the youth." This second case went to trial in September 1970, but the jury failed to reach a verdict. Prosecutors later dropped the charge rather than retry McKay, citing the length of his existing 30-year sentence.

A third accusation came in March 1972, when another inmate charged McKay with sexual assault. This incident mirrored his previous attacks in the prison. The charge surfaced during a 1975 Delaware Board of Pardons hearing where McKay requested a 10-year reduction of his 30-year sentence. During this hearing, Deputy Attorney General Harrison Turner opposed the request, citing McKay's violent history and problematic prison record.

Turner specifically referenced this third sodomy charge from 1972, noting that "since his incarceration, McKay has been charged three times by other inmates with sodomy." As with the other incidents, the allegations never resulted in a conviction, continuing the cycle of charges against McKay that prosecutors either dropped or failed to prove at trial.

The Board of Pardons denied McKay's request, with Turner arguing that "McKay's prior record is marked by crimes of violence and his record in prison has not been exemplary."

In August 1976, McKay's violence escalated when prison officials charged him and another inmate, Carlton E. Thornton, with raping a 23-year-old woman who was visiting the prison. According to Deputy Chief Horton, this was unprecedented in Delaware penal history—the first time a woman had allegedly been raped inside a state prison.

The incident revealed a disturbing level of manipulation. According to prison sources, McKay and Thornton had acted as "lookouts" while the woman conducted clandestine sexual visits with her inmate boyfriend. They later used that knowledge to pressure her into sex, threatening to harm her boyfriend if she refused. Fear of retaliation—and fear of punishment for the illegal visits—kept her from reporting the assault immediately.

Prosecutors dropped the charges, arguing that a trial served no purpose since both men were already serving long sentences.

McKay remained in the good graces of prison officials, not because of good behavior, but because he had something else to offer them. His favorable standing with prison authorities came from his role as an informant. Other inmates despised him as a "snitch," but prison officials valued the information he provided about his fellow prisoners.

Thomas H. Winsett, a prisoner serving a life term for the 1964 murder of a state policeman, explained to the *Morning News* on July 2, 1977:

"If a prisoner was violating some rule, he was well-advised not to let Luke [McKay's nickname] see him do it. If he was unlucky enough to be seen, he could count on a visit to the guard captain's office. Predictably, he's overbearing, cunning, cruel, and any other uncomplimentary thing that can be said about a person," Winsett continued. The *Morning News* reporter concluded: "There is, apparently, some advantage to having friends in the right places, even in prison."

The arrangement benefited prison officials, who relied on informants like McKay to maintain control within the facility. Horton acknowledged that McKay was "very cooperative with the officers... serving more or less as a runner within the prison." When asked directly if McKay was an informer, Horton responded evasively: "Any inmate that is cooperative creates that impression. It is very easy to have an individual labeled as an informer when, in fact, it is not true." But he did not deny it outright.

McKay's status as an informant earned him favor particularly with guards who relied on such information. McKay cultivated a special relationship with one of these guards, Curtis Powell of Felton. As Horton later acknowledged, "I believe their relationship was based on McKay being an informer and in prison, we depend to a certain extent upon informers."

McKay's reputation ultimately made him a target. On March 12, 1978, three inmates—Emanuel Redden, Joseph A. Colatriano, and Ronald Payne—attacked McKay during an exercise period, stabbing him in the thigh and arm. Prison Commissioner James T. Vaughn put it bluntly: "I think it's been stated before that he wasn't very popular with the inmates."

Years later, columnist Ralph Moyed called out the system that enabled McKay. Writing in the News Journal on April 12, 1990, he observed:

"When Aubrey McKay was arrested after raping 11 Wilmington women in 1977, I wrote that it wouldn't bother me if another convict stuck him with a shiv and minced his liver. A couple of weeks later, another convict stabbed McKay with a shiv, but the knife went astray and missed his liver and other arguably vital organs.

"I had mixed emotions about that. The knifing of Aubrey McKay had nothing to do with the crimes he committed. When he went on his rape spree, he was on furlough from the state penitentiary. He had killed a night watchman by slitting his throat during a burglary and, because of an evidentiary problem, had been allowed to cop a plea.

"Why was such a man released on furlough? It was not because he was a good risk. As I wrote at the time, authorities put the convicted killer on the streets as a reward for his finking on fellow inmates. Perhaps the people responsible should have been put on trial with McKay."

Deputy Chief Horton initially showed caution regarding McKay's ventures outside prison walls. In September 1975, Horton rejected a work-release recommendation for McKay, apparently recognizing the risk he posed. However, external pressure soon mounted. In December 1975, Littleton P. Mitchell, head of the state NAACP, and the Rev. Calvin Jones of Wilmington challenged these denials, requesting an investigation in a letter to then-Governor Sherman W. Tribbitt.

Rev. Jones had organized the New Hope Choir that McKay participated in and eventually headed. The Evening Journal noted on February 1, 1978 that McKay joined the choir, which toured churches and community meeting halls around Cheswold and Smyrna.

Despite his earlier reservations, Horton approved a 12-hour escorted furlough for McKay in April 1976—the first of many. Over the next year, prison officials kept releasing him, even with his long history of sexual violence, citing the need to reduce the prison population. His final furlough began on June 27, 1977. He was supposed to be staying with prison guard Curtis Powell in Felton, but instead he lived with his girlfriend, Lethia Cooper, in Wilmington—a clear violation of his furlough conditions that prison officials never caught.

From May to July 1977, McKay unleashed a reign of terror across Delaware and into New Jersey. Within the span of just two months, he attacked nine women—four of whom he raped—while systematically robbing his victims of jewelry, money, and personal possessions. His attacks followed a similar pattern: he would gain entry to a home, threaten his victim with either a hatchet or gun, bind and blindfold her, molest her, and then rob the premises.

The wave of violence began on May 17, 1977, when McKay broke into a west Wilmington home and confronted a woman with a hatchet as she started to do laundry in her basement. Her 19-month-old daughter sat in the living room, watching television. "Don't make a move or I'll split your head open," McKay told her.

He forced her to lie on the basement floor and hand over her watch and diamond ring after demanding to know their value. He then ordered her to strip off her clothes, and when she protested, told her, "Shut up, bitch," according to her court testimony. McKay tied her hands behind her and blindfolded her with her bra. The woman testified: "He told me, 'Now we're going upstairs and you're going to show me where your jewelry box is. If the kid makes a sound, she's dead.'" Once they reached the first floor, McKay rifled her purse and her husband's briefcase. When asked what she was thinking, the victim replied, "I was scared to death. I thought he would kill my baby and kill me."

McKay used the pistol stolen in this first attack for subsequent assaults. On June 13, he confronted another woman in a Wilmington parking garage at 12th and West Streets, forcing her to strip and blindfolding her with her bra before raping her in the back seat of a car. On June 29, he entered another home wearing a bandana mask, took the occupant upstairs at gunpoint, and raped her. As before, he bound and blindfolded the woman with her bra. After the rapist fled, she stumbled to a rooftop and screamed for help.

The following day, June 30, McKay approached another victim by asking to use her telephone. He pulled out a pistol, threatened her, and blindfolded her with a nightgown before raping her. "He told me if I shut up, he wouldn't hurt me. He asked me why I didn't want to die," this victim later testified in court. "I told him I wanted to see my little girls grow up. He asked me if I would do anything for my little girls. I told him yes."

By early July, Wilmington police had identified McKay as the suspect in this reign of terror. On July 2, as police prepared to arrest him at his girlfriend's home in the 200 block of East 28th Street, McKay got word and slipped away.

The circumstances surrounding McKay's escape became a matter of intense political controversy. Deputy Attorney General Edward C. Pankowski Jr. later alleged that Milton Horton had contributed to McKay's escape by making a telephone call to prison guard Curtis Powell, who in turn called McKay.

Why was McKay notified in advance? Pankowski put the question directly to law-makers during a legislative committee meeting on February 15, 1978 — a pointed accusation aimed at Milton B. Horton. An obviously stunned Horton shot back: "You're a damned liar, I didn't do any such thing."

The following week, Pankowski backed away from his allegation, stating: "Mr. Horton, I did not mean to criticize you. I apologize and I also apologize to the joint legislative committee on corrections for my remarks at last Wednesday's meeting in Dover."

Rep. Al O. Plant (D-Wilmington), however, continued to press the issue. At a public meeting in the City Council chamber on February 22, 1978, Plant accused both Horton and State Prison Commissioner James T. Vaughn of being responsible for McKay's escape.

According to Plant, Horton called prison guard Curtis Powell in Felton, where McKay was supposed to be staying on furlough, and instructed him to contact McKay. Powell phoned McKay in Wilmington and said, "I want to see you." Plant argued that the call gave McKay just enough warning to escape before police arrived on July 2.

"In other words, Horton tipped off McKay through Powell," Plant said. "And I blame

Horton and his superior, Vaughn, for this."

Horton, dismissed from his position shortly after these controversies, maintained that he had done nothing wrong. He insisted that when he called Powell, he simply instructed him to find out where McKay was and then go to the Wilmington police station to stand by if needed. Horton acknowledged that Powell had called McKay but claimed it was only to locate him, not to tip him off.

Regardless of the exact sequence of events, McKay managed to escape and flee to New Jersey, where he continued his crime spree.

"Don't make a move or I'll split your head open."

AUBREY MCKAY

Authorities recaptured him in Hoboken on July 22, after a multi-state manhunt. McKay attempted to rob 19-year-old Diane Youngclaus in a supermarket parking lot. Off-duty Port Authority officer Willie White heard her screams and tackled him.

By this time, authorities also pursued McKay for several similar crimes in New Jersey, including the kidnapping of a 27-year-old mother and her two children in Maplewood. During that assault, he allegedly held a knife to the throat of a six-week-old infant while he raped the woman.

McKay's arrest prompted officials to establish immediate policy changes. By September 1977, Milton Horton implemented new furlough rules that explicitly excluded anyone convicted of a sex offense from furlough eligibility. Other exclusions included prisoners with two adult felony convictions within the past 10 years and those who had escaped from an adult prison twice or more within five years.

As the full extent of McKay's crimes became known, Governor Pierre S. du Pont IV ordered a comprehensive review of the furlough system. This led to substantial reforms, including a bill signed by Governor du Pont in June 1978 ending furloughs for murderers, rapists, and kidnappers. Officials also recalled all five convicted murderers who had been on furlough.

Aubrey McKay's legal battles stretched into 1978, with two major trials resulting in five consecutive life sentences plus 320 years in prison. In the first trial, the court sentenced him to two life terms plus 170 years for the May 17 rape. A second trial in May 1978 resulted in three more consecutive life terms plus 150 years for the June 30 kidnap-rape.

In August 1978, McKay became part of a larger solution to Delaware's prison overcrowding crisis. U.S. District Court Judge Murray M. Schwartz ordered the Delaware Correctional Center to reduce its population to 650 inmates, a mandate that created intense pressure on prison officials. The prison's population had been fluctuating between 675 and 685, pushing administrators to find creative solutions.

Senator Joseph R. Biden Jr. negotiated an arrangement with Norman A. Carlson, director of the U.S. Bureau of Prisons, to transfer 40 inmates to federal facilities at a cost of $21 per day for each prisoner. Prison Commissioner Vaughn selected McKay among thirty-nine other high-profile inmates for this relocation—a move designed to address broader prison population issues rather than simply to isolate McKay.

Officials first moved McKay to the federal penitentiary in Lewisburg, Pennsylvania. Later, they transferred him to even more secure facilities, including the prison in Marion, Illinois, and ultimately to Soledad Prison in California.

The federal system ultimately provided the level of containment that Delaware's prisons had failed to maintain, ending his ability to victimize the public. The public financial burden had been substantial. As George A. Reddish, Delaware's chief of institutions, noted, while it cost taxpayers $20 a day to house the average prisoner at Delaware Correctional Center, McKay cost "considerably more" because he required close guarding for his own protection. "Before the McKay horror is finalized," noted columnist Bill Frank in the *Evening Journal* on January 27, 1986, "that the cost to the taxpayers will be close to a million dollars or more."

The McKay case laid bare deep failings in Delaware's criminal justice system. His status as an informant earned him protection and favor despite clear warning signs. Authorities repeatedly dismissed or minimized his history of sexual violence. Pressured by court-mandated population caps, prison officials prioritized compliance over public safety.

Like the farmer who saved the viper only to fall victim to its poisonous bite, Delaware extended privilege after privilege to McKay, ignoring his true nature. By the time he was locked away for good, his crime spree had shattered lives and forced the state to confront its naive assumptions about rehabilitation. Aubrey McKay's case reveals the fatal blindness of a system that refused to recognize what was evident all along—some predators cannot be reformed.

23

ART HEIST

A bold art theft revealed organized crime's sophistication.

" I thought to myself how one would feel to wake up in the middle of the night and realize that someone had gone through their house while they slept, or for that matter was possibly still in the house? I hoped she didn't wake up until daylight as I slithered back out the window."

A skilled burglar from the Matherly gang offered a glimpse into the uneasy thrill and risk built into their crimes, operations that gradually escalated into the Art Heist.

First, there were tractors—gleaming machines worth thousands, ripe for the taking across the fertile farmlands of Delaware and Pennsylvania. In the mid-1970s, Francis Matherly and his associates discovered a lucrative opportunity: farm equipment could be stolen, transported, and sold with surprising ease, turning agricultural machinery into quick cash.

On a crisp day in May 1976, a Lancaster County, Pennsylvania courtroom revealed the intricate machinations of the Matherly gang's tractor theft operation. James Mark, a West Grove farm machinery dealer, sat on the witness stand and methodically described how Francis R. Matherly had been supplying him stolen tractors at prices that seemed too good to be true.

"He promised new products at less than what I'd have to pay International Harvester," Mark testified, his voice steady and matter of fact, according to the *Intelligencer Journal* (May 19, 1976). The deals took place at Roy M. Myers' farm, near the Maryland-Chester County borders—a convenient meeting ground for criminal transactions.

The operation was surprisingly straightforward. Kenneth D. Howell, a Maryland convict, would steal the tractors. On one occasion, he stole two tractors from White Bros. in Middletown, Delaware, driving them directly to Myers' farm. Myers, along with Bruce and David Johnston, would be waiting to receive the stolen machinery.

The next month, Mark reportedly ordered two more tractors. This time, Howell, Myers, and the Johnston brothers drove to Ephrata, Pennsylvania, stole a U-Haul truck from a Citgo station, and lifted three tractors from a nearby International Harvester dealership. Mark would then purchase these stolen machines, completing the criminal cycle.

Not every potential buyer was willing. Wilmer D. Esbenshade recounted being offered a stolen tractor, noticing something off about the key. "I felt it might have been stolen merchandise," he told the court, "and I didn't want to jeopardize my farming operation." His neighbor, Gary G. Hauck, was less scrupulous and admitted to purchasing one of the stolen tractors, said the *Intelligencer Journal*.

The legal consequences were relatively mild. In May 1976, Francis Matherly faced multiple charges: six counts of receiving stolen property, six counts of criminal conspiracy, three counts of burglary, and three counts of theft. But the punishment seemed almost inconsequential compared to the scale of their venture.

By October the court sentenced Matherly to three consecutive terms of one to two years in the State Correctional Institution at Huntingdon, Pennsylvania. Prosecutors charged him with receiving two International Harvester tractors, two portable heaters, and another tractor—all valued at nearly $28,000. He promptly appealed, remaining free on $25,000 bail.

This early brush with the law did little to deter Matherly. Instead, it taught him valuable lessons about organizing theft rings and moving stolen goods through a network of buyers. Each member had a role: Howell would steal, Myers would receive, the Johnstons would facilitate, and Matherly would arrange the sales. It was a family affair, a criminal ecosystem that would grow more sophisticated with time. Little did anyone know that these tractor thefts were merely a prelude to far bolder crimes—setting the stage for a sensational art heist that captivated the Delaware Valley.

Other criminal organizations operated in the region beyond the Matherly gang, including their one-time associates, the Johnston brothers' gang, a violent outfit known for eliminating potential witnesses. Bruce A. Johnston Sr. even attempted to murder his own son, Bruce Jr., who had agreed to testify against his father and his uncles.

While Bruce Jr. survived the execution attempt, the assailants killed his 15-year-old fiancée, Robin Miller, during the attack. Despite this brutal attempt to silence him, Bruce Jr. went on to become the key witness who helped convict his father of six murders. The court sentenced his uncles, Norman and David Kirk Johnston, to multiple life terms for similar crimes.

Francis Matherly had refined his criminal operation into something more sophisticated as the 1970s drew to a close. Police sources described him as running two distinct gangs: one comprised of his own family—two brothers, a sister, three nephews, and their friends—and another of professional thieves, "cat" burglars and "second-story men" (a term for burglars who specialize in entering upper floors of buildings, typically through windows or by climbing, to avoid ground-level security) who had been stealing their entire lives.

Investigators described him as the brains behind most of the major burglaries committed in southeastern Pennsylvania and Delaware during the previous decade.

The family's criminal enterprise expanded beyond farm equipment. By 1980, they had graduated to more lucrative targets: wealthy estates in Delaware's so-called Chateau Country. "Who knows, maybe he stole all the silver around here and had to find something else," one investigator later quipped. In October of that year, they hit the home of Dr. Edward Olson, a dentist in Centreville. In June, they targeted Albert Heisler's home in Greenville. The combined haul was hefty—silver items, jewelry, and furs estimated at almost $100,000.

Noel Matherly, Francis's brother, played a crucial role in these operations. He had son Robert and nephew Gerald Madron scout targets before driving them to a chosen location. "My father would tell us he wanted us to do a burglary. He didn't care which house we hit as long as we did one and came back with something," Robert Matherly testified in court, according to the *Morning News* (September 4, 1982).

They would return the stolen goods to Noel's home after the burglary. There, he appraised the items and arranged for their sale—typically to Francis, who maintained an extensive network of black-market dealers ready to melt down silver, recut gems, or sell artwork without asking questions about their origins.

Intimidation kept the family's criminal enterprise running. When Robert Matherly refused to take part in a burglary, his father, Noel, beat him with an ax handle, hospitalizing him for three days. Noel denied the accusation, but the altercation set off a chain of events that unraveled the family enterprise. From his hospital bed, Robert called Pennsylvania state police. "When he wanted me to go out, I wasn't going to argue with him," Robert Matherly testified. "I didn't feel like hearing a bunch of argument," he told the Morning News (September 4, 1982).

To the Matherlys, crime was simply business. Investigators called Francis Matherly "an astute judge of valuable items." He moved stolen goods with expert precision.

The Matherly gang grew bold by 1982, seeking even more lucrative targets. No longer content with silver and jewelry, they set their sights on fine art. Their most brazen—and ultimately fatal—choice was the estate of Andrew Wyeth, one of America's most celebrated painters, renowned for his realist depictions of rural life.

The plan took shape in the weeks before the heist. Francis Matherly and William Porter, the gang's most skilled burglar, meticulously plotted their approach. Porter later bragged to FBI agents that he had committed between 1,000 and 1,500 burglaries throughout his criminal career. A burglar with an expert understanding of security systems, he also—ironically—owned a legitimate burglar alarm installation business in Tennessee.

On March 26, Matherly drove Porter to the Wyeth estate for their first attempt. When they arrived, a night watchman's presence initially forced them to hold back. After the watchman fell asleep, Porter carefully cased the Granary, the two-story stone building that served as Betsy Wyeth's office. He studied the building's layout, looking for entry points and potential alarm systems. The next night, Porter returned—this time, ready to break in.

On March 27, he arrived early, before the estate's night watchman was due at 9 p.m. He brought a ladder, radio equipment, and the cold precision of a professional thief. Matherly dropped him off near the property, then waited at the nearby Chadds Ford Inn, their communication maintained through walkie-talkies. With no security present yet, Porter moved methodically. He positioned the ladder against the Granary, carefully leaning it to the left of a second-floor window.

Porter aimed to transform his criminal exploits into literary profit. He drafted a manuscript titled *Art Burglary*, hoping to publish a first-hand account of the Wyeth heist. However, those book dreams collapsed when prosecutors entered the document into evidence during the trial of Guido Frezzo, a Pennsylvania businessman convicted of purchasing three of the stolen Wyeth paintings. Once it became part of the public record, anyone could read or copy Porter's meticulous confession, making it impossible to sell to publishers.

"As silently as possible, I pulled out the ladder to its full 16 feet and leaned it against the rock structure to the left of the window, just in case there happened to be someone inside," Porter wrote, according to the *Morning News* (March 3, 1985).

He paused at the top. "All seemed well. As below, there was also a light on upstairs. I could see several more pictures hanging on the wall. An antique bed, with a patchwork quilt, took up most of the floor space. Beside the bed was an antique table with a pitcher on it." From his vantage point, he saw no alarm devices. "Neither did I see any evidence of any wireless bugs."

Porter carefully removed the windowpane and felt around for an alarm device. Finding none, he climbed inside and headed straight for the panel that controlled the security system. "I saw no [motion] detector and with a sigh of relief I knew I was home free!" he wrote. "I could take my time and dismantle the keypad [alarm panel] and turn the alarm off, but as I approached the keypad, I realized it wasn't even turned on!"

To ensure a quick escape if needed, he went downstairs and slipped out the back door, moving the ladder into the meadows. Then he returned to work. "I decided to clean the upstairs walls off first so if someone did enter, they wouldn't know what was going on unless they came upstairs. To ensure that I didn't go away empty-handed, I carried the first three pictures out and laid them at the pick-up spot along the road."

With the first paintings readied for pickup by the roadside, he radioed Matherly, who arrived to load them into his truck.

The entire operation took less than two hours. The thieves removed fifteen paintings from Betsy Wyeth's personal collection—seven by Andrew Wyeth, five by Jamie Wyeth, two by lesser-known artists, and a lithograph. The value: $750,000.

The stolen works included seven of Andrew Wyeth's watercolors: "Writing Chair," "Thawing," "Saracen Helmet," "Block and Tackle," "Charlie Stone's Fish House," "Gray Mare," and "Baron Phillippe." Jamie Wyeth's pieces included two pencil sketches of ballet legend Rudolph Nureyev, a portrait of Andy Warhol, and two oil paintings—"Shorty" and "Whitewash." A lithograph titled "Moon and the Horse" rounded out the collection. While these fifteen pieces represented only a small fraction of the vast Wyeth catalog, their combined value made this one of the region's most substantial art thefts.

But stealing the paintings was only the first challenge. Selling proved to be an even more complex criminal undertaking.

Dr. Benedict LaCorte, another key member of the gang, drove to Matherly's home that night, where he, Porter, and Matherly discussed how to offload the stolen artwork. While he and LaCorte would seek buyers in Pennsylvania and Delaware, Porter loaded 11 paintings into his small Ford Mustang the following day and drove to Tennessee, hoping his connections there would bite. But no one was willing to purchase the stolen artwork.

Months later, LaCorte traveled to Tennessee and purchased all 11 paintings himself from Porter for $13,200. After the initial theft, the paintings became a hot potato. Douglas Fuller, one of the gang's associates, stored four of the stolen paintings in his attic, waiting for an opportunity to sell.

When LaCorte came to retrieve them, Fuller demanded payment for his risk. In response, LaCorte gave Fuller one of the paintings as compensation.

Of those four paintings, Fuller later sold the one he kept to John "Sadsbury Reds" Sorber, receiving $2,500 in cash and a $500 credit toward a gambling debt. Meanwhile, Matherly and LaCorte sold the remaining three to Guido Frezzo in exchange for a 1957 Chevrolet and $2,000. However, in a calculated double-cross, LaCorte later stole those three paintings back from Frezzo and resold them.

LaCorte had built a varied career. He started as a barber near the Wyeth estate (With a touch of dark humor, Andrew Wyeth told the *Evening Journal*, 'Benny used to cut my hair'). He then taught science before entering the chiropractic field. Guido Frezzo had helped fund LaCorte's new practice when LaCorte first established it. Ultimately, LaCorte brokered deals and laundered stolen goods as a crucial middleman in the Matherly operation.

By early 1982, this growing criminal enterprise had caught the attention of federal authorities, who noticed an uptick in house burglaries across southern Chester County and northern Delaware. The Wyeth art theft in late March became their most notorious crime and brought their entire network into sharp focus.

The first major police break came in August 1982, when agents arrested Francis Matherly at his home in Brookside Park, charging him with multiple counts of receiving stolen property and conspiracy. By January 1983, investigators moved to apprehend the remaining key players. With Porter and Sorber already in custody on other charges, FBI agents and Pennsylvania State Police arrested Guido Frezzo at his Avondale mushroom farm. That same night, Dr. Benedict LaCorte and Douglas Fuller surrendered to the FBI. The federal indictments, unsealed after all five men were in custody, detailed their specific roles in the theft and subsequent distribution of the stolen artwork.

As the investigation progressed, the Matherly family began to turn on itself. Robert Matherly's testimony against his father and uncle proved crucial. The very family bonds that had made the criminal enterprise possible now became its undoing.

The weight of their crimes bore down on them in different ways. For some, like Gerald Madron, the thought of facing prison again was too much. Twice, he attempted to take his own life—first by hanging, then by slashing his wrists—before authorities transferred him to Haverford State Mental Hospital in Pennsylvania.

Sitting uneasily in the witness box at the Kennett Square magistrate's court, Noel Matherly avoided looking at the relatives seated behind him. His eyes stayed on the floor or drifted to the side of the room as he spoke. "I decided to tell the truth in order not to make the charges more severe. I have to get this behind me," he said, his voice low, his posture penitential. He negotiated a plea bargain that gave him ten years in federal prison for the crimes he had committed across the tri-state. In exchange, he admitted, "I must tell the truth," reported the *Morning News* (August 7, 1982).

Francis Matherly likewise had made a deal with federal investigators by December 1982. Federal authorities promised him a relatively lenient 12-year sentence to be served in a minimum-security prison in Florida in exchange for helping recover the Wyeth paintings and providing testimony about his criminal activities. The government even promised protection for his wife and son.

With Matherly's cooperation, authorities were able to recover all fifteen stolen paintings. Upon learning of their recovery, Andrew Wyeth told reporters at an FBI news conference, "It is terrific! You know this seldom happens, that you get stolen art back." The Wyeths, while relieved at the paintings' recovery, had already taken steps to prevent future thefts. Betsy Wyeth confirmed that they installed a more sophisticated alarm system at the Granary. Andrew Wyeth struck a characteristic balance between caution and defiance: "I will not live in fear," he said. "I don't believe in that. But I'm not going to be foolish."

For the Matherly gang, the Wyeth heist represented both their most daring crime and the beginning of their end. What had seemed like a perfect criminal operation fell apart, thread by thread, testimony by testimony.

In the years that followed, the once-feared criminal network slowly disintegrated. Some would serve time; others would disappear into the cracks of the justice system. For Douglas Fuller, the walls closed in entirely. Rather than face what lay ahead, he took his own life—a stark punctuation to the collapse of the Matherly gang.

Those who survived faced their own reckonings. Assistant U.S. Attorney Walter S. Batty Jr. recommended that Francis Matherly and Dr. Benedict LaCorte serve their sentences at the federal penitentiary near Eglin Air Force Base in Florida.

Authorities identified Matherly, though never charged in the Wyeth burglary itself, as the head of burglary rings operating in southeastern Pennsylvania and northern Delaware for the past decade. He pleaded guilty to the interstate transportation of jewelry, furs, and other valuables stolen in Delaware before the Wyeth theft. After serving his time, his criminal empire in ruins, he declared bankruptcy in 1994. Four years later, the sheriff's office sold at auction a house he owned in Philadelphia—his final, ignominious fall from power.

LaCorte took a different approach in court. Facing sentencing, he told the judge he wanted "to apologize to society" and requested placement where he could "pay back society"—perhaps at a veterans' hospital or an old-age home.

Guido Frezzo did not fare as well. The court found him guilty of conspiracy and receiving stolen property transported across state lines, sentencing him to five years in prison, five years on probation, and a $20,000 fine. He began serving his sentence in December 1984. John "Sadsbury Reds" Sorber, on the other hand, escaped prison time. Tried and acquitted in 1983, he later returned to court under a grant of immunity, admitting that the jury had been wrong—he had indeed bought and resold the stolen paintings.

In the end, apologies, deals, and plea bargains could not erase the reality of what they had done. The Matherly gang had bet their futures on crime, and few walked away unscathed.

The Wyeth heist highlighted the vulnerabilities of private art collections, especially those belonging to prominent artists. The thieves struggled to sell the paintings, resorting to a tangle of small-time deals far below the art's true value. This case represents a rare triumph in art crime investigations—all fifteen stolen works recovered and an entire criminal network dismantled through coordinated law enforcement efforts.

No account of the Matherly gang would be complete without acknowledging News Journal staff reporter Jerry Hager's extraordinary investigative journalism.

DELAWARE BEHAVING BADLY

24

POWERFUL LAWYER KILLS GOVERNOR'S SECRETARY

A shocking murder marked by personal betrayal.

"He almost got away with murder—almost," said Charlie Boyer, a Wilmington resident who had known of Thomas Capano since schooldays. "If it wasn't for that fisherman, he would have."

Ken Chubb guided his fishing boat through the waters near the Delaware coast, about eight miles from shore. It was July 4, 1996, just days after Anne Marie Fahey had vanished without a trace. The morning was clear, the Atlantic stretching out around him as he scanned the water for signs of fish. Something unusual bobbing in the waves caught his eye. As his boat drew closer, the object sharpened into view: a large white Styrofoam cooler, its surface pitted with puncture holes and its edges chewed rough by the sea.

Chubb hauled the cooler aboard, not knowing its grim connection to Delaware's most high-profile missing person case. He took it home and repaired the damage, using it for over a year. Not until November 1997—after Thomas Capano's arrest made headlines—did a friend recognize the description of the cooler from news reports and urge Chubb to contact authorities.

The FBI took possession of the cooler after Chubb turned it in. A barcode printed on the cooler's side gave investigators their next lead. Working with the manufacturer, they traced the sale to a local retailer—and from there, confirmed that Capano had purchased the cooler himself. Forensic analysis confirmed their suspicions: this was the container Capano had used to transport Anne Marie Fahey's body. The woman who had disappeared into silence now had a tangible link to her killer. Chubb himself later called the discovery "a divine intervention."

On June 27, 1996, Anne Marie Fahey, scheduling secretary for Delaware Governor Tom Carper, met Thomas Capano for dinner at Ristorante Panorama in Philadelphia. They had a long, complicated history. Fahey had tried to end the affair, a relationship she described in her diary as toxic and suffocating. Capano, a married attorney and father of four teenage daughters, was a well-connected political insider. He had counseled a Delaware governor and served as legal counsel to the mayor of Wilmington.

The eldest son of a wealthy Italian custom home builder, Capano moved effortlessly through Delaware's most influential circles. Yet beneath his polished exterior simmered a dangerous intolerance for being thwarted. He was not the type of man who took rejection well. That night, they dined as if everything were normal. The restaurant's waitstaff later recalled nothing unusual, but Fahey's demeanor was subdued. At 9:30 p.m., they left the restaurant together. It was the last time anyone saw her alive.

Two nights later, when Fahey failed to show up for a planned dinner with her boyfriend at her brother's house, her family and friends grew alarmed. Her family called the police immediately. Anne Marie's landlord allowed them entry into her apartment at 1718 Washington St. in Wilmington, where they found no sign of a struggle—but they did find her diary. The handwritten pages revealed disturbing insights, offering a window into Fahey's increasingly desperate attempts to break free from Capano's influence.

"Now that I look back on that aspect of my life—I realize just how vulnerable I had become. ... For one whole year, I allowed someone to take control of my life," she had written. Two months before her disappearance, she had described Capano as a "controlling, manipulative, insecure, jealous maniac" who had stalked her.

Fahey's psychologist Dr. Neil Kaye, who had seen her the very afternoon she disappeared, later offered insights into the woman behind the headlines. "She was a remarkable, caring, family-oriented, vivacious person. She was very socially skilled, really a heart of gold. Yet like all of us, she carried her own secrets and demons and issues, which is why she was in treatment," Kaye recalled.

At 30, Fahey was 17 years younger than the 47-year-old Capano, a dynamic he exploited throughout their relationship. A constant struggle with bulimia and anorexia marked her adult life. She had begun dating a young banking executive at MBNA in recent months, a relationship that gave her the confidence to end things with Capano once and for all.

"She was definitely trying to break away from him," Kaye testified. "She had tried to break things off a number of times. This last time she had a new boyfriend. He was a contemporary, he was a good person, a good fit, if you would. I think she was going to leave him (Capano) that night."

Police knocked on the door of Capano's home at 2302 Grant Avenue at 3:30 a.m. on June 30. Despite the hour, he greeted them with remarkable composure—a calm demeanor that investigators would later find suspicious.

Capano provided a detailed account when questioned about Fahey's whereabouts. He acknowledged spending time with her on the 27th and taking her home after their Philadelphia dinner. He had gone inside her apartment to check her faulty air conditioner, according to his statement to police, before leaving around 10 p.m. That, he insisted, was the last he had seen of her.

As the interview continued, Capano suggested to officers that this was likely just a routine missing person's case. Perhaps she had run off, he offered. Maybe she was overwhelmed. The confidence with which he dismissed concerns left officers uneasy.

The police departed but returned later that same afternoon to conduct a more thorough search of both his house and his Jeep Grand Cherokee. They found nothing immediately incriminating despite their efforts. What they couldn't know then was how methodically Capano had already concealed evidence—a pattern that would come into sharper focus as the case unfolded.

Days passed. Then weeks. The investigation, initially classified as a missing-person inquiry, rapidly gained national attention. The disappearance of a governor's staff member—particularly one as well-liked as Fahey—drew media coverage far beyond Delaware's borders.

On July 5, 1996, just over a week after Fahey vanished, President Bill Clinton personally called Governor Tom Carper, offering FBI assistance in the search. The high-profile intervention from the White House underscored the gravity of the case—but the federal response revealed a curious disconnect in the machinery of law enforcement.

Colm F. Connolly, then a young assistant U.S. Attorney who would eventually lead the prosecution against Capano, later recounted a telling anecdote about this moment.

A Harvard-educated lawyer who had never before tried a murder case, Connolly found himself at the center of what would become Delaware's trial of the century.

"It was July Fourth weekend in 1996, and I was in the Acme Market on U.S. 202, and I ran into Judge Greg Sleet, who was the U.S. Attorney, my boss," Connolly recalled. "The lead story of the News Journal that day was President Clinton offered federal assistance [to find Anne Marie Fahey]. Judge Greg Sleet and I laughed, because Greg Sleet was the U.S. attorney, so he was the chief federal law enforcement officer, and nobody had contacted him. If you were really going to get the feds involved, you would contact him." Sleet's response was pragmatic: "Well, I'll call over to Wilmington, and we'll offer our services." The next working day, July 8, the FBI finally made contact.

The bureaucratic fumble might have been comical under different circumstances. For the Fahey family, however, each passing day deepened their anguish and diminished hopes of finding Anne Marie alive.

The inquiry shifted on July 31, when a federal search team led by Connolly conducted an exhaustive 11-hour search of Capano's home, his Jeep Grand Cherokee, and his wife's Chevy Suburban. The meticulous examination yielded a crucial discovery: two tiny spots of blood on a baseboard in Capano's home. DNA analysis later confirmed what investigators suspected—the blood belonged to Anne Marie Fahey. With this evidence, the FBI officially classified the investigation as a federal kidnapping probe.

On November 8, 1997, after more than a year of mounting pressure, Thomas Capano's brother, Gerard "Gerry" Capano, finally broke his silence. Facing charges for cocaine and illegal weapons possession found during an October 8 raid on his home, Gerard made a grim confession to prosecutors that shattered his brother's carefully constructed alibi.

Gerard revealed that on June 28, 1996—the day after Anne Marie's disappearance—he had helped his brother Thomas transport a large cooler containing Fahey's body. They had taken Gerard's 25-foot fishing boat approximately 60 miles off the Atlantic coast, to a stretch of water known for its shark population—a chilling calculation that suggested Thomas had researched the optimal location to dispose of human remains.

Once they reached their destination, the brothers heaved the cooler overboard, expecting it to disappear beneath the waves. But the Styrofoam container refused to go under. In growing desperation, Gerard himself took aim with a gun and shot holes into the cooler, trying to make it fill with water and slip beneath the surface. The cooler stubbornly floated across the ocean's surface despite their efforts to sink it.

Thomas then made a crucial decision, according to Gerard's testimony. Retrieving the cooler, he removed Fahey's body, wrapped it in chains, and released it directly into the depths. This time, weighted by the metal links, the body plunged into the dark waters, never to be recovered. The brothers then tossed the cooler overboard, allowing it to drift away on the ocean currents.

Gerard also admitted to helping Thomas dispose of additional evidence. They had discarded a sofa stained with blood in a trash bin at their brother Louis Capano's construction site that same day. Perhaps most tellingly, Gerard confessed that despite his pleas for Thomas to surrender to authorities, his brother had steadfastly refused. Prosecutors later cited that refusal as evidence of Capano's consciousness of guilt.

Four days after Gerard's damning confession, on November 12, 1997, FBI agents intercepted Thomas Capano on Interstate 95 as he was driving his brother Joseph and sister-in-law to Philadelphia International Airport. The timing was strategic; while Thomas was being taken into custody, his brothers Louis and Gerard were testifying before a federal grand jury.

Although Louis Capano Jr. had remained silent for more than a year, he came forward just two days after Gerard's confession. He confirmed key parts of his brother's story and added new details about the disposal of evidence. Beyond the blood-stained sofa already known to investigators, Louis admitted that Fahey's nightgown and other personal items had also been discarded in his company's trash bins. Each brother's testimony strengthened the case, revealing the calculated nature of Thomas's attempts to eliminate all traces of his crime.

Court officials arraigned Capano on state murder charges that same night and sent him to Wilmington's Gander Hill prison without bail. Though largely circumstantial, the evidence had grown so overwhelming that prosecutors believed the case had reached critical mass. Prosecutors had blood evidence and damning testimony from two brothers, but they still lacked physical proof linking Capano directly to the disposal of Fahey's body.

Then, just two days after Capano's arrest, the case took an unexpected turn. Ken Chubb turned the damaged cooler over to the FBI. Prosecutors considered the cooler—the same one Gerard Capano had described—the most powerful piece of physical evidence in their case.

Capano's trial began on October 6, 1998. The defense team, led by flamboyant Boston attorney Joseph S. Oteri, faced an uphill battle against mounting evidence. In a sharp departure from their initial denials, the defense admitted that Capano had disposed of Fahey's body—but painted it as a tragic accident.

The relationship between Capano and his counsel was visibly strained. "I made a bad mistake in taking a lawyer for a client," Oteri later confessed, describing how Capano refused to heed legal advice. "You're paying me an enormous fee and you're not listening to me. How stupid can you be?"

Capano insisted on taking the stand despite his entire defense team's objections. Over eight days of testimony, he told the jury that Deborah MacIntyre—his longtime mistress—had discovered him and Fahey together and, in her distress, had tried to commit suicide. According to his version, "In the struggle, Fahey had accidentally been shot and killed." He claimed to have panicked, disposing of the body only to protect MacIntyre. She denied being at Capano's house that night and testified she had purchased the gun at Capano's request, claiming he told her that someone had made threats against him.

The jury didn't buy it. They had already seen the cooler, which prosecutors Colm Connolly and Ferris Wharton had dramatically presented to the courtroom: "Ferris and I walked it out as if we were walking a coffin out of church," Connolly recalled. Capano contradicted his initial statements to police with an elaborate story that later collapsed during cross-examination. When pressed by prosecutor Connolly, Capano erupted, calling him a "heartless, gutless, soulless disgrace for a human being"—an explosion that got him temporarily ejected from the courtroom.

On January 17, 1999, after three days of intense deliberations that began with a deadlocked vote, the jury returned with a verdict: guilty of first-degree murder. During that time, jurors conducted a chilling experiment, with Erin Reilly Lee, a 28-year-old juror, climbing into an identical cooler to test Capano's account of disposing of Fahey's body.

When the lid wouldn't close, jurors concluded that Capano must have broken Fahey's bones to make her fit inside. The experience was so traumatic that Lee asked to be escorted to her hotel room, where she wept and whispered to Fahey's memory, "I'm just so sorry. I'm so sorry that this happened to you." The jury recommended the death penalty in a 10-2 vote. In March, Judge William Swain Lee sentenced Capano to execution.

The Delaware Supreme Court overturned Capano's death sentence in 2006, ruling that the way the jury had reached that decision failed to meet constitutional requirements established by the Ring v. Arizona decision. In the subsequent resentencing trial, a new jury's 11-1 vote for the death penalty failed to provide the unanimous agreement on aggravating circumstances now required by law. As a result, Capano was sentenced to life in prison without parole.

Prison officials kept him in solitary confinement for twelve years, a circumstance that might have broken a lesser man. Ed Sacks, a former lawyer who had worked briefly with Capano at a Wilmington firm in the 1970s, visited him shortly before his death.

"Frankly, I don't know how anybody could survive being in solitary confinement for 13 years and not go crazy, and he didn't," Sacks recalled. During their visit, they discussed Sacks' new granddaughter, the movie Avalon, Capano's memories of his grandfather, and current political tensions in Washington.

Capano spent his days reading historical fiction, watching news and movies, and receiving visits from his daughters. However, the isolation and confinement took their physical toll.

On September 19, 2011, guards found Capano unresponsive in his cell at Vaughn Correctional Center in Smyrna, having suffered a heart attack. He was just 61 years old, an age that echoed his father's premature mortality. The once-powerful attorney who had manipulated the highest echelons of Delaware politics—and believed himself untouchable—died alone in a prison infirmary. It was a final, ignominious chapter in his fall from grace.

Prosecutor Ferris Wharton later reflected that Capano's death surprised no one who had watched his long physical decline behind bars. Judge William Swain Lee, who had originally sentenced Capano, later observed with a mix of clinical detachment and contempt: "He ate himself to death; there's no question about it."

For the Fahey family—the five Fahey siblings who had weathered the grinding judicial process together, Robert, Kathleen, and their three brothers and sisters—Capano's death brought neither joy nor closure. "Every religion I'm familiar with requires some sort of atonement for one's sins for forgiveness," Robert Fahey observed after learning of Capano's death. "Since he never apologized to any of the many people whose lives he destroyed, nor did he admit any guilt for Anne Marie's murder, my guess is that he went straight to hell today. That's where he belongs."

"It's bittersweet," her sister Kathleen Fahey-Hosey said upon hearing of Capano's death. "You knew it would happen one day but this kind of brings it all back."

The Atlantic depths never yielded Anne Marie Fahey's remains. Her life cut tragically short at 30, Anne Marie left behind siblings who had already endured the early deaths of their parents. To the public, she would forever be associated with "Delaware's trial of the century," her memory often reduced to headlines and courtroom exhibits. But to her family, she was simply their beloved youngest sister—someone with a vibrant spirit and warm heart, who encountered a predator disguised as a respectable man.

25

CONFIDENCE MEN

Con artists defrauded Delaware's elite.

On March 14, 2006, Wilmington's News Journal reported the sentencing of George W. Blood, a Maryland resident who had defrauded investors of more than a million dollars through a Ponzi scheme. The newspaper called him "a confidence man without conscience," reviving a phrase rarely heard in modern crime reporting.

While Blood's 21st-century fraud drew headlines, Delaware history offers many earlier examples of similar cons—deceptions that exploited moments when trust broke down easily.

Americans poured into cities and large towns by the early 1900s, where anonymity replaced familiarity and life rewarded bold risk. In this fluid, often impersonal environment, strangers approached each other as opportunities. People no longer relied on church ties, family reputation, or small-town vigilance to guide their judgments. If you could sell yourself, you could sell anything. Confidence men thrived in that atmosphere.

The term "confidence man" has an antiquated ring, conjuring images of old-time tricksters rather than modern white-collar criminals. The phrase dates to July 1849, when The New York Herald reported on the arrest of a New York City swindler named William Thompson under the headline "Arrest of the Confidence Man." Thompson had gained brief notoriety for approaching well-dressed strangers on the street and asking, "Have you the confidence to lend me your watch until tomorrow?" The term caught the public's imagination, appeared in newspaper headlines across the country, and soon entered common speech as shorthand for any smooth-talking deceiver.

Thompson's case did more than introduce a catchy expression—it clarified the public's understanding of a criminal who relied on charm rather than force. Novelist Herman Melville immortalized the concept in his 1857 novel The Confidence-Man, which emphasized the theatrical, performative nature of such deceptions. As one character observes, "Ah, sir, they may talk of the courage of truth, but my trade teaches me that truth sometimes is sheepish. Lies, lies, sir, brave lies are the lions!" People commonly used "confidence man" as the standard term throughout the late 19th century and often abbreviated it to "con man" in more casual usage.

The term "con artist" emerged in the early 20th century as a variation on "con man," underscoring the element of calculated self-presentation in the deception. Swindlers were not just thieves—they were skilled manipulators, often presenting themselves as legitimate professionals, investors, or even philanthropists. "Con man" had largely supplanted "confidence man" in everyday language by the mid-20th century, though law enforcement and newspapers occasionally retained the older terminology, as the 2006 description of George Blood demonstrates.

Alongside "confidence man," another colorful term entered the American lexicon of deception. "Flim-flam" described both the act of swindling and the swindle itself, with its rhythmic sound suggesting the rapid, confusing movements that often distracted victims.

Senator Chauncey Depew of New York offered a memorable definition in 1905, explaining that "to flim-flam" is "to confuse a man's mind to such a degree that he actually consents to and concurs in his own cheating." To illustrate the concept, Depew shared a story: A boy asks a grocer to put molasses in his pitcher. After the grocer does so, the boy points out some molasses still clinging to the measure. The grocer replies, "That's all right, sonny. There was some in the measure before." Satisfied with this nonsensical explanation, "the flimflammed boy goes off, content."

Delaware newspapers documented con artists who returned again and again, deploying familiar dodges with relentless energy. Their tales show that while the details varied, the core strategy remained constant: exploiting trust for personal gain.

Jack Meredith ranked as one of Delaware's most notorious con artists, who eluded authorities in the 1940s through his prolific use of aliases. A 1944 *Morning News* article called him "the man with a hundred names," notorious for writing bad checks and swindling Wilmington businessmen out of thousands.

"Meredith recently has been concentrating on used car dealers and has succeeded in obtaining dozens of automobiles fraudulently," Special Agent John W. Vincent warned. Meredith opened fraudulent bank accounts using approximately 100 aliases, used counterfeit credit to impress his victims, and left them stuck with worthless checks.

His criminal repertoire didn't end there. Posing as a construction company owner, he contracted for heavy machinery, paying with worthless checks. Even more audaciously, after escaping from a western state penitentiary, he impersonated a Parole Board member and purchasing agent for the very prison from which he had fled. At a country club dinner in Iowa, Meredith—still pretending to be a Parole Board member—gave a talk on "The Birds of Passage," stories he claimed described criminals who had appeared before his board. In reality, he was describing fellow inmates from the prison he had escaped.

Decades before Meredith's ruses, Wilmington merchants had already fallen victim to similar deceptions. In May 1920, another con man swept through the city preying on local grocers. Introducing himself as a Cleveland merchant, he charmed his targets and presented his business card. He talked groceries to ingratiate himself, then asked for check-cashing favors, claiming he needed money to buy groceries for his niece, who refused to accept payment for his room and meals at her home. The Cleveland merchant then used the proceeds to purchase a small number of food items, keeping the remainder.

His trickery extended to hiring a local woman as an unwitting accomplice. He convinced her that he was a federal agent, and that the government had hired her to help gather evidence against "food profiteers." The Cleveland merchant used her presence to legitimize his deception, thereby further disarming his victims. According to the newspaper account, "five local grocers are known to have been victimized out of $25," though the swindler likely entrapped others in the same swindle.

Confidence hustles often became more elaborate when targeting wealthier marks, sometimes crossing state lines to bring their operations into Delaware. In 1893, a scam targeting John J. Franey of Shenandoah, Pennsylvania, unfolded in stages that would soon involve Wilmington as well. Two impostors presented themselves to Franey as wealthy mine owners from the West. One called himself Walter J. Philips, the other Charles Brown of San Francisco. Philips initiated contact by pretending to search for his uncle, supposedly named James Franey, and showing a slip of paper with that name. This created an artificial connection that opened the door to conversation.

The pair soon invited Franey to Baltimore to discuss purchasing mining claims in the "Idaho mining district of Colorado" for $12,000. However, Franey grew suspicious when he observed contradictions in Philips' behavior—the man claimed illiteracy, but Franey spotted him reading a newspaper and signing documents. Once confronted, Philips disappeared, sending a telegram to Franey: "I have received reliable and valuable information from Colorado about my property; my property is not for sale under any circumstances. I leave for Colorado tonight."

Before departing from Baltimore, Philips hinted he might travel to Wilmington, a possibility that immediately concerned John J. Franey. Even more troubling, Philips' accomplice Brown had specifically stated he would register at the Clayton House in Wilmington. Franey alerted Wilmington's Chief of Police, John F. Dolan, who issued a general order instructing his officers to arrest the impostors if they found them in the city. But Every Evening suggested such a warning might be unnecessary, noting that Wilmington's businessmen were unlikely to give the confidence men "a very warm reception at their hands." Whether authorities ever apprehended the two remains unclear.

Unlike the impostors who targeted Franey, "Bruce" Chateaubriand dispensed with anonymity. He established himself openly in Dover in 1888, complete with a wife and child to enhance his credibility. Claiming secret detective work, he told those who questioned his mysterious behavior that he was monitoring a potential elopement involving a student at the Peninsula Conference Academy.

Chateaubriand went even further: he created a fictional "Detective Agency on the Mutual Benefit plan" and listed prominent Dover citizens as officers without their knowledge. New members paid $25, half of which went directly to Chateaubriand. According to the Daily Republican, he collected fees from approximately 125 members, a staggering $3,125 (equivalent to more than $100,000 today), before disappearing. The Daily Republican drew a curious distinction. While Chateaubriand pocketed approximately $3,125 from his bogus detective agency (what the paper called "a good little speculation"), it reserved the label "real crookedness" for a different offense entirely. Chateaubriand had accepted $5 from an English firm to collect a debt from a Philadelphia company, money he pocketed without performing any service. In the newspaper's view, sharp dealing was one thing; breaking a direct contract was another.

While some confidence men created elaborate machinations, others relied on simpler methods. George Hagany, known as "Slim Jim," exemplified this style. Known to Wilmington police as early as the 1880s, he used sleight-of-hand tricks to separate victims from their valuables. In one notable 1882 incident, Slim Jim smoothly robbed a countryman in a Race Street saloon: "I'll show you how we do things here. Now you see it and now you don't," he said, making the victim's watch disappear right before his eyes. Such audacity made him infamous, yet somehow, he repeatedly evaded serious punishment, remaining a familiar menace in Wilmington, Philadelphia, and Baltimore.

"To flim-flam is to confuse a man's mind to such a degree that he actually consents to and concurs in his own cheating."

SENATOR CHAUNCEY DEPEW

The Joseph and Robert Baker case from 1964 demonstrates the remarkable persistence of simple confidence techniques. The brothers visited stores on Market Street in Wilmington, purchased minor items like shoe polish, then confused clerks with a rapid exchange of bills. As Lt. Walter Purnell explained, the technique was "an old one," where a confidence man uses a $10 bill to buy something for less than a dollar. When called back for his change, he would ask for a $20 bill in exchange for two tens, then ask for his original $10 back while offering another in exchange for a twenty. "This is accompanied by much shuffling of a roll of bills and fast patter," creating confusion that left the clerk short on cash. Joseph Baker received two concurrent one-year sentences for this gambit, while authorities dropped the charges against his brother and ordered him to leave Wilmington immediately.

Confidence men often targeted the most vulnerable. A 1927 *Evening Journal* editorial lamented how con artists had turned to "the widow with recently acquired insurance and property left by her husband's will as the most lucrative of sources for easy money." These predators would present themselves as bankers or brokers, offering "sure thing" investments to trusting widows. Some would even marry their victims to gain control of their fortunes before vanishing. Despite warnings from bankers, attorneys, and courthouse officials, the "honeyed words of the confidence man" often proved irresistible.

This predatory pattern did not end there, and shows no sign of disappearing. In December 1966, the *Morning News* reported on a particularly cruel case: a man posing as a bank investigator convinced a 67-year-old woman—who had saved $3,500 through "considerable sacrifice"—to withdraw her entire savings and turn it over to him. He and her money disappeared immediately. Commentators described such flim-flam moves as "one of the most vicious confidence games because it preys on the aged and the credulous."

The opportunistic nature of con artists is perfectly illustrated in the curious case of Linwood Mort. In 1933, he received a telegram signed "Jack Coyne," a man he knew who had recently traveled to Haverstraw, Massachusetts, for a funeral. The message asked Mort to wire $35 to a New York address, with no explanation. Suspicious that the telegram had been sent from Philadelphia—not Haverstraw—Mort began investigating.

He confirmed that Coyne hadn't sent the message, but the real Coyne did recall meeting a stranger on the train—someone to whom he had casually revealed personal details. That man had evidently used the information to impersonate Coyne and target Mort. Mort's alertness prevented the ploy and gave authorities a chance to capture the swindler when he attempted to collect the money in New York.

Captain Beverly, as he called himself, demonstrated similar opportunism in 1901 when he extracted "several hundred dollars" from New Castle residents by claiming he wanted to establish a naval school there. He cashed several worthless checks before departing, and according to the Middletown Transcript, Altoona, Pennsylvania police also wanted him for passing a check for $10,000 that "afterward proved to be worthless."

John P. Carroll's 1928 case was even more dramatic. Newspapers described him as a "suave thief and confidence man" who operated in Wilmington. Carroll's criminal repertoire extended far beyond simple burglary. He had escaped from Leavenworth Penitentiary, where authorities had sentenced him to 14 years for a $500,000 train robbery. He first charmed a prison official, then escaped by hiding inside a mattress crate. He sent his imprisoned wife "a hacksaw, ropes, and instructions" to assist her escape from the Missouri Women's State Reformatory, where authorities had incarcerated her as his accomplice, after gaining his own freedom.

In Philadelphia, he used multiple aliases—H.A. Murphy, R.H. Hyatt, and Allen Kerbie—and in Wilmington, he rented a room at 819 Jefferson Street from Mrs. Mary A. Porter, using the name "Williams." According to press accounts, he appeared well-dressed and respectable, and "nothing was thought wrong until after he had left."

"One of his plans was to pose as a wealthy man and become acquainted with wealthy people whom he would visit at their homes," explained Detective Inspector William L. Connelly. "He then exhibited a large quantity of jewelry, prompting his new friends to show theirs. Shortly after, their jewelry would disappear." This social engineering approach of using false identity, manufactured wealth, and strategic displays of jewelry to gain both access and information epitomized the confidence man's craft.

Carroll's criminal activities were diverse and prolific. Beyond his home burglaries, police discovered "a number of stolen money order books" and believed that "he has cashed in thousands of dollars through postal frauds." He eventually admitted to "ten post office robberies and a number of house robberies."

Authorities eventually caught Carroll in Philadelphia on the relatively minor charge of "having given a bogus check in payment for an expensive wristwatch for a woman." When they apprehended him, his persuasive abilities remained sharp. Carroll, believing he could manipulate his way to freedom, "talked to [detectives] of the fortune he would give them as soon as an opportunity occurred to make a break for liberty." To exploit that bravado, Detective Inspector William L. Connelly placed himself in an adjoining cell, posing as another prisoner. There, he "gained the man's confidence and secured information disclosing the hiding places of a quantity of the stolen property."

Carroll revealed the locations of hidden valuables worth approximately $33,000, including items he had taken from Richard C. McMullen's Wilmington home. He complained of a "tough break" in his Philadelphia confession about this particular robbery: "A daughter of the family came home unexpectedly while I was robbing the house, and I had to make a getaway with only $40,000 of the stuff."

Carroll's intricate social manipulations highlighted one dimension of confidence games. However, Delaware's historical records reveal another troubling aspect—ethnic prejudice—often coloring the public's perception of deception. In July 1922, Antonio Cagnetto of Newark reported that "two gypsy women who passed through here last week" robbed him of $14 using what the newspaper described as "flim-flam methods." Cagnetto followed the women to Wilmington and had them arrested, but authorities released them after they promised to return the money. This brief account reveals how certain groups were often associated with particular forms of deception in the public imagination.

As transportation improved and populations became more mobile in the late 19th century, confidence men found fertile hunting grounds around railroad stations. An 1897 account from The Sun described a "tall, fine-looking man, wearing a long light ulster, black derby and patent leather shoes" attempting to lure a farmer named Hiram Watkins near the Philadelphia, Wilmington & Baltimore Railroad station in Wilmington.

The article specifically identified this well-dressed stranger as a "bunco-steerer"—a specialist in the confidence world who would identify potential marks and steer them toward swindling operations. These front men would engage victims in conversation, gain their trust, and then lead them to places where other accomplices would complete the swindle. The term "bunco" described a confidence game similar to three-card monte, popular in 19th century America.

In this case, the bunco-steerer claimed that Watkins' son in New York was in trouble and needed money, offering to deliver it personally. Two bystanders, noticing the suspicious interaction, intervened and warned Watkins, causing the confidence man to flee into the Clayton House hotel before disappearing entirely.

By 1899, the problem had grown so severe that Philadelphia authorities began targeting known criminals well beyond the city limits. One high-profile example came during the Electrical Exhibition that year, when police deployed elaborate measures to intercept swindlers traveling through Wilmington and other points along the rail lines.

Captain Miller deployed detectives from cities across the country, creating a "dead line" around Philadelphia that extended to Wilmington and Chester. The *Wilmington Daily Republican* reported that these officers would "search every railroad and trolley car coming in the direction of the city" and that the Pullman Palace Car Company had given them permission to "enter and search all its sleepers, parlor, buffet, and dining room cars."

Detecting and apprehending confidence men has remained challenging throughout history. An 1874 Smyrna Times editorial expressed frustration that "all the teachings of experience and all the daily clamor of the press seem to be unavailing to convince a certain class of visitors from the interior that if they make sudden friendships in the city, they will regret it." The writer concluded that "unless every stranger learns the lesson of wholesome distrust, he would do well to stay away from large cities," offering a simple rule: "A man who forces himself upon your acquaintance with offers of friendship and service, intends to rob or swindle you."

Despite such warnings, confidence ploys thrived because they exploited fundamental human weaknesses. As Senator Chauncey Depew astutely observed in 1905, vanity often trumps caution: "To say to the average mortal, 'I like your looks,' in the phrase and manner suited to his degree of cultivation, is the surest way to convince him of your own taste and candor." The confidence man's entire business model relied on this vulnerability—making people believe their "prepossessing appearance" had attracted the swindler's attention.

This calculated manipulation of human psychology formed the foundation of countless confidence rackets. A well-executed con created artificial connections, established false trust, and led victims down a carefully constructed path to deception. The William Ferris case from 1905 perfectly illustrates these principles.

Two confidence men approached Ferris, who was nearly ninety years old, on Eighth Street in Wilmington. One introduced himself as Hill, claiming to seek investment advice. Walking together, they "coincidentally" met the second swindler, who introduced himself as Winchester, claiming to be the brother of James C. Winchester, president of the First National Bank.

After gaining Ferris's trust through this fabricated connection, they invited him to a house where they attempted to convince him to bring $1,000 in cash to match their own supposed investment. Fortunately, Ferris verified Winchester's claim at the First National Bank and discovered the deception before handing over any money. When police arrived at the house on Tatnall Street where the plot had unfolded, the swindlers had vanished, leaving behind only "a sheet of paper with some figures on it."

The Ferris incident underscores how con artists flourished by preying on enduring human vulnerabilities such as pride, sympathy, or desire for easy gain, adapting their deceptions to fit the times. While men dominated these criminal enterprises, women also appeared as accomplices, distractions, or even primary operators, equally adept at exploiting human trust. Newspapers over decades documented these crimes in detail, but the public's appetite for easy wealth or quick returns continued to blind them to risk.

The phrase "confidence man" may have faded, but the swindler never left. From William Thompson in the 1840s to George Blood in the early 2000s, con artists have thrived by exploiting the same human weaknesses—vanity, trust, and greed. History shows that only vigilance offers real protection. Where those fail, the con artist endures.

26

INSIDERS SELL DUPONT SECRETS TO KOREA

The dark side of corporate espionage.

Edward Schulz had spent more than three decades at DuPont. Thirty years climbing the corporate ladder, thirty years immersed in the secret world of Kevlar — the miracle fiber that could stop bullets but couldn't, as it turned out, stop corporate betrayal. DuPont developed Kevlar in 1965, and its billions in annual sales "represented American innovation at its finest." When he retired around 2000, the 72-year-old scientist didn't leave empty-handed. Despite the non-disclosure agreements bearing his signature, Schulz quietly tucked away confidential DuPont documents, taking with him the accumulated secrets of one of America's most inventive companies. While at DuPont, Schulz had been responsible for technical research and development related to Kevlar, giving him intimate knowledge of the fiber's manufacturing process.

Michael David Mitchell had a shorter tenure, but no less access. As a DuPont engineer and later Kevlar marketing manager, the 52-year-old from Chesterfield, Virginia had been entrusted with the company's crown jewels: closely guarded manufacturing processes, sensitive data on Kevlar production capacity, and technical specifications. This information had cost DuPont millions to develop and provided a detailed blueprint of the company's manufacturing strengths and limitations. After DuPont fired Mitchell in 2006, he, too, decided to keep what wasn't his. Mitchell, who held a master's degree in chemical engineering and had worked at DuPont for almost 24 years, formed his own synthetic-fiber consulting business, Aramid Fiber Systems LLC, after leaving the company.

The theft particularly stung because Kevlar wasn't just any product. Invented in Wilmington and manufactured in Richmond, Virginia, as well as Columbia, South Carolina, Kevlar had become a cornerstone of DuPont's industrial empire. Manufacturers incorporated Kevlar into fiber-optic cables, brake pads, tires, sports equipment, and a host of other industrial materials. Sales of Kevlar and its cousin material Nomex (a heat-resistant fiber used in firefighting gear) generated approximately $1.4 billion annually for DuPont.

Neither Shulz nor Mitchell knew it then, but a South Korean fiber manufacturer named Kolon Industries was already plotting to steal what it couldn't create. Struggling to perfect Heracron, its own aramid fiber designed to compete with Kevlar,

Kolon devised a systematic plan to acquire DuPont's confidential technology by recruiting former employees with knowledge of the fiber's production. And these two former DuPont employees would soon become the perfect accomplices in a plot to breach the para-aramid fiber market, where DuPont controlled more than 70 percent of U.S. sales.

For Schulz, the call came in 2006. Kolon Industries needed an insider with deep technical knowledge of Kevlar's manufacturing secrets. The company approached the retired scientist with an offer: become a "consultant" and share what he knew. The proposition was as tempting as it was illegal.

Schulz agreed. He began meeting with Kolon representatives, turning over the very documents he had smuggled out of DuPont years earlier. Divulging each trade secret violated trust and constituted a federal crime under the Economic Espionage Act. But for the veteran scientist, these considerations apparently meant little compared to Kolon's consulting fees.

Mitchell's path to betrayal began after his termination in 2006. Rather than surrendering DuPont's restricted information as required, he held onto it—a ticking time bomb of sensitive material waiting to be exploited. By 2007, Mitchell, too, had found a willing buyer in Kolon Industries. The South Korean company hired him as a consultant as well, and the floodgates opened.

Mitchell didn't just provide historical information. He actively worked to extract fresh intelligence from DuPont. He emailed Kolon updated spreadsheets detailing Kevlar production capacities and process data — a direct violation of his non-disclosure agreement. These transmissions did not go unnoticed. DuPont's security team, already suspicious of Kolon's rapid advances, traced the leaks back to Mitchell.

By 2009, both the civil and criminal consequences mounted. DuPont filed a lawsuit against Kolon in February, alleging closely guarded technology theft. Simultaneously, the company alerted federal authorities, triggering an FBI investigation that would eventually ensnare both Mitchell and Schulz. This wasn't just a civil dispute over intellectual property—the case carried the potential for serious federal criminal penalties, including up to 10 years in prison and $5 million in fines per offense. The stakes had escalated dramatically for both men.

Mitchell, perhaps sensing trouble, made a critical mistake. He attempted to cover his tracks by destroying evidence and even threatened to expose Kolon unless he received additional payment. This desperate move only added obstruction of justice to his growing list of crimes.

The FBI moved with precision, executing search warrants and seizing documents from Mitchell's home. They set up undercover meetings with Kolon representatives, building an airtight case. In one particularly damning operation in 2008, agents arranged for a meeting at the Doubletree Hotel near Richmond International Airport, where an unidentified cooperator posed as a disgruntled DuPont scientist willing to sell secrets. Agents surreptitiously recorded the meeting, capturing Kolon representatives discussing the theft of proprietary information. During this meeting, the cooperator emphasized that the information they sought was "highly sensitive 'trade secret' information owned by DuPont, and that the need for secrecy was critical."

The FBI's careful evidence gathering, including the damning Doubletree Hotel meeting, ultimately created an overwhelming case against Mitchell. Confronted with the extensive evidence of his activities, Mitchell saw no way out. In December 2009, he waived indictment and pleaded guilty to a two-count charge of theft of trade secrets and obstruction of justice.

Schulz's day of reckoning came later. The investigation eventually uncovered his role in the conspiracy, and in 2014, he too found himself facing federal charges. Like Mitchell before him, Schulz pleaded guilty — in his case, to conspiracy to steal trade secrets.

For their betrayals, both men paid prices that surely exceeded whatever Kolon had paid them.

A federal judge sentenced Mitchell in March 2010 to 18 months in prison. A year and a half to contemplate how selling out his former employer had led to a felony conviction and the destruction of his reputation. Adding financial insult to his professional injury, the court ordered Mitchell to pay approximately $187,000 in restitution to cover DuPont's legal expenses resulting from his actions. At his sentencing hearing, prosecutor Brian R. Hood emphasized the severity of Mitchell's crimes, telling the judge, "It is a billion-dollar product by any measure.... We are talking about a serious offense, Your Honor."

Throughout the proceedings, Mitchell maintained a telling silence. When given the opportunity to speak at his sentencing—a moment when many defendants express remorse or offer explanations—"Mitchell declined to speak shortly before he was sentenced by U.S. District Judge James R. Spencer." His silence spoke volumes, revealing either shame or an inability to justify selling out decades of trust. The man once eager to share DuPont's secrets with Kolon now had nothing to say in his own defense.

After initially resisting cooperation with authorities, Mitchell eventually agreed to assist the government's case against Kolon. "He was something of a handful to manage," Hood later told the judge, noting that Mitchell's willingness to help improved only after he pleaded guilty. Nevertheless, his eventual assistance proved valuable in building the case against the South Korean company.

Schulz's case followed a similar pattern of public silence. Throughout his legal proceedings, no statements or explanations from the former scientist appeared in any public record. Like Mitchell, Schulz offered no public justification for turning against the company where he had spent three decades building his career. Schulz, perhaps benefiting from his age and collaboration with authorities, received a somewhat lighter sentence in June 2015: two years of probation. But the court still imposed a $75,000 fine and ordered 500 hours of community service—a substantial penalty for a retiree and a permanent reminder of his misdeeds.

Meanwhile, on the civil front, DuPont pushed its lawsuit against Kolon forward with dramatic results. In September 2011, a jury in a Richmond federal court deliberated for about 10 hours before returning a verdict: Kolon had willfully and maliciously misappropriated DuPont's trade secrets. The jury awarded DuPont $919.9 million in damages, the third-largest U.S. jury verdict of that year. The massive award validated DuPont's claims and dealt a crushing blow to Kolon.

"This case was the most egregious case of trade-secret theft that we've experienced in my 35 years of representing the DuPont Company," said Thomas L. Sager, senior vice president and general counsel at DuPont. Company executives celebrated the judgment as a major victory in their global battles to protect lucrative corporate secrets.

The court subsequently went further, issuing a remarkable 20-year injunction that barred Kolon from producing or selling its Heracron fiber entirely. That ruling effectively delivered a mortal blow to Kolon's flagship product. Kolon asked the court in response to put the injunction on hold while it appealed, arguing that the ban would cause the "uncompensated death" of an entire business and result in irreparable harm.

The company maintained that it "had no need for and did not solicit any trade secrets or proprietary information of DuPont," and claimed that many of the alleged "secrets" were actually public knowledge. The South Korean manufacturer also filed its own countersuit, alleging that DuPont was attempting to monopolize the market for para-aramid fiber through anti-competitive practices, including requiring high-volume customers to buy 80 to 100 percent of the product from DuPont.

In a surprising turn of events, Kolon's persistence in challenging the verdict eventually paid off. In April 2014, the U.S. Court of Appeals in Richmond threw out the massive $919.9 million award. The appeals court ruled that the jury verdict could not stand because the trial judge had wrongfully excluded evidence relevant to Kolon's defense. The court ordered a new trial and, in an unusual step, directed that a new judge be assigned to the case. The court also put the 20-year injunction on hold, preventing it from ever taking effect.

But Kolon's legal troubles were far from over. On the criminal side, the case had been building steadily. In August 2012, a federal grand jury in Virginia indicted Kolon Industries and five of its executives on multiple felony counts, including conspiracy to convert trade secrets, theft of trade secrets, and obstruction of justice. The indictment included a "forfeiture claim" seeking at least $225 million in alleged criminal proceeds from Kolon.

This legal action marked a landmark moment in the prosecution of international intellectual property theft. Using an international treaty, U.S. prosecutors successfully served a foreign corporation with no U.S. presence for the first time. That move forced the company to respond in U.S. court. It also put other overseas firms on notice that distance offered no immunity if they engaged in stealing American technology.

Although the five indicted Kolon executives remained in South Korea, safely beyond U.S. jurisdiction, the case against the corporation itself moved forward. After years of legal maneuvering, including challenges to U.S. jurisdiction and efforts to avoid being served with legal papers, Kolon Industries finally admitted guilt. In April 2015, the company pleaded guilty to conspiracy to steal trade secrets.

The price tag for their industrial espionage campaign was staggering: a total of $360 million, including $275 million in restitution to DuPont and an $85 million criminal fine. This resolution coincided with a settlement of the civil case for a similar amount of $275 million, effectively closing both legal fronts of the battle.

Meanwhile, the five Kolon executives indicted alongside the company effectively became international fugitives, choosing to remain abroad rather than face prosecution and the prison sentence Mitchell received. U.S. authorities would have required either their extradition or voluntary travel to the U.S. to prosecute them, neither of which had occurred.

DuPont insiders Edward Schulz and Michael David Mitchell—like so many before and after them—discovered too late that the temporary financial gain from selling company secrets rarely outweighs the permanent consequences.

"This indictment should send a strong message to companies around the world that industrial espionage is not a business strategy," U.S. Attorney Neil MacBride declared when announcing charges against Kolon. Prison sentences, court orders, and financial penalties—not press releases—delivered that message.

DuPont eventually closed ranks, but not before the breach inflicted lasting damage. "DuPont's investment in developing this information, amounting to hundreds of millions of dollars over many years, was thereby essentially lost," the company stated in a court filing. "Kolon is now able to compete against DuPont in the aramid market using DuPont's own information against it."

"Protecting the trade secrets of American businesses sustains the integrity and competitiveness of the American economy," Assistant Attorney General Leslie Caldwell noted after Kolon's guilty plea.

DuPont v. Kolon Industries, Inc. revealed both the vulnerability of valuable intellectual property and the lengths to which competitors might go to steal it. More importantly, it exposed the human element. Some insiders were willing to sell loyalty for the right price. Mitchell and Schulz got the wrong one—prison, debt, and disgrace.

27

PEDIATRICIAN BETRAYS HUNDREDS OF CHILDREN

The unmasking of a trusted professional.

A small army of volunteer contractors and heavy equipment operators descended upon the BayBees Pediatrics complex on Route 1 near Lewes, on October 10, 2011. The buildings had stood vacant for nearly two years, the property a cursed landscape. Vandals smashed its windows. Trespassers defaced the walls. Looters stripped the once-cheerful interiors, stealing electronics, power tools, and even Disney collectible figurines. Beyond the physical decay lay something worse. A deeper corruption seemed to permeate the very foundation of the place; a residue of the unspeakable crimes Dr. Earl Bradley had committed against his most vulnerable patients.

When the BayBees Pediatrics property went to sheriff's sale in May 2011, no one placed a bid, despite the site's prime commercial location on one of Delaware's busiest highways. "The best thing to do if you buy it is burn it," local property investor Bill Mervine had remarked at the auction. His colleague Jay Swartzentruber added bluntly, "The dirt is worth more than the building itself."

The foreclosure process left Fulton Bank with no choice but to buy back the property for $78,500, a fraction of its commercial value. Potential buyers wanted no part of it. Millsboro contractor Harry Caswell described the place as "like a haunted house."

For the work crews who finally arrived that October morning to demolish the complex, this was no ordinary job. It was an act of communal exorcism, a way to help heal a deeply wounded community. The property's new owner, Bruce Geyer, had purchased it from the bank with one primary objective: "We're just chomping at the bit to get the thing torn down and taken away from there," he told News Journal reporter Dan Shortridge.

Offers of help poured in from local builders and tradesmen eager to get involved. "I've got a whole file full of people that want to be part of this," said Caswell. "People are just calling up saying, 'Can I lend a hammer?'" Their grim assignment was clear: to obliterate every trace of the suffering that had taken place within those walls. Attorney General Beau Biden vowed the building would be "wiped off the face of the earth."

Leveling Bradley's property marked the final step in erasing his physical presence.

Earlier that year, on January 19, state police and DelDOT employees confiscated and destroyed Bradley's personal effects from a storage unit in Rehoboth Beach. The Delaware Attorney General's Office had intervened to halt a scheduled auction, citing community sensitivity. Instead, DelDOT crews crushed the items — including photo viewers, a pair of swords, power tools, various arcade games, and a Mountain Dew vending machine — with heavy equipment. Attorney General Beau Biden said the state wanted to ensure the objects would never enter public circulation as morbid collectibles, profiting off the suffering of Lewes families.

By sunset on October 10, bulldozers had reduced Bradley's infamous "palace of horrors" to rubble. They left behind an empty lot, and a community still scarred by his crimes.

Born on May 10, 1953, in Philadelphia, Earl B. Bradley pursued a career in pediatrics, earning his medical degree from Temple University School of Medicine in 1983. He completed his residency at Thomas Jefferson University Hospital in 1986 before working at Frankford-Torresdale Hospital and later establishing a private practice in Northeast Philadelphia.

Bradley abruptly relocated to Lewes in 1994 after Beebe Medical Center offered him a position. His move followed an unresolved molestation allegation in Pennsylvania involving a 21-month-old girl—an investigation that ended without charges. This lack of resolution effectively allowed Bradley to leave the state without scrutiny and begin practicing in Delaware with a clean slate.

The Delaware Board of Medical Practice, which had licensed Bradley, received Pennsylvania's disclosure of the earlier molestation allegation against him. However, the Delaware board failed to conduct its own inquiry, which the board was supposed to treat as standard procedure. This marked the first of many institutional failures that enabled Bradley's predatory behavior for years to come.

Once in Delaware, Bradley quickly gained a reputation as an accommodating pediatrician, crafting an environment designed to put children at ease. His office complex, with its miniature Ferris wheel, carousel, and Disney-themed examination rooms, appeared to be the creation of a doctor who genuinely cared about making medical visits less frightening for children. Parents were drawn to his practice, appreciating his willingness to see patients on short notice, and his seemingly child-friendly approach. A former Bradley employee told reporter Wade Malcolm of the News Journal, "He would always say, 'I don't want the children to be afraid of me. Kids always think going to the doctor is going to a monster, and I don't want them to think of me that way'."

Behind this carefully constructed façade of whimsy and care lurked a tragic irony: Bradley meticulously created an environment that facilitated his predatory behavior. The playful décor served as both lure and camouflage, disarming parents and children alike. The secluded rooms and outbuildings gave him the privacy he needed to commit his crimes.

Journalists Cris Barrish, Dan Shortridge, and Wade Malcolm of the News Journal doggedly uncovered a disturbing pattern of allegations, warnings, and missed opportunities that spanned Bradley's entire career in Delaware. Their investigative coverage revealed how institutions that should have protected children instead failed them repeatedly, allowing Bradley to continue practicing despite numerous red flags.

Complaints about Bradley accumulated, but authorities repeatedly dismissed them. Beebe Medical Center examined Bradley in 1996 after a nurse reported concerns about his use of catheterizations and inappropriate physical contact. She specifically described how he positioned older patients on their hands and knees, according to Barrish. The nurse also expressed alarm that Bradley made girls undress before routine exams, kissed and hugged them, and remarked about attractive mothers. Even with these warning signs, Beebe concluded Bradley's behavior was "within the mainstream of current pediatric practices." The hospital's CEO Jeffrey M. Fried later said he considered the complaint "clinical," not sexual.

Bradley left Beebe in 1997 for private practice but retained his privileges to attend to births and see patients who were hospitalized, right up until his arrest eleven years later. This turned out to be yet another opportunity that authorities missed to stop his predation.

A seven-year-old's grandmother reported Bradley had pulled down the girl's underwear and violated her with his hand during a 2003 physical. In 2004, a parent reported to Milford police, after a visit to Bradley's satellite office there, that her daughter complained he "gives her too many kisses," as reporter Dan Shortridge detailed. Milford police investigated and wanted to charge Bradley with offensive touching, but prosecutors decided they did not have enough evidence to proceed. Another mother said her three-year-old claimed Bradley "kissed her tongue" when he took her to a room alone. Bradley often used candy or toys he kept in non-examination rooms as a ploy to get children alone, court records show.

No one formally reported Bradley to the medical disciplinary board, despite a state law that obligates the Attorney General's Office, police, doctors, and nurses to report any physician they believe guilty of unprofessional conduct to that board.

In 2008, police and prosecutors missed yet another chance to lock up Bradley when a handful of parents told state police of inappropriate vaginal exams.

A twelve-year-old girl who saw Bradley for a sore throat and pink eye said he gave her a vaginal exam and penetrated her with his fingers.

A six-year-old seeking evaluation for possible attention-deficit disorder said Bradley allegedly gave her a physical and touched her genital area. After the exam, Bradley repeatedly kissed her several times and asked if she wanted to stay overnight with him.

An eight-year-old who sought treatment for excessive urination received three vaginal exams over several weeks. Bradley did not wear gloves, kissed her on the lips, and afterward gave her a prize, police said.

Throughout this period, Bradley's sister and former office manager, Lynda Barnes, had grown increasingly concerned about her brother's behavior. In 2004, she wrote to the Medical Society of Delaware about Bradley's physical and emotional deterioration, including his use of drugs from patient samples and allegations of inappropriate touching of patients. The society claimed a malfunctioning fax machine cut off part of her two-page letter.

Dr. Carol A. Tavani, who chaired a society committee that helped impaired physicians, said she never knew of the touching allegation, and Dr. James P. Marvel Jr., a former society president, later told police he didn't investigate Barnes' complaint because it was a "family matter." No one from the society reported these concerns to the Delaware Board of Medical Practice.

Police finally arrested Bradley on December 16, 2009, after the parents of a two-year-old girl reported that their daughter said he hurt her genital area when he took her to a basement to get candy. The girl's father said she had made a similar complaint two months earlier after she got a flu shot. Unlike previous complaints, this one led to immediate action, with police executing a search warrant at Bradley's office complex the same day.

On the day of the arrest, many parents and colleagues suspected the accusations were bogus. One thought it might be a "smear campaign." When police searched Bradley's office complex, however, detectives were stunned to find dozens of explicit rape videos of little girls, many still in diapers.

In an interview with reporter Cris Barrish, State Police Detective Scott Garland, a veteran computer forensic sex-crime investigator, described one video of an attack on a two-year-old girl as "the most violent and brutal attack on a child of any age that I have ever seen captured on video." Garland recounted the horrific evidence in a haunted voice, noting that he had never seen anything like it and had never been prepared for it during his years investigating sexual crimes.

Garland testified that Bradley forced oral sex on the young victims so violently that some girls appeared to choke or suffocate, becoming "ashen gray" from near-choking. During these assaults, Bradley would perform mouth-to-mouth resuscitation to revive the children who had stopped breathing, then casually tell them, "Let's go get a popsicle," before returning them to their unsuspecting parents. The detective noted that Bradley used "very high definition" camcorders and mini cameras disguised as ballpoint pens to meticulously document these attacks.

Wade Malcolm of the News Journal reported that the Delaware Attorney General's Office believed Bradley's crimes dated back at least 11 years. Prosecutors later charged him with sexually abusing more than 100 children—some as young as three months old. The average age of his victims was just three years old.

The case's ghastly nature and the sheer number of victims shocked the community and drew national attention.

Bradley waived his right to a jury trial, choosing a stipulated trial—a legal process that allowed the court to reach a verdict based on agreed-upon evidence. This approach spared the victims and their families from having to relive the attacks in open court.

Judge William C. Carpenter Jr. found Bradley guilty on all 24 counts of rape, assault, and sexual exploitation of a child. On August 26, 2011, he sentenced Bradley to 14 life sentences plus an additional 164 years, ensuring he would never again walk free. Carpenter condemned Bradley for betraying the profound trust that society places in physicians, and prosecutors labeled him a "monster," emphasizing the lasting trauma inflicted upon victims and their families, reported Cris Barrish (News Journal, August 27, 2011).

In Bradley's sentencing statement, prosecutor Paula Ryan did not mince words: "Earl Bradley committed unspeakable acts upon those who could not speak for themselves. He deliberately manipulated the parents of these children. He manipulated those who worked with him, and he repeatedly and intentionally—without remorse or hesitation—attacked and sexually assaulted toddlers and nonverbal children.

"To make indescribable and horrific matters even worse," Ryan added, "he videotaped these incidents for his own perverse pleasure, endlessly editing and copying, permanently memorializing his attacks on these children for his own twisted collection."

Bradley received the harshest punishment possible under Delaware law. Even so, many in the community believed no sentence could match the enormity of his crimes or undo the damage he had done. "You have shamed your profession," Judge William C. Carpenter Jr. declared at sentencing.

The Bradley case exposed catastrophic failures at multiple levels of Delaware's medical and legal systems. Complaints about Bradley had emerged as early as 1994, yet each time, institutions failed to take decisive action.

In the wake of these revelations, Delaware swiftly enacted legal reforms to address systemic failures. In June 2010, the General Assembly passed nine bills aimed at strengthening oversight of healthcare professionals and preventing similar abuses. These laws mandated that the Board of Medical Licensure and Discipline permanently revoke the license of any physician convicted of a felony sexual crime. They also required doctors applying for a license or renewal to disclose all prior investigations into their behavior, not just those resulting in formal punishment. Additionally, the law now required the medical board to hold disciplinary hearings in public, and physicians who failed to report suspected misconduct by a colleague could face fines up to $10,000 and possible suspension or revocation of their own licenses, reported Cris Barrish.

Further tightening the system, the General Assembly introduced three additional bills in March 2011, expanding these protections beyond physicians. The proposed legislation barred convicted sexual felons from obtaining licenses in various healthcare fields, including nursing, dentistry, psychology, physician assistance, clinical social work, and chemical dependency counseling. The new law also instituted permanent license revocation for anyone in these fields whom a court had convicted of a felony sexual crime. Lawmakers described these reforms as long overdue, acknowledging the failure of existing policies to prevent Bradley's prolonged predation despite years of concerns raised, then disregarded.

State leaders framed these reforms as an unequivocal commitment to protecting patients. "What we learned from the Bradley situation was that we must all be held accountable," Rep. Mike Barbieri (D-Newark), a licensed social worker who sponsored several of the new measures, told reporter Barrish. "Ignoring inappropriate behavior by a professional colleague is a dereliction of duty and makes us just as culpable as the person committing the act."

The reforms had an immediate impact. Delaware's Board of Medical Licensure and Discipline drastically increased serious disciplinary actions from just a handful in 2009 to 22 in 2010, marking a 400 percent rise. Delaware's ranking for doctor discipline jumped from 35th to 13th in the nation in Public Citizen's Health Research Group annual survey. By mid-2011, the board had already taken seven more serious actions against physicians. The increased scrutiny sent a clear message: regulators would no longer tolerate lax oversight.

At the national level, the American Academy of Pediatrics released its first policy on protecting children from abuse by health care providers, citing the Bradley case directly. The policy urged pediatricians to screen employees for past records of abuse, develop protocols for chaperoned medical exams, and establish formal reporting systems for complaints.

The ripple effects of the Bradley case extended far beyond the courtroom. Victims and their families continued to struggle with the trauma years after his arrest. Children whom Bradley had sexually abused faced a difficult path to healing. Some began showing symptoms of post-traumatic stress disorder, becoming aggressive or exhibiting sexualized behavior. Others seemed outwardly unaffected, their trauma hidden beneath the surface.

However, as Cathy Rose, clinical coordinator at a Lewes-area child counseling agency, explained, healing was possible. "It doesn't have to define them," she said of the children she worked with. "What really needs to be avoided is that they'll be forever walking around as a 'Bradley victim'."

Parents grappled with overwhelming guilt, despite having no way to know what Bradley did behind closed doors. "I took her to him," one mother said, her voice quavering. "I brought her there." Many families faced financial hardship as they turned to therapy for their children or dealt with their own emotional repercussions. Some marriages dissolved under the strain, and the experience shattered their sense of safety in the medical system.

Families also sought justice through civil means, filing more than 150 civil lawsuits against Bradley, Beebe Medical Center, the Medical Society of Delaware, and individual doctors accused of negligence for not reporting Bradley's suspicious behavior. The court granted these lawsuits class-action status in April 2011, allowing victims to pursue collective legal action.

The community's reaction was complex and deeply personal. News Journal reporter Wade Malcolm captured the rawness of emotion in a May 29, 2011 article, describing a handwritten note tied with a black ribbon to the banister of the checkerboard-patterned building where many of Bradley's assaults took place. Written on a fast-food napkin in blue ink, it read:

"I can't even begin to tell you what a sick son of a bitch you are. You have taken my daughter and so many other children's innocence away. You don't deserve any protection. Our children didn't have any. Why the hell should you? I speak for all families when I say that you are a coward, you are a sick perverted freak, and I hope you get the ultimate punishment possible!"

That anonymous cry of anguish, perhaps more than anything, captured the essence of what Earl Bradley had done to a community that once placed their faith in him to care for their most precious treasure—their children. Bradley's crimes vanished from sight after BayBees Pediatrics disappeared in October 2011. But the damage endured, scarring families, shaking trust in institutions, and reminding Delaware how predators thrive when accountability fails. This story belongs to the victims who endured the unimaginable, and to the journalists who refused to look away.

A Special Note of Gratitude

History does not always offer comfort. Some chapters bruise more than they illuminate. Still, the stories in this book—however grim, absurd, or unsettling—tell us something essential about the place we live. They chart the boundaries of power and pain, of privilege and punishment. They reveal what happens when ambition outruns conscience, when institutions turn their backs, when communities choose silence over truth. It's a painful journey at times, but in tracing these darker contours, we also come closer to clarity.

You've read about shell games and shattered trusts, public betrayals and private terrors. You've followed doomed escapes, con artists in silk ties, and lawmen who bent with the wind. These cases tested Delaware's patience and, at times, its very sense of decency. But in telling them, we sharpen our understanding of how a state defines wrongdoing—and what it's willing to forgive.

To finish this book is to complete a journey through the shadowed side of civic life. It's not always easy terrain. So thank you—for your curiosity, your stamina, and your willingness to face these uncomfortable moments alongside me. That company matters.

Because if Delaware's history teaches anything, it's this: justice is rarely tidy. But paying attention is its own kind of accountability. And sometimes, it's the only one we get.

Notes on Sources

When Spells Became Criminal Acts

"Community Alarmed over Witchcraft Accusation." Daily Republican (September 10, 1883).

"Believed to Be Under Preternatural Influence." Daily Republican (July 5, 1888).

"Baldwins Accused of Necromancy." Daily Republican (March 19, 1895).

"Letter to the Editor: Chickens, Witchcraft, and a Failed Sacrifice." Delaware Tribune (March 11, 1869).

"An Alleged Conjuror in Court." Every Evening (April 14, 1891).

"Witchcraft Case Dismissed in Modern Court." Every Evening (September 22, 1895).

"Daniel Hector Sentenced for Voodoo Practices." Every Evening (March 3, 1905).

"Charm Powder Case Involving Mary Burke." Every Evening (February 5, 1921).

"Pardon Granted in Witchcraft Case." Milford Chronicle (February 2, 1906).

"Witchcraft Beliefs and Remedies on the Frontier." Rev. Joseph Doddridge, Notes on the Settlement and Indian Wars in Pennsylvania and Virginia (1824).

"Witchcraft Act of 1604 Quoted in Legal Commentary." [Legal excerpt, no publication] (1604).

Cheney Clow's Rebellion

"Rebellion or Myth? Cheney Clow Revisited." Cheney Clow's Rebellion by Joseph Brown Turner (1912).

"Historical Sketch of Cheney Clow's Execution." The Cincinnati Enquirer (October 18, 1881).

"Clow's Trial and Execution." Delaware Register and Farmers' Magazine, Vol. 1 (1838).

"The Tory Fort at Little Creek." Delaware Continentals, 1776–1783 by Christopher L.

Ward (1941).

"Cheney Clow's Political Trial." *Every Evening* (September 10, 1930).

"Petition for Mercy in Cheney Clow Case." *The Freeman's Journal* (September 3, 1783).

"Delaware's Revolutionary Conflicts." *A History of Delaware* by Walter A. Powell (1928).

"Cheney Clow: Political Prisoner of the Revolution." *Journal-Every Evening* (September 27, 1934).

"The Execution and Legacy of Cheney Clow." *Journal-Every Evening* (September 27, 1934).

"Clow's Treason Trial and the Militia Clash." *News Journal* (July 4, 1997).

"The Last Days of Cheney Clow." *News Journal* (January 17, 1999).

"Reflections on Cheney Clow's Death Warrant." *News Journal* (January 17, 1999).

"Justice Deferred: Cheney Clow and the Mob." *News Journal* (June 9, 2024).

"Report of Cheney Clow's Arrest and Resistance." *The Philadelphia Times* (June 19, 1892).

Patty Cannon, Queen of the Kidnappers

"The Abominable Crime of Man Stealing." *Baltimore Morning Chronicle* (July 23, 1827)

"Outlaws of the Eastern Shore: The Patty Cannon Legacy." *Baltimore Sun* (September 9, 1930).

"Indictments in the Cannon Case." *Delaware Register and Farmers' Magazine* (May 16, 1829).

The Entailed Hat; or, Patty Cannon's Times: A Romance. George Alfred Townsend (1884).

"Patty Cannon and the Border Atrocities." *Every Evening* (September 29, 1930).

The Infamous Patty Cannon in History and Legend. Jerry Shields (1990).

Narratives and Confessions of Lucretia P. Cannon. Clinton Jackson and Erastus E. Barclay (1841).

"Bones in a Chest: A Shocking Discovery in Sussex." *National Gazette* (April 14, 1829).

"The Detailed Narrative of Peter Hook." *National Gazette* (January 27, 1827).

"Details Emerge and Some Kidnapped Boys Are Returned." *National Gazette* (June 30,

1826).

"George Alfred Townsend on Patty Cannon." Smyrna Times (March 15, 1882).

Tales of Old Maryland: History and Romance on the Eastern Shore of Maryland. J. H. K. Shannahan, Jr. (1907).

"Trial Developments and Additional Graves." United States Gazette (April 21, 1829).

"More Details of the Kidnapped Boys Returned." United States Gazette (July 4, 1826).

"Description of Mary Fisher, the Kidnapped Woman." United States Gazette (March 3, 1826).

"Southern Planters Write to Alert Mayor Joseph Watson." United States Gazette (May 22, 1829).

"Cyrus James Confesses to Multiple Murders." Gazette and Watchman (April 29, 1829).

"Philadelphia Mayor Offers Reward for Patty Cannon Gang." United States Gazette (July 15, 1828).

"Constable Garrigues Apprehends John Purnel." National Gazette (October 4, 1828).

"Returned Children from New Orleans Identified." Philadelphia Inquirer (January 23, 1829).

"Shocking Depravity Unearthed on Patty Cannon Farm." Wilmington Watchman (April 10, 1829).

The Dover Eight

"Dover Eight's Dramatic Escape Nearly Forgotten." News Journal (September 18, 2012).

"Excitement in Delaware—Unsuccessful Attempt to Capture Fugitive Slaves." The Dover Reporter (March 13, 1857).

"Larson Captures Life of Tubman." News Journal (August 11, 2003).

"Asanti Daughter of Zion." in Harriet Tubman: A Reference Guide to Her Life and Works by Kate Clifford Larson, Westport, CT: Greenwood Press, (2004).

Bound for the Promised Land: Harriet Tubman, Portrait of an American Hero. Kate Clifford Larson. New York: Ballantine Books, 2004.

"Harriet Tubman and the Dover Eight." National Park Service. https://www.nps.gov/hart/faqs.htm

"Stories: Dover Eight." Black and Education Project. https://blackandeducation.org/stories/2017/2/4/j8gx2wzt3p6vxsoxfovkd1lr05vu97-t26ks

"Pritchett Meredith Farm Site." Harriet Tubman Underground Railroad Byway. https://harriettubmanbyway.org/pritchett-meredith-farm/

"Samuel Green and the Fight for Freedom." *Star Democrat* (September 2, 2007).

"Patriotism and Peril in Dover Jail." *The Post-Standard* (April 17, 2005).

"Indictments in the Dover Eight Case." *Baltimore Sun* (March 11, 1857).

"Letter from Thomas Garrett to Samuel Rhoads, March 13, 1857." in *The Underground Railroad* by William Still. Philadelphia: Porter & Coates, 1872.

"Letter from William Brinkly to Philadelphia Vigilance Committee, March 23, 1857." in *The Underground Railroad* by William Still. Philadelphia: Porter & Coates, 1872.

The Underground Railroad: A Record of Facts, Authentic Narratives, Letters, &c. William Still. Philadelphia: Porter & Coates, 1872.

"Biographical Series: Henry Predeaux, Denard Hughes, and Thomas Elliott." Maryland State Archives.

Decapitation for Insurance Money

"The Dover Delaware Tragedy." *Baltimore Sun* (June 12, 1873).

"The Verdict in the West Murder Case." Reprinted from the *Philadelphia Enquirer* in The *Daily Evening Express* (June 11, 1873).

"The West Case Verdict." *Delaware Gazette and State Journal* (June 14, 1873).

"The West Trial—A Brief Resumé of the Case." *The Daily Gazette* (June 3, 1873).

"The West Trial—Second Day." *The Daily Gazette* (June 6, 1873).

"The People's Column." *The Daily Gazette* (June 11, 1873).

"The Dover Butchery." *Every Evening* (June 4, 1873).

"Trial of Dr. Isaac C. West." *Middletown Transcript* (June 7, 1873).

"The Skinned Negro." New York Daily Herald (June 6, 1873).

"A Multitude of Witnesses on the Question of Gas." New York Daily Herald (June 7, 1873).

"The Theory of Self-Defense and Insanity." New York Daily Herald (June 10, 1873).

"Why He Butchered Turner." New York Daily Herald (June 11, 1873).

"The Man Who Killed and Skinned a Negro Declared Not Guilty." New York Daily Herald (June 12, 1873).

"The West Murder Trial." Wilmington Daily Commercial (June 6, 1873).

"The Verdict in the West Case." Wilmington Daily Commercial (July 8, 1873).

Smugglers in Lewes

"Marshal Dunn's Rejection by the Senate." Baltimore Sun (March 27, 1878).

"Pilots and Smuggling Protested." Delaware Gazette (January 30, 1816).

"Lewes Smugglers Apprehended." The Daily Gazette (July 8, 1874).

"Final Hearing for Lewes Smugglers." The Daily Gazette (September 9, 1874).

"Lewes Smugglers Released from Jail." The Daily Gazette (June 18, 1875).

"Fine Flavor of Romance in Lewes Smuggling." Every Evening (July 10, 1874).

"Morris Retained Amid Service Cuts." Every Evening (August 29, 1876).

"Another Smuggler Arrested." Middletown Transcript (July 15, 1876).

"Smuggling Returns to Lewes." Milford Chronicle (January 26, 1883).

"Captain Williams and Andrew Baker Arrested." Smyrna Times (January 26, 1876).

"Lighthouse Changes and Jenkins Resigns." Smyrna Times (September 19, 1877).

"Vessels Seized in Mahon's Creek." Smyrna Times (January 9, 1878).

"Major Morris Accuses Lighthouse Keeper." Wilmington Daily Commercial (July 28, 1876).

"Marshal Dunn's Expedition to Lewes." Wilmington Daily Gazette (July 8, 1874).

"Longtime Smuggling Ring Finally Confronted." Wilmington Morning Herald (January 21, 1876).

Rail Hero Wannabe

"Brown's Motive and Confession." *The Daily Gazette* (July 2, 1878).

"Coroner's Jury Travels to Crash Site." *The Daily Gazette* (July 1, 1878).

"Inquest Concludes with Jury Verdict." *The Daily Gazette* (July 3, 1878).

"Brown Released, Returns to Family Life." *Delaware Gazette and State Journal* (January 31, 1884).

"Trial of Harley Brown: Mental State Considered." *Delaware Gazette and State Journal* (December 7, 1878).

Harley G. Brown Find a Grave memorial (ID 10548008) https://www.findagrave.com/memorial/10548008/harley-g-brown

"Wreck at Claymont Recalled in Retrospective Profile." *Journal-Every Evening* (February 16, 1934).

"Brown's Return to Wilmington Revisited." *Middletown Transcript* (December 14, 1883).

"Brown Sentenced to Five Years." *Morning Herald* (December 9, 1878).

"Courtroom Packed as Trial Begins." *Morning Herald* (December 6, 1878).

"Legal Debate over Brown's Indictment." *Morning Herald* (December 7, 1878).

"Public Sympathy for the Defendant." *Smyrna Times* (July 3, 1878).

Prostitution and the Brothel Era

"Divorce Testimony Reveals Vice in Philadelphia." *Daily Republican* (May 24, 1866).

"Increase in City Saloons Tied to Brothel Licenses." *Delaware Gazette and State Journal* (August 1, 1867).

"Police Raid Colored Brothel on Marsh Lane." *Every Evening* (October 4, 1875).

"Children Rescued from Vice Den." *Every Evening* (August 3, 1888).

"Authorities Clash Over Who Should Close Brothel." *Every Evening* (May 21, 1891).

"Wilmington Vice: Sadie Miller Fined." *Evening Journal* (June 18, 1925).

"Edna Powell Convicted in Bartlett Death Case." *Journal-Every Evening* (July 30, 1936).

"Sailors Rioted at Green House Brothel." *Morning Herald* (December 13, 1875).

"Mayor's Police Accused of Brothel Patronage." *Morning News* (December 3, 1880).

"Sadie Miller Convicted for Disorderly House." *Morning News* (March 3, 1919).

"Red Light District Tolerated by Officials." *Morning News* (October 3, 1941).

"Powell Testimony Prompts Police Shake-Up." *Journal-Every Evening* (December 5, 1936).

"Wilmington's Brothel Era Remembered." *Evening Journal* (July 5, 1973).

"Smithsonian Exhibit Acknowledges Wilmington Madams." *News Journal* (March 11, 1983).

"Daughter Rescued from House of Ill Fame." *Seaford Citizen* (February 28, 1874).

"Public Sentiment Needed to Enforce Vice Laws." *Smyrna Times* (April 16, 1879).

"Kate Mackey Ordered to Vacate Brothel." *Wilmington Daily Commercial* (August 10, 1874).

Mutilated Body Sparks Town Investigation

"Noah Benson's Murderers." *Daily Republican* (January 4, 1892).

"Miller Captured After Disappearing Post-Murder." *Daily Republican* (March 14, 1892).

"Expert Witness Formad Describes Human Blood Corpuscles." *Daily Republican* (June 2, 1892).

"Defense Challenges Blood Evidence." *Daily Republican* (June 3, 1892).

"Convicted Defendants Maintain Innocence." *Daily Republican* (June 6, 1892).

"Editorial: Justice for the Poor or Mere Conviction?" *Daily Republican* (September 24, 1894).

"Letter from Hutt Claims Injustice." *Delaware Gazette and State Journal* (May 23, 1901).

"Renewed Appeal for Pardon from Hutt." *Delaware Gazette and State Journal* (June 6, 1901).

"Murder Defendants Arraigned and Evidence Presented." *Evening Journal* (January 6, 1892).

"Trial Opens in Noah Benson Murder." *Evening Journal* (May 31, 1892).

"Opening Arguments: Circumstantial Evidence at Center." *Evening Journal* (May 31, 1892).

"Trial Resumes; Tugboat Testimony Introduced." *Evening Journal* (June 1, 1892).

"Dr. Formad's Expert Blood Analysis." *Evening Journal* (June 2, 1892).

"Court Debates Validity of Garment Evidence." *Evening Journal* (June 3, 1892).

"Petition for New Trial Filed." *Evening Journal* (June 9, 1892).

"Miller, Hutt, and Johnson Sentenced." *Evening Journal* (June 15, 1892).

"Governor Reynolds Urged to Intervene." *Evening Journal* (January 17, 1893).

"Governor Declines Clemency Petition." *Evening Journal* (September 11, 1893).

"Inquest Yields New Leads in Benson Case." *Morning News* (January 1, 1892).

"Detectives Discover Additional Evidence in Delaware City." *Morning News* (January 5, 1892).

"Witness Burgher Recants and Names Crowd." *Morning News* (January 8, 1892).

"State Rests; Defense Attacks Forensic Claims." *Morning News* (June 3, 1892).

"Retrospective: The Benson Case." *Morning News* (February 29, 1908).

Insider Vanishes with Bank's Fortune

"Four Accomplices to Pay the Penalty." *Baltimore Sun* (February 19, 1898).

"Boggs Declines to Reveal Whereabouts." *Baltimore Sun* (February 20, 1898).

"Boggs Testifies in Kenney Trial." *Baltimore Sun* (July 13, 1898).

"Cotter Sentenced for Role in Bank Fraud." *Evening Journal* (April 13, 1899).

"Boggs and Co-defendants Arraigned." *Evening Journal* (January 18, 1902).

"Roosevelt Commutes Boggs's Sentence." *Evening Journal* (April 25, 1902).

"President Grants Pardon at Wife's Plea." *Middletown Transcript* (January 25, 1902).

"Clark Convicted, Sentenced to Trenton." *Morning News* (June 30, 1898).

"Final Arguments in Kenney Trial." *Morning News* (December 16, 1898).

"Kenney Acquitted in Second Trial." *Morning News* (December 19, 1898).

"Chronological Record of William N. Boggs's Crime." *Morning News* (May 12, 1899).

"Pardon of William E. Cotter Announced." *Morning News* (February 6, 1900).

"Boggs Comments on Banking System." *Morning News* (May 7, 1902).

"Bach Letter to Mrs. Boggs Sparks Controversy." *Morning News* (September 30, 1902).

"Bank President Richardson Assumes Responsibility." *Morning News* (January 15, 1907).

"Boggs Hired as Bookkeeper After Release." *Smyrna Times* (May 7, 1902).

Oyster Pirates

"Attack on Lighthouse Keeper by Poachers." *Baltimore Sun* (October 17, 1901).

"Detective Ratledge Pursues Pirates in Mahon's Ditch." *Delaware Gazette and State Journal* (October 17, 1901).

"Raid on Oyster Pirates Near Mispillion." *Delaware Gazette and State Journal* (October 24, 1901).

"Oystermen Petition Legislature for Guard Boat Reform." *Every Evening* (January 23, 1907).

"Oscar Hann of Turkey Point Captured." *Evening Journal* (September 16, 1896).

"Little Creek Captain Condemns Enforcement Failures." *Evening Journal* (March 11, 1907).

"Federal Dumping Threatens Oyster Shoals." *Evening Journal* (April 20, 1907).

"State Plans Purchase of Modern Patrol Vessel." *Evening Journal* (June 22, 1909).

"Dover Oystermen Alarmed by Pirate Threats." *Milford Chronicle* (January 23, 1959).

"Delaware Oyster Industry at Risk, Says Fennimore." *Morning News* (April 18, 1906).

"New Guard Boat 'Protector' Commissioned." *Morning News* (May 16, 1906).

"Private Enforcement Patrol Launched by Oystermen." *Morning News* (April 17, 1913).

"James Munsey and Isaac Burris Plead Guilty." *Smyrna Times* (October 23, 1901).

Double Lives Exposed

"Rev. Taylor's Bigamy Case Exposes Legal Loophole." *Every Evening* (December 16, 1903).

"Null Held on Multiple Charges Including Bigamy." *Every Evening* (January 21, 1924).

"Elmer Oeschler Accused by Three Wives." *Every Evening* (January 16, 1928).

"Wilmington Woman Arrested in Bigamy Case." *Every Evening* (October 16, 1930).

"Clifton Faces Bigamy Charge from Two Wives." *Every Evening* (January 24, 1934).

"Rev. Taylor Arrested on Desertion Charges." *Morning News* (November 21, 1903).

"Sheriff from Iowa Arrives for Rev. Taylor Extradition." *Morning News* (January 15, 1904).

"George A. Christopher Confronted by Two Wives." *Morning News* (March 25, 1904).

"Rev. Taylor Sentenced in Iowa for Bigamy." *Morning News* (April 25, 1904).

"Lightcap Testifies to Being Used as Gambling Collateral." *Morning News* (December 22, 1924).

"Wilmington Policeman Convicted of Bigamy." *Morning News* (December 31, 1947).

"Stanback Charged After Secret Marriage Exposed." *Morning News* (July 15, 1976).

"Reeves Indicted for Bigamy Despite Warning." *Morning News* (March 4, 1988).

"Glover Held in Florida, Bigamy Warrant Filed." *Journal-Every Evening* (February 11, 1960).

"Joan Beech and John Waller Charged." *Journal-Every Evening* (October 28, 1960).

"Paoletti Pleads Guilty to False Statement." *News Journal* (September 3, 2011).

"Wilbur Justice Pleads Guilty to Misstatement." *News Journal* (June 7, 2013).

"Robbins Convicted and Branded for Bigamy." *Smyrna Times* (April 21, 1859).

Moonshiners

"Pierce and Smith Arrested in Seaford Raid." *Every Evening* (October 25, 1921).

"Judge Warns Drinkers About Lethal Moonshine." *Every Evening* (January 13, 1922).

"Bloodhounds Proposed to Track Moonshiners." *Every Evening* (April 21, 1922).

"Delaware's Largest Still Found Near Roxana." *Every Evening* (May 1, 1922).

"Iron Bootleggers and the Psychology of Prohibition." *Every Evening* (November 13, 1922).

"Ku Klux Klan Issues Warning to Sellers." *Every Evening* (January 8, 1923).

"Marker Arrested by Federal Investigator." *Milford Chronicle* (February 3, 1922).

"New Moonshine Operations Near Milford." *Milford Chronicle* (January 25, 1929).

"Delaware Moonshine Wins Jersey Market." *Milford Chronicle* (September 2, 1932).

"Delaware Beer Sales and Intoxication Down." *Milford Chronicle* (August 4, 1933).

"Law Enforcement Backed by Growing Public Sentiment." *Smyrna Times* (May 3, 1922).

"Massive Multi-County Moonshine Raid Nets Eight." *Smyrna Times* (August 2, 1922).

"Gooding Blamed for Hit-and-Run During Raid." *Smyrna Times* (August 2, 1922).

"Moonshiners' 'Spy Network' Thwarts Arrests." *Smyrna Times* (July 13, 1927).

"Ongoing Surveillance of Lewes-Rehoboth Camps." *Smyrna Times* (November 2, 1927).

"Agents Face Gunfire in Kent County Battle." *Smyrna Times* (January 16, 1929).

"Dry Agents Seize 1185 Pints Near Smyrna." *Smyrna Times* (July 22, 1931).

"Whittaker Claims Still for Medical Use." *Wilmington Daily Commercial* (August 27, 1921).

KKK Intimidation Finally Fails

"First Klan Rally Since 1928 Draws Thousands." *Evening Journal* (August 2, 1965).

"Civil Rights Leader Calls for Klan Exposure." *Evening Journal* (August 16, 1965).

"Revived Klan Elects New Grand Dragon." *Evening Journal* (August 27, 1965).

"Delaware Klan Claims 1,000 Members." *Evening Journal* (September 16, 1965).

"Smyrna Legislator Defends Ku Klux Klan." *Evening Journal* (October 13, 1965).

"Editorial: News Media Must Expose the Klan." *Evening Journal* (October 16, 1965).

"Governor Calls for Klan Investigation." *Evening Journal* (October 20, 1965).

"Delaware Klan Holds Torch Rally Outside Dover." *Evening Journal* (October 25, 1965).

"Delaware House Passes Anti-Klan Mask Law." *Evening Journal* (March 26, 1982).

"Opinion: Don't Legislate by Whim of the Hooded." *Evening Journal* (June 8, 1982).

"Senate Approves Bill to Unmask Hate Groups." *Evening Journal* (June 18, 1982). "State Human Relations Chair Denounces Klan." *Morning News* (October 22, 1965).

"Missionary Condemns Delaware Klan as Global Embarrassment." *Morning News* (October 22, 1965).

"Governor Signs Anti-Mask Law." *Morning News* (July 14, 1982).

"Wilmington NAACP Chief Criticizes Klan Activity." *Morning News* (February 28, 1988).

"Klansman Details Rise of Newport Dens." *Morning News* (February 28, 1988).

"Klansmen Draw Jeers at Hedgeville Rally." *News Journal* (June 30, 1997).

Kidnappers Take Young Hilda Brodsky

"Romano Discharged After Family Refuses to Testify." *Courier Post* (August 14, 1936).

"Kidnappers Release Hilda Brodsky Without Ransom." *Every Evening* (April 19, 1932).

"Detectives Track Wrong Suspects to Bedford." *Every Evening* (May 30, 1932).

"Cohen's Arrest Sparks Renewed Investigation." *Evening Journal and Every Evening* (June 26, 1933).

"Cohen's Extradition Blocked After Court Testimony." *Evening Journal and Every Evening* (July 18, 1933).

"Police Believe Cohen Altered Appearance Via Surgery." *Evening Journal and Every Evening* (September 25, 1933).

"Hilda Again Fails to Identify Cohen." *Evening Journal and Every Evening* (September 26, 1933).

"Attorney General Green Seeks Romano Extradition." *Journal-Every Evening* (August 7, 1936).

"Early Investigations Hampered by Family Secrecy." *Morning News* (April 16, 1932).

"Brodsky Family Struggles to Recover." *Morning News* (April 20, 1932).

"Threats of a Second Kidnapping Stir Panic." *Morning News* (May 4, 1932).

"Michael Cohen Arrested; Brodsky Child Fails to Identify." *Morning News* (July 18, 1933).

"Romano Linked to Kidnap Car." *Morning News* (August 7, 1936).

"Philadelphia Editorial Praises Police Courage." *Philadelphia Evening Bulletin* (April 19, 1932).

"Romano Freed; Tearful Court Scene." *Wilkes-Barre Times Leader* (August 13, 1936).

Mothers Kill Children

"Experts Debate Andrea Yates Death Penalty." Associated Press (August 10, 2001).

"Filicide Patterns Cut Across Class and Race." Associated Press (April 7, 2011).

"How Could She? Society's Blind Spots on Filicide." Associated Press (April 7, 2011).

"Sunday School Teacher Drowns Sons in Bathtub." *Every Evening* (March 24, 1931).

"Mother Kills Three Children in Garage." *Evening Journal* (January 8, 1980).

"Mother Kills Son, Dogs Before Taking Own Life." *Journal-Every Evening* (February 6, 1960).

"Mother's Jealousy Blamed for Murder-Suicide." *Morning News* (August 1, 1933).

"Psychiatrist Analyzes Infanticide Motives." *Morning News* (August 22, 1969).

"Crime Data: Ten Children Killed by Parents." *News Journal* (April 20, 1997).

"Grossberg Defense May Rely on Medical Evidence." *News Journal* (April 20, 1997).

"Grossberg Pleads Guilty in Baby Death." *News Journal* (April 21, 1998).

"Infanticide Often Treated as Manslaughter." *News Journal* (April 21, 1998).

"Peterson Testimony Undermines Grossberg Defense." *News Journal* (April 21, 1998).

"Judge Hints Custody Shift Motivated Mother's Actions." *News Journal* (March 31, 2019).

Hammond's Family Burden

"Alonzo Hammond Charged in Domestic Assault." *Every Evening* (January 26, 1932).

"Grand Jury Declines to Indict Alonzo Hammond." *Every Evening* (February 4, 1932).

"Mother and Child Drown as Car Plunges from Ferry." *Journal-Every Evening* (December 8, 1937).

"Hammond Fires on Officer; Posse Hunts Fugitive." *Milford Chronicle* (July 28, 1939).

"Escaped Prisoners Captured After Multi-State Chase." *Milford Chronicle* (January 17, 1941).

"Three Inmates Escape Using Smuggled Saw Blades." *Milford Chronicle* (February 14, 1941).

"Fire Destroys Joseph Gray Property near Lincoln." *Milford Chronicle* (September 23, 1960).

"Father and Son Convicted in Milford Auto Theft." *Morning News* (December 12, 1932).

"Wife Missing After Domestic Dispute in Milford." *Morning News* (October 9, 1975).

"Courtroom Farce as Arson Indictment Delivered." *Journal-Every Evening* (September 21, 1960).

"Psychiatric Evaluation Follows Shotgun Incident." *Evening Journal* (October 17, 1973).

"Police Detain Hammond in Domestic Shooting Case." *Evening Journal* (October 18, 1973).

"Body of Myrtle Hammond Found in Cornfield." *Evening Journal* (October 8, 1975).

"Guard Stabbed During Kent County Jailbreak." *Smyrna Times* (October 19, 1939).

Ration Coupon Counterfeiters

"Three Arrested in Wilmington for Possession of 1,200 Counterfeit Coupons." *Every Evening* (September 27, 1943).

"Gasoline Coupons Seized in Philadelphia Raid." *Every Evening* (October 5, 1943).

"Twelve Dealers Summoned in OPA Coupon Probe." *Every Evening* (October 12, 1943).

"Leahy Orders Independent Review in Coupon Case." *Every Evening* (January 13, 1944).

"OPA Plans New Spot Checks on Gas Coupons." *Every Evening* (March 3, 1944).

"Federal Agents Arrest Ten in Gas Black Market Ring." *Every Evening* (May 18, 1944).

"OPA Official: Food Coupon Counterfeiting Now the Focus." *Every Evening* (February 19, 1945).

"McKinley Jones Pleads Guilty in Gas Stamp Case." *Every Evening* (June 5, 1945).

"Kornblum and Cardinale Held in Meat Coupon Conspiracy." *Every Evening* (September 26, 1945).

"Arguments Heard in Kornblum Probation Appeal." *Every Evening* (January 15, 1946).

"Judge Denies Kornblum's Parole; Sentence Upheld." *Every Evening* (January 16, 1946).

"Dealer Suspended After Using Counterfeit Sugar Coupons." *Every Evening* (May 7, 1946).

"Five Stations Cited for Ration Irregularities." *Milford Chronicle* (October 8, 1943).

"Government Shuts Down Wilmington Sugar Ration Office." *Milford Chronicle* (January 17, 1947).

"Dennis A. Hill Sentenced in Philadelphia Counterfeiting Case." *Morning News* (December 10, 1943).

"Cohen Warns Dealers of New High-Quality Counterfeits." *Morning News* (March 3, 1944).

"Gasoline Black Market Draining Millions of Gallons Daily." *Morning News* (March 15, 1944).

"Wadman, Stewart, Papes Arraigned in Federal Court." *Morning News* (May 19, 1944).

Lonely Hearts

"Mrs. Brennan Seeks Parole in Lonely Hearts Case." *Evening Journal* (November 19, 1964).

"Texas Rangers Hold Brennan Son in Connection with Murders." *Journal-Every Evening* (April 21, 1949).

"Brennan Trio Arraigned in Courtroom Drama." *Journal-Every Evening* (April 22, 1949).

"FBI Confirms Human Remains in Evidence." *Journal-Every Evening* (April 25, 1949).

"Raymond and George Brennan Released on Bail." *Journal-Every Evening* (May 17, 1949).

"Defense Seeks Venue Change in Lonely Hearts Trial." *Journal-Every Evening* (May 27, 1949).

"Court Overrules Change of Venue in Brennan Case." *Journal-Every Evening* (June 10, 1949).

"Brennan Trial to Begin July 18 in Dover." *Journal-Every Evening* (June 22, 1949).

"Brennan Sons Change Pleas in Court." *Journal-Every Evening* (March 1, 1950).

"Brennan Sons Denied Bail in Murder Case." *Milford Chronicle* (April 22, 1949).

"Delaware Police Dig for More Victims on Brennan Farm." *Milford Chronicle* (April 29, 1949).

"Mrs. Brennan Allegedly Admits Killing Wooldridge." *Milford Chronicle* (September 23, 1949).

"Confessions Lead Police to Dover Dump Remains." *Morning News* (April 18, 1949).

"Testimony Voided by Court Technicality in Murder Trial." *Morning News* (September 13, 1949).

Clarence Welch Steals Company Millions

"Welch Disappearance Baffles Friends, Family." *Journal-Every Evening* (November 16, 1953).

"Bank Buys Welch Firm at Auction for $175,000." *Journal-Every Evening* (November 20, 1953).

"Welch Found Alive in New York After Disappearance." *Journal-Every Evening* (November 23, 1953).

"Welch's Psychiatric State Cited in Business Collapse." *Journal-Every Evening* (December 9, 1953).

"Clarence Welch, Jr. Missing; Family Fears Foul Play." *Milford Chronicle* (November 20, 1953).

"Welch Located in NYC; Hospitalized After Breakdown." *Milford Chronicle* (November 27, 1953).

"Search Intensifies for Milford Manufacturer." *Morning News* (November 16, 1953).

"Farmers Bank Acquires Welch Company Stock." *Morning News* (November 20, 1953).

"Welch Suicide Attempt Fails; Committed to Bellevue." *Morning News* (November 23, 1953).

"Welch Released from Hospital, Recuperating in Milford." *Morning News* (December 9, 1953).

"Welch Disappearance Prompts 13-State Manhunt." *Salisbury Daily Times* (November 23, 1953).

Bookies

"Clarence Mitten Denies Bookie Charges in Court." *Journal-Every Evening* (November 23, 1934).

"Undercover Probe Exposes Wilmington Bookie Network." *Evening Journal* (August 28, 1961).

"DA Links PA Gamblers to Wilmington Bookie Banks." *Evening Journal* (November 18,

1961).

"Delaware Mafia Presence Denied by Mayor; Challenged by U.S. Attorney." *Evening Journal* (April 25, 1970).

"Numbers Racket and Race Bets Tied to Organized Crime." *Evening Journal* (August 14, 1971).

"Gambling Racket Targeted in Senate Hearings." *Journal-Every Evening* (October 25, 1957).

"Commentary: My Bookie." *Morning News* (May 10, 1950).

"Editorial Letter: Realist Pushes for Open Gambling in Delaware." *Morning News* (February 21, 1956).

"Bookie Busted in Manor Park Hideout." *Morning News* (August 25, 1960).

"Wilmington Commissioner Endorses Legalized Gambling—Except Slots." *Morning News* (August 18, 1965).

"Police Undercover Informants Fuel Bookie Rivalries." *Morning News* (September 26, 1974).

"Prominent Gambler Eyes Retirement from Numbers Game." *Morning News* (September 26, 1974).

"Boyd the Bookie: Inside Wilmington's Backroom Betting Operation." *Morning News* (June 10, 1975).

"Bookies Predict Boost from Legal Sports Betting Surge." *News Journal* (May 7, 2004).

"Illegal Gambling Persists as Enforcement Lags." *News Journal* (September 13, 2009).

Serial Rapist Unmasked

"McKay Case Prompts Criticism of Furlough Oversight." *Evening Journal* (March 24, 1970).

"Pardons Board Rejects McKay Sentence Reduction Request." *Evening Journal* (January 2, 1975).

"New Rape Linked to McKay Triggers Renewed Outcry." *Evening Journal* (August 31, 1976).

"Citizen Group Demands End to Violent Offender Furloughs." *Evening Journal* (September 10, 1976).

"Furloughed McKay Suspected in Four Rapes." *Evening Journal* (July 5, 1977).

"Editorial Slams Furlough Policy After McKay's Arrest." *Evening Journal* (July 11, 1977).

"Prisoner Abuse Claims Follow McKay Return." *Evening Journal* (July 12, 1977).

"McKay Indicted on 35 Charges Following Capture." *Evening Journal* (July 27, 1977).

"Inmate Jury Selection Begins in McKay Rape Trial." *Evening Journal* (January 26, 1978).

"Editorial Questions McKay's Pretrial Detention Status." *Evening Journal* (February 1, 1978).

"Attorney General Personally Prosecutes McKay." *Evening Journal* (February 16, 1978).

"Wilmington Man Testifies McKay Confessed to Rapes." *Evening Journal* (February 23, 1978).

"Editorial Decries Lapses in Prison Management." *Evening Journal* (March 14, 1978).

"Letters to Editor Demand Prison Reform After McKay." *Evening Journal* (May 10, 1978).

"Bill Revokes Furloughs for Class A Felons." *Evening Journal* (June 29, 1978).

"Years Later, McKay Case Still Haunts Wilmington." *Evening Journal* (January 27, 1986).

"McKay's Early Record Cited in Prison Oversight Debate." *Morning News* (October 7, 1969).

"Prosecutor Vows Investigation in McKay Furlough Case." *Morning News* (March 25, 1970).

"McKay Identified in String of Wilmington Rapes." *Morning News* (August 31, 1976).

"Guard Denies Knowing McKay Was on Furlough." *Morning News* (July 6, 1977).

"McKay Charged with 22 Additional Crimes." *Morning News* (July 23, 1977).

"Lawmakers Demand Prison Accountability After McKay Crimes." *Morning News* (August 31, 1977).

"Grand Jury Indicts McKay in Pretrial Assault." *Morning News* (January 26, 1978).

"Victim Testifies in McKay Trial on Rape Charges." *Morning News* (February 16, 1978).

"McKay Found Guilty on Eight Felony Counts." *Morning News* (February 22, 1978).

"McKay Stabbed by Inmates; Prison Security Questioned." Morning News (March 13, 1978).

"McKay Sentenced to Life Plus 150 Years in Second Trial." Morning News (May 25, 1978).

"New Measures Proposed for Delaware Prison Reform." News Journal (April 12, 1990).

Art Heist

"Federal Indictments in Wyeth Art Heist Made Public." Chronicle Tribune (January 28, 1983).

"Matherly Testimony Secures Recovery of Wyeth Art." Evening Journal (January 26, 1983).

"Federal Grand Jury Details Wyeth Heist Indictments." Evening Journal (January 27, 1983).

"Wyeth Paintings Theft Revealed as Regional Burglary Network." Evening Journal (January 28, 1983).

"Heist Plotters Failed to Find Buyer, Turned Government Witness." Evening Journal (January 30, 1983).

"Wyeth Heist Witness Attempts Suicide After Mental Evaluation." Evening Journal (April 27, 1983).

"Brothers Indicted for Perjury in Matherly Theft Case." Evening Journal (October 9, 1986).

"Trial Begins for Five Accused in Tractor Theft Ring." Intelligencer Journal (May 18, 1976).

"Dealer Identifies Matherly as Member of Tractor Theft Ring." Intelligencer Journal (May 19, 1976).

"Matherly Sentenced in Tractor Theft Case; Appeals Filed." Intelligencer Journal (May 20, 1976).

"Family Testifies Against Matherly in Burglary Ring Trial." Morning News (August 7, 1982).

"Noel and Robert Matherly Link Brother to Stolen Goods." Morning News (September 4, 1982).

"Francis Matherly Leads FBI to Stolen Wyeth Paintings." Morning News (January 23, 1983).

"Porter Testifies in Spadaro Arson and Blackmail Case." Morning News (January 24,

1984).

"Burglar Pens Tell-All Memoir on Wyeth Heist." *Morning News* (March 3, 1985).

"Pa. Supreme Court Orders New Trial in Johnston Gang Theft Case." *Philadelphia Inquirer* (July 6, 1979).

Powerful Lawyer Kills Governor's Secretary

"Capano's Arrest Follows Brother's Shocking Confession." CBS News (October 14, 1999).

"Capano Loses Final Appeal, Remains on Death Row." CBS News (July 5, 2002).

"Trial Cast Shared Reflections from Wilmington's Most Notorious Case." *Daily Times* (September 22, 2011).

"Thomas Capano's Fall from Power to Convicted Killer Recalled." *Daily Times* (November 20, 2017).

"Capano Guilty in Fahey Murder After Gripping Trial." *News Journal* (January 18, 1999).

"Fahey Murder: Conviction, Trial Details, and Legal Aftermath." *News Journal* (January 12, 2006).

"Capano Dies in Prison, Ending One of Delaware's Darkest Chapters." *News Journal* (September 20, 2011).

"Capano Case Remembered for Its Legal Drama and Tragedy." *News Journal* (November 20, 2017).

"Twenty Years Later: Capano Conviction Still Resonates in Delaware's Legal Memory." *News Journal* (January 16, 2019).

"Thomas Capano, Convicted Killer in Fahey Case, Found Dead in Prison Cell." *Philadelphia Daily News* (September 20, 2011).

"Capano, Convicted in Mistress's Death, Dies at 61." *Philadelphia Inquirer* (September 20, 2011).

Confidence Men

"Sharp-Eyed Bystanders Prevent Farmer's Loss." *Baltimore Sun* (November 11, 1897).

"Confidence Man Robs Countryman in Race Street Saloon." *Daily Gazette* (December 2, 1882).

"Slim Jim Arrested Again for Burglary." *Daily Republican* (January 26, 1885).

"Detective Con Man Fleeces Dover Residents, Disappears." *Daily Republican* (December 18, 1888).

"Mining Scam Nearly Traps Businessman." *Every Evening* (June 20, 1893).

"Elderly Man Escapes $1,000 Confidence Scam." *Every Evening* (September 30, 1905).

"Millionaire Bandit Carroll Tied to Local Robberies." *Every Evening* (June 18, 1928).

"Medicine Man's Legacy Lives On in Modern Scams." *Milford Chronicle* (January 31, 1958).

"Check Scam Targets Wilmington Grocers." *Morning News* (May 24, 1920).

"Suspicious Telegram Foils Impostor's Scheme." *Morning News* (November 4, 1933).

"FBI Issues Warning on Con Artist Jack Meredith." *Morning News* (March 15, 1944).

"Fast-Talking Con Men Swindle Market Street Shops." *Morning News* (November 6, 1964).

"Bank Flim-Flam Leaves Woman Penniless." *Morning News* (December 28, 1966).

"Ponzi Scheme Nets Delaware Con Man 6½ Years." *News Journal* (March 14, 2006).

"Marriage Used as Cover in Confidence Swindle." *Smyrna Times* (January 16, 1856).

"Visitors Warned Against Urban Con Men." *Smyrna Times* (May 27, 1874).

"Old Con Man Uses Woman and Child to Dupe Merchants." *Wilmington Daily Commercial* (April 3, 1920).

Insiders Sell DuPont Secrets to Korea

"Kolon Sentenced to $360M in Trade Secrets Case." *Chemical & Engineering News* (August 22, 2015).

"Jury Awards DuPont $920M for Kevlar Secrets Theft." *Daily Telegraph* (September 16, 2011).

"FBI: Ex-DuPont Engineer Gave Secrets to Kolon." *Daily Times* (March 16, 2011).

"Schulz Sentenced to Probation for Role in Kevlar Plot." *Martinsville Bulletin* (August 18, 2015).

"DuPont Sues Kolon for Alleged Theft of Kevlar Trade Secrets." *News Journal* (February 4, 2009).

"Kolon Must Face DuPont Antitrust Suit, Court Rules." *News Journal* (March 15, 2011).

"DuPont Wins $920M Verdict in Kevlar Trade Secrets Case." *News Journal* (September 15, 2011).

"Judge Refuses to Overturn $919M Verdict in DuPont Case." *News Journal* (January 31, 2012).

"Kolon Indicted on Conspiracy and Trade Secrets Charges." *News Journal* (October 19, 2012).

"Court Throws Out DuPont Award in Trade Secrets Trial." *News Journal* (April 4, 2014).

"DuPont Launches New Kevlar Innovations in Asia." *News Journal* (April 16, 2014).

"Former DuPont Employee Sentenced in Trade Theft Case." *News Journal* (August 18, 2015).

"Kolon and Executives Indicted for Industrial Espionage." *News Virginian* (October 19, 2012).

"Engineer Sentenced to Prison in Kevlar Espionage Case." *Richmond Times-Dispatch* (March 19, 2010).

"Federal Judge Denies Kolon Motion in Trade Secrets Trial." *Richmond Times-Dispatch* (January 31, 2012).

"Court Overturns $920M DuPont Verdict Against Kolon." *Richmond Times-Dispatch* (April 4, 2014).

"Kolon Executives Indicted in DuPont Espionage Case." *Richmond Times-Dispatch* (August 22, 2015).

"Federal Court Issues 20-Year Ban on Kolon Fiber Production." *Telegraph Journal* (September 1, 2012).

Pediatrician Betrays Hundreds of Children

"Bradley's Storage Locker Toys Destroyed by State Following Auction Cancellation." News

Journal (January 25, 2011).

"New Bills Seek to Bar Sexual Felons from Licensure." News Journal (March 22, 2011).

"Civil Lawsuits Against Bradley Gain Class-Action Status." News Journal (April 12, 2011).

"Mental Illness Defense Weighed by Bradley's Attorneys." News Journal (April 21, 2011).

"Bradley Declines Jury Trial, Case May Return to Sussex." News Journal (May 10, 2011).

"Bradley Property Becomes Bank-Owned in Public Auction." News Journal (May 18, 2011).

"Medical Oversight Laws Toughened After Bradley Case." News Journal (May 29, 2011).

"Trial Ends in One Day as Bradley Concedes to Child Rape Charges." News Journal (June 7, 2011).

"Victim's Parents Still Struggling Two Years Later." News Journal (June 12, 2011).

"Judge Finds Bradley Guilty on All Counts." News Journal (June 24, 2011).

"Bradley Faces Sentencing after Conviction on 24 Counts." News Journal (August 6, 2011).

"Bradley Sentenced to Life Without Parole for Raping 86 Children." News Journal (August 27, 2011).

"State to Raze Bradley Buildings to Erase Public Trauma." News Journal (September 16, 2011).

"Doctor's Office Where Bradley Abused Children to Be Demolished." News Journal (October 9, 2011).

"Background Checks No Guarantee of Protection from Abusers." News Journal (November 28, 2011).

"Former Patients Begin Long Recovery after Bradley Conviction." News Journal (December 12, 2011).

BOOKS BY DAVE TABLER

List of Titles

Delaware Before the Railroads	2022
Delaware from Railways to Freeways	2023
Delaware from Freeways to E-ways	2024
Delaware at Christmas	2025

Made in the USA
Middletown, DE
10 January 2026